The Repenter is the Beloved of God

I0453575

Āyatullāh Bashīr Ḥusayn al-Najafī

AL-BURĀQ

Copyright

Copyright © 2025 al-Burāq Publications.
All rights reserved. No part of this publication may be reproduced, distributed, or transmitted in any form or by any means, including photocopying, recording, or other electronic or mechanical methods, without the prior written permission of the publisher, except in the case of brief quotations embodied in critical reviews and certain other noncommercial uses permitted by copyright law. For permission requests, write to the publisher, addressed "Attention: Permissions [The Repenter is the Beloved of God]," at the email address below.

ISBN: 978-1-956276-63-3
Printed and published by al-Burāq Publications.
Arabic transcription by Shaykh Muḥammad al-Jāsim.
Translated and annotated by al-Burāq Publications. Where needed, context and transliterations were added. Some minor edits were made to the translated Arabic text.

Ordering Information
We offer discounts and promotions for wholesale purchases, non-profit organizations, and other educational institutions. Contact us at the email below for further information.

www.al-Buraq.org
publications@al-Buraq.org

First Edition | March 2025 | Layālī al-Qadr

Dedication

The publication of this book was made possible through the generous support of our donors.

Please recite *Sūrat al-Fātiḥah* and ask God for the Divine reward (*thawāb*) to be conferred upon the donors and also the souls of all the deceased in whose memory their loved ones have contributed graciously towards the publication of *The Repenter is the Beloved of God*.

We begin by giving all praise and thanks to God ﷻ for giving us the *tawfiq* to translate this book. He has guided us and without Him, we would not have been guided to the straight path embodied by the Prophet Muḥammad ﷺ and the Ahl al-Bayt عليهم السلام.

This book is dedicated to all the scholars, martyrs and believers who worked tirelessly to promote the pure Muḥammadan path.

We want to also give our thanks and appreciation to all believers from around the world and acknowledge the team which helped al-Burāq Publications complete this work, spending countless hours to make its publication possible. Please recite Sūrat al-Fātiḥah on behalf of them, their families, and their marḥūmīn.

This book is dedicated in honor of the following individuals. Please remember them in your prayers and may God ﷻ have mercy on them and their loved ones.

Ali Akbar Khoyee

Ali Ftouni

Ali Mansoor Zaydi

Ali Reza Razmi

Alya Agemy

Aya Nasrallah

Bande Khuda

Bokhari Marḥūm

Fatima Raza

Ḥajj Ahmad Sheet

Ḥajj Hassan Sobh

Ḥajj Sami Ftouni

Ḥājjī Amneh Sobh-Ftouni

Ḥājjī Hiam Hojeije

Ḥājjī Imane Srour

Ḥājjī Majida Fakherddine

Hasan Zaheer

Ibtissam Fouani

Imām al-Mahdī عجل الله تعالى فرجه الشريف

Iskandar ʿAbbās

Juman Alyousif

Khaldoon Alsaee

Layth al-Wilzi

Leila Mansour

Mahmoud Tiba

Mallak Jaber

Muttaqi Daniels

Nikbakht Yosofi

Rosetta Troupe

Sakina Alfani

Sayyid Sobh H. Sobh

Turfah Sobh

Yousuf Ali Rizvi

Du'ā' al-Ḥujjah

اللهم كن لوليك الحجة بن الحسن صلواتك
عليه وعلى آبائه في هذه الساعة وفي كل
ساعة وليا وحافظا وقائدا وناصرا ودليلا
وعينا حتى تسكنه أرضك طوعا وتمتعه فيها طويلا

O God, be, for Your representative, the Ḥujjat (proof), son of al-Ḥasan, Your blessings be upon him and his forefathers, in this hour and in every hour: a guardian, a protector, a leader, a helper, a proof, and an eye - until You make him live on the Earth, in obedience (to You), and cause him to live in it for a long time.

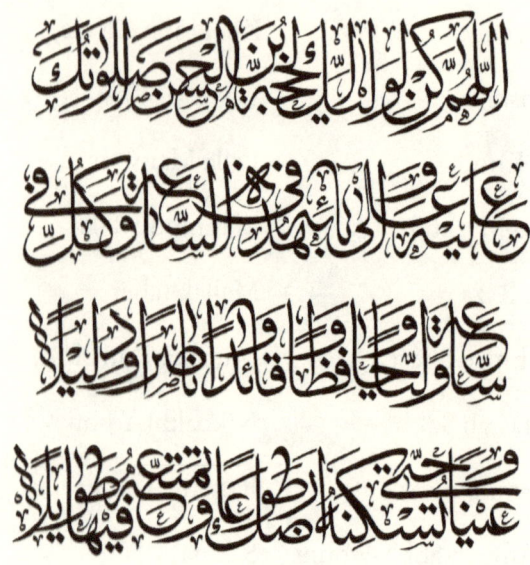

Terms of Respect

The following Arabic phrases have been used throughout this book in their respective places to show the reverence which the noble personalities deserve.

عزّ وجلّ

Used for God, meaning:
Exalted and Sublime (Perfect) is He

صلى الله عليه وآله

Used for Prophet Muḥammad, meaning:
Blessings from God be upon him and his family

عليه السلام

Used for a man (singular) of a high status, meaning:
Peace be upon him

عليها السلام

Used for a woman (singular) of a high status, meaning:
Peace be upon her

عليهما السلام

Used for men/women (dual) of a high status, meaning:
Peace be upon them both

عليهم السلام

Used for men and/or women (plural) of a high status, meaning:
Peace be upon them all

عجل الله تعالى فرجه الشريف

Used for Imām Muḥammad al-Mahdī, meaning:
May God hasten his return

قدس سره

Used for a deceased scholar, meaning:
May his resting [burial] place remain pure

Transliteration Table

The method of transliteration of Islāmic terminology from the Arabic language has been carried out according to the standard transliteration table below.

ء	ʾ	ر	r	ف	f
ا	a	ز	z	ق	q
ب	b	س	s	ك	k
ت	t	ش	sh	ل	l
ث	th	ص	ṣ	م	m
ج	j	ض	ḍ	ن	n
ح	ḥ	ط	ṭ	و	w
خ	kh	ظ	ẓ	هـ	h
د	d	ع	ʿ	ي	y
ذ	dh	غ	gh		
Long Vowels					
ا	ā	و	ū	ي	ī
Short Vowels					
ـَ	a	ـُ	u	ـِ	i

Table of Contents

بسم الله الرحمن الرحيم

In the Name of God, the Beneficent, the Merciful

God ﷻ said:

﴿إِنَّ ٱللَّهَ يُحِبُّ ٱلتَّوَّٰبِينَ وَيُحِبُّ ٱلْمُتَطَهِّرِينَ﴾

﴿inna llāha yuḥibbu t-tawwābīna wa-yuḥibbu l-mutaṭahhirīna﴾

﴿Indeed God loves the penitent and He loves those who keep clean﴾[1]

﴿إِنَّمَا ٱلتَّوْبَةُ عَلَى ٱللَّهِ لِلَّذِينَ يَعْمَلُونَ ٱلسُّوٓءَ بِجَهَٰلَةٍ ثُمَّ يَتُوبُونَ مِن قَرِيبٍ
فَأُوْلَٰٓئِكَ يَتُوبُ ٱللَّهُ عَلَيْهِمْ ۗ وَكَانَ ٱللَّهُ عَلِيمًا حَكِيمًا﴾

﴿innamā t-tawbatu ʿalā llāhi li-lladhīna yaʿmalūna s-sūʾa bi-jahālatin thumma yatūbūna min qarībin fa-ʾulāʾika yatūbu llāhu ʿalayhim wa-kāna llāhu ʿalīman ḥakīman﴾

﴿[Acceptance of] repentance by God is only for those who commit evil out of ignorance and then repent promptly. It is such whose repentance God will accept, and God is Knowing, Wise﴾[2]

---

[1] Sūrat al-Baqarah, Verse 222.

[2] Sūrat an-Nisāʾ, Verse 17.

Introduction

بسم الله الرحمن الرحيم

In the Name of God, the Beneficent, the Merciful

Praise be to God, Who revealed to His servant the Holy Book as a warning for all the worlds, and peace and blessings be upon he who was sent as a mercy to the worlds and on his blessed progeny, and curses be upon their enemies until the Day of Judgement.

It was out of the kindness of the Creator and His mercy for His servants that He bestowed upon them the blessing of existence and paved for them the path to reach the highest of ranks and attain closeness to the Divine. As such, He sent forth prophets and messengers and revealed books and scriptures to guide them to the [righteous] deeds and ways that bring them closer to Him and win His favor. God ﷻ said,

﴿وَمَا خَلَقْتُ ٱلْجِنَّ وَٱلْإِنسَ إِلَّا لِيَعْبُدُونِ﴾

﴾wa-mā khalaqtu l-jinna wa-l-ʾinsa ʾillā li-yaʿbudūni﴿

﴾I did not create the jinn and the humans
except that they may worship Me﴿[3]

[3] Sūrat ad-Dhāriyāt, Verse 56.

He does not need the worship of His servants; no servant's mistake nor the sins of the disobedient affect Him or bring Him any harm. Out of His care and kindness, He placed them in this world, afflicted them, and tested them with various forms of obligation, aiming to cleanse their souls and purify their hearts. The ultimate wisdom behind this is for His servants to grow close to Him by striving on the spiritual and mental level, through which they attain His mercy and pleasure. Therefore, obligations were outlined in which the servant was called to commit to certain beliefs within the faith in God ﷻ and His books and messengers and the leaders, vicegerents, and Imāms appointed by Him. These obligations also include actions to be carried out physically, which He conveyed to His prophets and messengers via revelation and which the pure Imāms clarified to their students and wise scholars, benefiting them with their light of guidance. Similarly, other obligations involve forbidding certain things, for the Creator knows what harm and afflictions such things contain and the barriers they can create between the servant and his Lord. As per His wisdom, God set the servant free after He showed him good from evil, clarifying the paths that lead to Him and warning him of the forbidden and unlawful that corrupts him and distances him from the Divine. In this way, the servant has the freedom of choice, and He has given him the [righteous] way; either he becomes grateful and of good behavior, or he becomes ungrateful and of wicked conduct. As such, the servant is well-informed in whichever choice he makes. Glory be to the Innovator, the Guider, the Compassionate, the Beneficent whose giving is limitless and whose kindness and generosity are endless; verily, He is the Blessed, the One Who gives abundantly.

His vast mercy encompasses those who have stumbled in their way and fallen prey to vice and the traps of Shayṭān due to their poor choices, slipping into the darkness of disobedience in beliefs or other aspects of religion. Hence, God opened doors to His mercy for them, too, and paved the way for them to return to His care and compassion through repentance and seeking forgiveness. Repentance is a door that God ﷻ opened for His servants whose souls strayed and got lost, sinking in the darkness of vice, and so, the Divine Mercy came to save them from despair and remind them to fear God, encouraging them to think of returning to Him. God relieves them of this hardship as He says,

﴿قُلْ يَٰعِبَادِيَ ٱلَّذِينَ أَسْرَفُوا۟ عَلَىٰٓ أَنفُسِهِمْ لَا تَقْنَطُوا۟ مِن رَّحْمَةِ ٱللَّهِ ۚ إِنَّ ٱللَّهَ يَغْفِرُ ٱلذُّنُوبَ جَمِيعًا ۚ إِنَّهُۥ هُوَ ٱلْغَفُورُ ٱلرَّحِيمُ﴾

﴿qul yā-ʿibādiya lladhīna ʾasrafū ʿalā ʾanfusihim lā taqnaṭū min raḥmati llāhi ʾinna llāha yaghfiru dh-dhunūba jamīʿan ʾinnahū huwa l-ghafūru r-raḥīmᵘ﴾

﴿Say [that God declares,] 'O My servants who have committed excesses against their own souls, do not despair of

the mercy of God. Indeed God will forgive all sins. Indeed, He is the Forgiving, the Merciful﴾[4]

Furthermore, His mercy does not suffice with the promise of forgiveness. Rather, it encompasses unimaginable compassion and care as He obliged them to seek repentance and forgiveness to gain closeness to Him by instilling in them a desire to contemplate repentance, equipping them with all requirements of returning to Him, and providing them with the strength to do so. Ultimately, He has prohibited all that may lead to sinning and removed the obstacles [that may prevent repentance]; glory be to Him.

[4] Sūrat az-Zumar, Verse 53.

The Meaning of Repentance and Its Necessity

Linguistically, repentance means to return if it refers to the servant. If it refers to God ﷻ, it means the return of His compassion over His servant, including him in His mercy and care and accepting him in the ranks of those who submit to His commands and abide by what He forbids.

When the servant sins, he grows further away from the Divine. An abundance of sustenance increases this distance and deepens his arrogance. When man sees that all his affairs are going well and he does not feel hindered in his desires and wants, he will continue his disobedience. He will continue distancing himself from his Lord, failing to realize that all his blessings—health, wealth, children, and the good state of his life affairs—are bestowed upon him by God ﷻ. Perhaps this may also lure him as God ﷻ says,

﴿فَذَرْنِي وَمَن يُكَذِّبُ بِهَٰذَا ٱلْحَدِيثِ ۖ سَنَسْتَدْرِجُهُم مِّنْ حَيْثُ لَا يَعْلَمُونَ﴾

﴾sa-nastadrijuhum min haythu lā yaʿlamūn[a]﴿

﴾We will draw them imperceptibly [into ruin], whence they do not know﴿[5]

If the servant were to persist in his sin and misguidance, then he might meet his death while in that state, and this is what God refers to in this verse,

---

[5] Sūrat al-Qalam, Verse 44.

﴿فَلَمَّا نَسُوا۟ مَا ذُكِّرُوا۟ بِهِۦ فَتَحْنَا عَلَيْهِمْ أَبْوَٰبَ كُلِّ شَىْءٍ حَتَّىٰٓ إِذَا فَرِحُوا۟ بِمَآ أُوتُوٓا۟ أَخَذْنَـٰهُم بَغْتَةً فَإِذَا هُم مُّبْلِسُونَ﴾

﴿fa-lammā nasū mā dhukkirū bihī fataḥnā ʿalayhim ʾabwāba kulli shayʾin ḥattā ʾidhā fariḥū bi-mā ʾūtū ʾakhadhnāhum baghtatan fa-ʾidhā hum mublisūna﴾

﴿فَقُطِعَ دَابِرُ ٱلْقَوْمِ ٱلَّذِينَ ظَلَمُوا۟ ۚ وَٱلْحَمْدُ لِلَّهِ رَبِّ ٱلْعَـٰلَمِينَ﴾

﴿fa-quṭiʿa dābiru l-qawmi lladhīna ẓalamū wa-l-ḥamdu li-llāhi rabbi l-ʿālamīna﴾

﴿So when they forgot what they had been admonished of, We opened for them the gates of all [good] things. When they became proud of what they were given, We seized them suddenly, whereat, behold, they were despondent. Thus the wrongdoing lot were rooted out, and all praise belongs to God, the Lord of all the worlds﴾[6]

It is not wise for a man to be deceived by the pleasures of the worldly life, for worldly blessings are wonderful and numbs his senses, beautifying the path toward vice. Nonetheless, God ﷻ loves His servant, so He gave him the blessing of existence, health, and well-being, equipped him with internal and external senses, and gave him the power and freedom to choose whatever he wants without prior entitlement. All these are indicators of the love of the ﷻ for

---

[6] Sūrat al-Anʿām, Verses 44–45.

this servant, for He did not leave him in this world defenseless against wild desires. Rather, He bestowed upon him the power of the mind and rationality to enable him to distinguish between good and evil, what benefits him and what harms him, and He sent forth messengers and revealed books, establishing signs at every crossroad in man's daily life and means to guide him to the righteous path. Examples of such signs and means are health and disease, birth and death, for when man sees that caravans of people enter this world every day and that caravans leave this life, he remembers God ﷻ. He realizes he cannot escape Him and shall return to his Originator. Ultimately, all this is to remind the servant of what he forgot under the influence of the wonderful pleasures of this world.

Possessing a sound intellect requires one to distance oneself from all ugly acts and commit to reaching what is better; hence, it is prudent that man adheres to the right path and obeys God ﷻ. A sound intellect requires one to worship and be among those who obey [God] for him to come out of the darkness and into the light. As such, repentance is one of man's most prominent duties.

In principle, repentance can be interpreted as the feeling of regret that pushes a servant to it, for a rational man will certainly feel regret if he reflects upon himself and considers the state of sin, loss, and disobedience in his life. At the same time, he serves his desires and self that steers him toward wickedness, as described in this verse:

﴿أَفَرَءَيْتَ مَنِ ٱتَّخَذَ إِلَـٰهَهُۥ هَوَىٰهُ﴾

﴿*a-fa-ra'ayta mani ttakhadha 'ilāhahū hawāhu*﴾

﴿*Have you seen him who has taken his desire to be his god*﴾[7]

Owing to the reminders and warnings from God ﷻ, whose care and compassion continuously seek to save man from the crushing darkness, if a rational man were to heed this, he would feel regret and sorry for what he had taken for granted in the presence of His mercy and for how he had wasted his life while seeking distance from God ﷻ. This power of the mind thus drives him to search for what he lost and return to Whom he distanced himself from. In this way, regret, sorrow, and anguish serve as factors that push him back into His care and mercy. For, the main contributing factor and the real driver is realizing his loss that resulted from him responding to his desires uninhibited, which thus pushes him to think about how to return to the Originator ﷻ.

[7] Sūrat al-Jāthiyah, Verse 23.

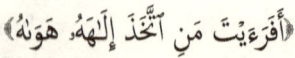

The Conditions of Repentance

We established that repentance is man's return to the path of worship and his reinstatement in the ranks of those who obey God ﷻ. In light of this, repentance can only be achieved through a set of conditions, which are many. We. We will mention the most important conditions that form the base of repentance.

The First Condition

It is to regret the sins, the wrongs, and the acts of disobedience one committed.

Regret is for one's heart to overflow with sorrow, sadness, and grief in a way that disturbs his peace and tranquility and shakes his previously stable reality. Thus, he can only regain this peace and stability by seeking the forgiveness of God ﷻ and acceptance into the ranks of those who have hope in His forgiveness, ask for His mercy, and obey His commands.

It is narrated that Imām Jaʿfar aṣ-Ṣādiq عليه السلام said,

> Amīr al-Mu'minīn عليه السلام said:
>
> > Regretting an act of evil requires one to refrain from it.

Imām Muḥammad al-Bāqir ※ also said,

> Regret suffices as repentance.[8]

Furthermore, we must familiarize ourselves with the four most important roots of this meaning of regret:

First Root

It is to realize that one's value in people's hearts diminishes and that one loses social status. If one were to feel that people object to him and realize that he was or almost got cast out by people, he would feel regret. He would buckle under the pressure of this loss and the piercing words of people who chase him who chase him wherever he goes.

Such a kind of regret furthers the distance between man and God ※ because it reveals his love for this world and his status in the people's hearts. In this way, he has sunk into an abyss of corruption by surrendering to the love of the self via pretending virtuousness [riyāʾ], which is a part or branch of the branches of shirk [polytheism]. In this regard, it is narrated that Imām ʿAlī ※ said,

> Verily, the least amount of riyāʾ [pretending to be virtuous] equals shirk [polytheism].[9]

---

[8] Kulaynī, Shaykh Muḥammad b. Yaʿqūb, *al-Kāfī*, Vol. 2, p. 426.

[9] Sharīf Raḍī, Muḥammad b. al-Ḥusayn, *Nahj al-Balāghah*, Sermon 86.

Furthermore, it is narrated that Imām Jaʿfar aṣ-Ṣādiq عليه السلام said,

> Pretending to be virtuous equals shirk [polytheism]. Whoever works [in terms of worship] for the people, his reward is upon the people, and whoever strives for God, his reward is from God.[10]

It is also narrated that he عليه السلام said,

> God عزّ وجلّ said,
>
> ﴿فَمَن كَانَ يَرْجُوا۟ لِقَآءَ رَبِّهِۦ فَلْيَعْمَلْ عَمَلًا صَـٰلِحًا وَلَا يُشْرِكْ بِعِبَادَةِ رَبِّهِۦٓ أَحَدًا﴾
>
> ﴿*fa-man kāna yarjū liqāʾa rabbihī fa-l-yaʿmal ʿamalan ṣāliḥan wa-lā yushrik bi-ʿibādati rabbihī ʾaḥada*^{n}﴾
>
> ﴿*So whoever expects to encounter his Lord—let him act righteously, and not associate anyone with the worship of his Lord*﴾[11]

The Imām عليه السلام comments on this,

> [Some] men strive to do good deeds not for God, but to gain the commendation of people and let the people

[10] Kulaynī, Shaykh Muḥammad b. Yaʿqūb, *al-Kāfī*, Vol. 2, p. 293.

[11] Sūrat al-Kahf, Verse 110.

> know [of their good deeds]. Such men have engaged in shirk [polytheism] in the worship of their Lord.

He then continues,

> No man hides a good deed except that God shows him goodness, and no man hides an evil deed except that God shows him evil.[12]

It is also narrated that the Imām ﷺ said,

> The Messenger of God ﷺ said:
>
> > There will come a time when people will be filthy from the inside but good-looking from the outside due to worldly greed. They will not have any intention of seeking the rewards with God. Their religion will be merely for showoff [riyā'] and not for fear [of the Hereafter]. God will punish them universally, even though they may pray like a drowning person [in desperation], but it will not be accepted.[13]

In this sense, the ugliness of this type of regret is followed by man's grief and guilt over what he has done out of the fear that he strayed from the path toward worldly

---

[12] Kulaynī, Shaykh Muḥammad b. Ya'qūb, *al-Kāfi*, Vol. 2, pp. 293–294.

[13] Ibid., p. 296.

leadership and status—even if disguised in a religious cover. It is narrated that Abū Hasan 🕮 mentioned a man who desires leadership and ruling over others. He said,

> Two ravenous wolves set free in a flock of sheep whose shepherd is absent are not more dangerous to a man's religion than his love for leadership [desire to rule over others].[14]

Moreover, it is narrated that Imām Ja'far aṣ-Ṣādiq 🕮 said,

> Beware of these leaders who pretend to be leaders. I swear by God, people have never marched behind [such] a man except that he destroys [them] and [he] is destroyed.[15]

It appears that what is referred to in these two narrations is the pursuit of leadership without rightful entitlement, similar to what Amīr al-Mu'minīn 🕮 said,

> Beware! By God, the son of Abū Quḥāfah [Abū Bakr] dressed himself with it [the Caliphate] while he certainly knew that my position about it was the same as the position of the axis about the hand-mill...[16]

---

14 Ibid., p. 297.

15 Ibid.

16 Sharīf Raḍī, Muḥammad b. al-Ḥusayn, *Nahj al-Balāghah*, Sermon 3. Majlisī, 'Allāmah Muḥammad Bāqir, *Biḥār al-Anwār*, Vol. 29, p. 497. Ṭabrisī, Shaykh Aḥmad b. 'Alī Ṭabrisī, *al-Iḥtijāj*, Vol. 1, p. 192.

As for the rightful people of leadership, they do not desire leadership for what it is. Rather, they seek it as a means to uphold truth and vanquish falsehood, as evidenced by what Amīr al-Mu'minīn ؑ said,

> Behold, by Him Who split the grain [to grow] and created living beings, if people had not come to me and supporters had not exhausted the argument and if there had been no pledge of God with the learned to the effect that they should not acquiesce in the gluttony of the oppressor and the hunger of the oppressed, I would have cast the rope of Caliphate on its shoulders and would have given the last one the same treatment as to the first one. Then you would have seen that, in my view, this world of yours is no better than the sneezing of a goat...[17]

In another sermon of his ؑ when he set out for war with the people of Baṣrah, 'Abdullāh b. 'Abbās said,

> I entered upon Amīr al-Mu'minīn ؑ at Dhīqār and saw that he was stitching his shoe.
>
> He said to me:
>
>> What is the value of this shoe?

---

[17] Sharīf Raḍī, Muḥammad b. al-Ḥusayn, *Nahj al-Balāghah*, Sermon 3. Majlisī, 'Allāmah Muḥammad Bāqir, *Biḥār al-Anwār*, Vol. 29, p. 497. Ṭabrisī, Shaykh Aḥmad b. 'Alī Ṭabrisī, *al-Iḥtijāj*, Vol. 1, p. 192.

I said:

> It has no value now.

He then said:

> By God, it should have been more dear to me than ruling over you, except that I have to establish right and ward off wrong.[18]

Second Root

In this root of regret, after indulging in much disobedience or his life darkened with the ugliness of sin, the servant realizes that he has invoked the Almighty's wrath against him and has become deserving of His punishment and admonishment. In such a state, if he comes across a verse about punishment or hears the words of someone seeking advice or a righteous, wise person, his mind flashes with the images of Hellfire, and he almost feels its heat on his face, death all around him at the bottom of Hell, yet he is not dead. As a result, intense feelings of regret and grief overwhelm him, and sadness over what he took for granted at the side of God washes over him, fearing the worst of punishments.

While this is a decent form of regret, his return to obedience to God, motivated by this regret, puts him

---

[18] Sharīf Raḍī, Muḥammad b. al-Ḥusayn, *Nahj al-Balāghah*, Sermon 33.

among those who obey God because they fear His punishment or want to avoid a bad turn of fate. This form of regret is praised, as evidenced by how Amīr al-Mu'minīn عليه السلام describes the pious people,

> To them, Hell is also as if they see it and are suffering punishment in it.[19]

In this same sermon, the Imām عليه السلام also said regarding such people of piety,

> When they come across a verse that frightens them of [Hell], they heed it with their hearts and feel as though the sounds of Hell and its cries are reaching their ears. They bend themselves from their backs and prostrate themselves on their foreheads, their palms, their knees, and their toes praying ardently to God to release them [from Hell].[20]

This same notion is highlighted in the following saying of God عز وجل and other verses that remind us of the ugliness that awaits the disobedient,

﴿قُوٓاْ أَنفُسَكُمۡ وَأَهۡلِيكُمۡ نَارٗا وَقُودُهَا ٱلنَّاسُ وَٱلۡحِجَارَةُ﴾

﴾*qū 'anfusakum wa-'ahlīkum nāran waqūduhā n-nāsu wa-l-ḥijāratu*﴿

---

[19] Ibid., Sermon 191.

[20] Ibid., Sermon 191.

﴾Save yourselves and your families from a Fire whose fuel will be people and stones﴿[21]

Third Root

In this form of regret, the disobedient becomes aware of the rewards that he lost and that he has become deserving of being distanced from and denied Paradise and its bliss—its rivers and orchards, its pleasures and delights. That is because it is meant only for those who are pious. Hence, he mourns the greatness of these blessings, which are referenced in the verse:

﴿وَإِذَا رَأَيْتَ ثَمَّ رَأَيْتَ نَعِيمًا وَمُلْكًا كَبِيرًا﴾

﴾wa-'idhā ra'ayta thamma ra'ayta na'īman wa-mulkan kabīran﴿

﴾As you look on, you will see there bliss and a great kingdom﴿[22]

The same is highlighted in Amīr al-Mu'minīn's عليه السلام description of the pious people:

[21] Sūrat at-Taḥrīm, Verse 6.

[22] Sūrat al-Insān, Verse 20.

> They feel Paradise as if it is in front of them and they are in utter bliss in it.[23]

With the power of his mind and insight that God bestowed upon him, he thus realizes that he incurred a great loss and that he deserves to be denied those blessings; he had sought to replace these blessings with a fleeting finite pleasure that led him in the end into a world of grief, regret, and sorrow. He does not know how to regain his right to these blessings or how much crying and sadness could benefit him. Even though regret is the basis of repentance and God promised to accept it—and God does not break His promises—the servant does not know and does not realize that he has been granted repentance and that he achieved it in the sense that is required of him. So, he does not feel reassured, his tears do not cease rolling down his face, and the burden of heartbreak and grief does not lessen. Many righteous servants have slipped up and mistakenly committed some form of disobedience, and their regret and tears have gone on endlessly as they know that whoever has not sinned is better than one who has. So, they cry and seek forgiveness but do not feel they can reach it for certain.

Fourth Root

This form of regret is the highest and noblest of all. The servant reflects upon himself and contemplates what he has done, realizing that he deserves to be rejected from the

---

[23] Sharīf Raḍī, Muḥammad b. al-Ḥusayn, *Nahj al-Balāghah*, Sermon 191.

Lord's door and denied closeness to Him and His pleasure, forbidden from knocking at His door and nearing Him. With his insight, he sees the devoted servants of God who were allowed great ranks of closeness to Him. This, in turn, squeezes his heart with sorrow and pain as he sees himself being cast out from the side of the Divine and forbidden from trying to approach Him. In his mind, sin has cost him the sweetness of conversing with Him and robbed him of the means to ascend to the heights of His mercy. He deserved to lose the pleasure of the Divine, which is more beloved to the servants of God ﷻ than Paradise and is dearer to their hearts than widening the distance between themselves and Hellfire. This notion is evidenced in the verse,

﴿وَرِضْوَانٌ مِّنَ ٱللَّهِ أَكْبَرُ﴾

﴾*wa-riḍwānun mina llāhi 'akbaru*﴿

﴾*Yet God's pleasure is greater [than all these]*﴿[24]

Furthermore, it is narrated that Imām 'Alī ؑ said,

> Sitting in the masjid is more beloved to me than sitting in Paradise, for sitting in Paradise pleases myself, while sitting in the masjid pleases my Lord, and His pleasure is more beloved to me than the pleasure of my self.

[24] Sūrat at-Tawbah, Verse 72.

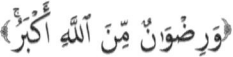

A man should know that the closest of means and shortest of paths toward God ﷻ is his love for Him. Love has been defined as the inclination toward the beloved, and this is an interpretation of necessity because its reality necessitates this inclination and drive to the Beloved and closeness to Him. It may arise from certain actions or activities. It may be a gift from the Grantor of Existence, resulting in attraction between the two who love each other or attraction towards the beloved and the realization of the perfection of the beloved and then being affected by it.

The lover may be attracted to a person or an entity, but he may not distinguish what stands between him and the beloved. So, he merely identifies this feeling of love, imagining that it is all there is to the matter. For instance, the concept of creation proposes that an innate attraction pulls the servant-given existence toward the Granter of Existence and His blessings. However, he may be ignorant of the source of these blessings so that he may attribute them to others or associate equals to God, Who granted him these blessings through his ignorance, thus going astray and losing his way. As such, it becomes clear that knowledge of the source of all good and all honor saves a person from this ambiguity, and we realize the extent of the delusion and confusion that have come to surround the definitions of love and its purpose.

Attention:

Instincts might overpower the mind, and the sound soul or the power of imagination may take over, leading to the person getting lost in the blur of temporary desires and the darkness of mortal pleasures. Hence, he perceives all things that satisfy these desires to be good. For instance, his sexual instinct may stir, making anything that might cater to it appear appealing and attractive—this is similar to realistic love. But after the night clears, this feeling fades. Reality sets in: he finally sees the ugliness of what he had initially perceived as beautiful and realizes how it is, in fact, not suitable for him as he had thought, and what he had thought to be an oasis of water turned out to be a mirage. Ultimately, one can only be rid of the shackles of imagination and instinct through the guidance of God ﷻ, or he must be a human of holy status, such as Imām ʿAlī ؑ, who said:

> Get away from me, O world. Your rein is on your shoulders as I have released myself from your claws, removed myself from your snares, and avoided walking into your slippery places. Where are those whom you have deceived by your jokes? Where are those communities whom you have enticed with your embellishments? They are all confined to graves and hidden in burial places. By God, if you had been a visible personality and a body capable of feeling, I would have awarded you the penalties fixed by God because of the people whom you seduced through

desires, the communities whom you threw into destruction, and the rulers whom you consigned to ruin and drove to places of distress after which there is neither going nor returning. Indeed, whoever stepped on your slippery place slipped, rode your waves were drowned, and evaded your snares received inward support. He who keeps himself safe from you does not worry even though his affairs may be straitened, and the world to him is like a near-expiring day. Get away from me, for, by God, I do not bow before you so that you may humiliate me, nor do I let loose the reins for you so that you may drive me away. I swear by God an oath wherein I, except for the will of God, shall so train myself that it will feel joyful if it gets one loaf for eating and be content with only salt to season it. I shall let my eyes empty themselves of tears like the stream whose water has flown away. Should ʿAlī eat whatever he has and fall asleep like the cattle who fill their stomachs from the pasture land and lie down, or as the goats (who) graze, eat the green grass and go into their pen! His eyes may die if he, after long years, follows loose cattle and pasturing animals. Blessed is he who discharges his obligations towards God and endures his hardships, allows himself no sleep in the night, but when sleep overpowers him, lies down on the ground using his hand as a pillow, along with those who keep their eyes wakeful in fear of the Day of Judgement, whose bodies are ever away from beds, whose lips are humming in remembrance of God and whose sins have been erased through their prolonged beseechings for forgiveness.

﴿أُوْلَٰٓئِكَ حِزْبُ ٱللَّهِ أَلَآ إِنَّ حِزْبَ ٱللَّهِ هُمُ ٱلْمُفْلِحُونَ﴾

﴿*ulā'ika ḥizbu llāhi 'a-lā 'inna ḥizba llāhi humu l-mufliḥūna*﴾

﴿*They are God's confederates. Look! The confederates of God are indeed felicitous!*﴾[25] [26]

As love has been established as the compatibility and suitability that leads to attraction, much has been said about what accompanies it. For instance, it has been reported that love is a type of will and that the servants' love for their Lord involves obeying Him, seeking His pleasure, and avoiding what brings forth His wrath and punishment. As for the love of God ﷻ for His servants, we see it in the way He wants to honor them and reward them, to be pleased with them and preserve them from sin,[27] all of which are the results of His love.

---

[25] Sūrat al-Mujādilah, Verse 22,

[26] Sharīf Raḍī, Muḥammad b. al-Ḥusayn, *Nahj al-Balāghah*, part of Imām 'Alī's letter to his governor of Baṣrah, 'Uthmān b. Ḥunayf al-Anṣārī, letter number 45.

[27] Al-Ḥusaynī, Sayyid 'Alī Khān, *Riyāḍ al-Sālikīn*, Vol. 2, p. 254.

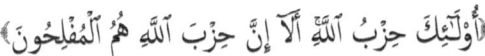

Similarly, we also defined love as the perception of perfection, which is a main influence; the greater the realization and the more perfect the beloved, the deeper and more complete the love.[28] This is also a result of love, for this realization is an action that stems from love.

Many other well-known interpretations of love exist. For instance, it is defined as the heart forgetting about everything else besides the beloved, and it is clear that love precedes this annihilation of everything else. Similarly, it is said that love is a fire that burns everything except the desired beloved. Another saying is that love is agreement in all cases and situations, and another states that it is investing effort and that the lover does what he wants. It is also said that love is being inclined toward something in your entirety, then preferring it over yourself, then favoring it in secret and public in both what pleases and displeases you, and then knowing that you have failed in its right. Another saying is that a bad act cannot diminish that love, cannot be increased with goodness, cannot be forgotten with nearness, nor diverted with distance. Ultimately, all these meanings stem from one thing: love.

Furthermore, some dignitaries have stated that love depends on knowledge and perception, which is divided according to the various divisions of senses and tangibles. Every sense perceives one form of tangible elements, and each brings forth a unique pleasure related to the

---

[28] Ibid.

component it perceives, eliciting an inclination toward it like the perceiver. Thus, they become beloved to the person of a sound nature, for the pleasure of the eye is in seeing and perceiving beautiful things, the joy of the ear is hearing sweet and soothing tunes, the joy of the nose is smelling sweet scents, the pleasure of the tongue is in tasting good food. The joy of the skin is in touching something soft and smooth. Once the senses perceive elements as pleasurable, they become beloved, creating an inclination toward them in the person of a sound nature. This is evidenced in the saying of Prophet Muḥammad ﷺ,

> What I love the most in this world are women and perfume [in the context of encouraging marriage], and praying lights up my eyes.[29]

He provided examples of the reasons that drive [such] inclination, including the inclination toward always existing and the repulsion from not existing and perishing. Another example is benevolence and how man is a slave for benevolence, for a heart beats with love for those who do good to it. This is supported by the narration that reports that Prophet Muḥammad ﷺ said,

---

[29] Fayḍ Kāshānī, Mullā Muḥammad b. Murtaḍā, *al-Maḥajja al-Bayḍā' fī Tahdhīb al-Iḥyā'*, Vol. 8, pp. 8–9.

> O God, do not make the immoral lend me a hand [do good to me] such that my heart grows to love him.[30]

Man is inclined toward the beloved's self owing to their beauty and goodness, and perhaps the love is cemented once the souls find themselves matching and compatible. It is reported that the Prophet ﷺ said,

> Souls are grouped in batches; they feel familiar with those whom they know well and disagree with those whom they disapprove of.

However, it is prudent that we know that the Holy Prophet ﷺ related the reasons for love to its consequences of inclination toward the beloved, and he made these reasons to be the source of pleasure via perception. But if you were to contemplate the meaning of love, you would find that this perception and pleasure are consequences of love and not reasons that lead to it.

Moreover, I am surprised that he considers man's true love for the Creator and his inclination toward Him to be driven by pleasure, whichever way it is interpreted.

What should be said is that love is compatibility and suitability that lead to attraction, and this is a universal aspect that happens at some of its levels by way of divine decree and predestination and other levels by gaining it

---

30 Majlisī, ʿAllāmah Muḥammad Bāqir, *Biḥār al-Anwār*, Vol. 83, p. 186.

through worship, obedience, and actions that lead to the outcome and meaning of love [for God] we highlighted. As we are [by nature] ignorant of the ways that lead us to this meaning, we must be provided with these ways and actions, and this is the wisdom and reason behind the existence of legitimate, decreed acts of worship. Perhaps this is what the following Qudsi ḥadīth refers to:

> Whoever insults any of My friends has waged a war against Me. Whoever of the servants seeks closeness to Me should know that there is nothing in that matter more beloved to Me than his fulfilling his obligations, and he should seek nearness to Me by performing optional acts so I may love him; when I love him, I will be his ears with which he will hear, his eyes with which he will see, his tongue with which he will speak and his hands with which he will perform his activities. Whenever he prays, I answer. Whenever he asks for help, I will help him. I have not so much hesitated in all that I do as my hesitation at the time of the death of a believer who dislikes death, and I dislike disappointing him.[31]

This is in addition to what has been narrated,

> My servant, obey Me so that you become like Me...

[31] Kulaynī, Shaykh Muḥammad b. Yaʿqūb, *al-Kāfī*, Vol. 2, p. 352.

All in all, this was a comprehensive overview of the first condition.

Second Condition

It is to abstain from the sin and resolve not to return it.

Know that abstaining from sin, resolving not to return to it, and regretting it can only be achieved after familiarizing yourself with it. In this regard, sins are divided into two categories:

The first is obvious and apparent; it is the sin that we know or can be known among the sins mentioned in Islāmic Law and prohibited by the Islāmic legislator. Scholars have highlighted and interpreted these sins in detailed books specific to them.

The second is the hidden, and it is the sin that man commits due to the ugliness of his heart [inner self] and wicked behavior. He thus returns again and again to his ugly path and fate, and most of the time, he remains ignorant [of this state and these sins] all his life unless God protects him and alerts him of his ignorance. His mercy and compassion guide him away from his faults and protect him from his stumble in the dark.

Often, a man busies himself with worship, exhausting himself and investing in all his time and energy, claiming all this to be genuine worship. Yet, in its core and reality, it is disobedience, increasing only distance from God ﷻ no matter how long he engages in it. That is because he is doing these acts of worship while thinking he is fulfilling his obligatory duty to the fullest; that is, he believes he has perfectly obeyed God. If you, dear reader, were to contemplate your deeds, you would find that many of them are also done in this way; you think that you performed ablution in the required way, that you made ghusl in the way that is needed, or that you prayed in the way that is needed. The mere act of suspecting and thinking that one is worshiping God perfectly as needed and the ignorance that afflicts the ignorants and those who are lost in life lead them to slip into disobedience and leave the boundaries of servitude and obedience. Even the infallible ﵇ did not adopt such a mindset; the following is recited in the supplications reported from Imām Zayn al-ʿĀbidīn ﵇:

> O God, no one reaches a limit in thanking You without acquiring that of Your beneficence which enjoins upon him thanksgiving, nor does anyone reach a degree in obeying You, even if he strives without falling short of what You deserve because of Your bounty. The most thankful of Your servants cannot thank You, and the most worshipful of them fall short of obeying You. None of them is due Your forgiveness through what he deserves or Your good pleasure for his merit. When You forgive someone, it is through Your graciousness, and

> when You are pleased with someone, it is through Your bounty.[32]

The same is also highlighted by the Master of the Martyrs Imām al-Ḥusayn ﷺ in his Du'ā' 'Arafah:

> ...[by all that I bear witness] that if I try my best and strive throughout all ages and all times, if I live them, to thank properly only one of Your favors, I will not be able to do that, except through a favor of You, which also requires me to thank You for it, once again with new thanking and with praise that is newly acquired and newly prepared. True is this! And if I try hard, as well as the counters from Your creatures, to count the scope of Your favoring, both the past and the present, we shall never be able to calculate it in number or count it in time. Too far is this! How can it be? While it is You Who has informed in Your rational Book and true news:

﴿وَإِن تَعُدُّواْ نِعۡمَةَ ٱللَّهِ لَا تُحۡصُوهَآ﴾

﴾wa-'in ta'uddū ni'mata llāhi lā tuḥṣūhā﴿

﴾If you enumerate God's blessings, you will not be able to count them﴿[33]

[32] Imām Zayn al-'Ābidīn ﷺ, *al-Ṣaḥīfah al-Sajjādīyyah*, the Imām's supplication when confessing his shortcomings in giving thanks.

[33] Sūrat an-Naḥl, Verse 18.

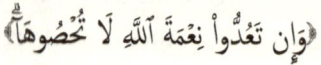

> True is Your book, O God, and Your informing. Your Prophets and Messengers have conveyed what You revealed to them, from Your Revelation, and what You have made plain for them and through them Your religion.[34]

If you were to contemplate your acts of worship, you would find the danger of this ugliness in its beginning, middle, or end, and it is an astonishing concept that destroys whoever is afflicted with it. If you were to think frankly, you would find that all your worship falls under this disobedience. Then you realize the extent of the Almighty's kindness and benevolence as He overlooks you [the disobedience in your worship], includes you among those who are obedient to Him, and allows you to stand in the line of His righteous servants. He will enable His servants to label you with the characteristics of the pious ones, such as the one who prays, the one who fasts, an educated person, a scholar, and so on, although He knows what you truly are and your reality.

Continuing with such a thought and mindset is continuing with sin and persistence in misguidance. That is why the pious disavow such possibilities [of thought] and ask God for help and aid to get rid of the pitfalls of the consequences of such a mindset and belief, as highlighted by Imām ʿAlī ﷺ in his description of the pious,

---

[34] See books on supplication, including the chapter on deeds for the day of ʿArafah in Mafātīḥ al-Jinān.

When anyone of them is spoken of highly, he says:

> I know myself better than others, and my Lord knows me better than I know. O God, do not deal with me according to what they say, and make me better than they think of me and forgive me (for those shortcomings) which they do not know.[35]

As previously established, repentance is to turn back from sin to the One Who conceals faults and knows the unseen, but this return differs according to the disobedience committed. For instance, there are two types of sin. First, regarding sins considered disobedience between the servant and his Lord, such as refraining from praying, fasting, and other similar obligatory duties, one returns from them and repents through regret over what has been done and is determined not to repeat what he has committed. This type of disobedience is also divided into two categories:

The first category of these sins is the one that does not need to be made up for with action, meaning that one does not have to do Qaḍāʾ [compensation] for it. It is sufficient to abstain from committing it, feel regret, be determined to turn back from it, and seek forgiveness from God over what he did—this will later be highlighted.

---

[35] Sharīf Raḍī, Muḥammad b. al-Ḥusayn, *Nahj al-Balāghah*, from the Sermon of Hammām, which is known for the characteristics of the pious, no. 191.

The second category of these sins is the one that must be made up for with Qaḍā', such as prayer, fasting, and pilgrimage. One who abandons any of these obligatory duties can only repent by feeling regret as expressed previously, being determined to commit to the right path of obedience, and compensating for what he missed in his duties [making Qaḍā' prayer, fasting, etc.].

That is regarding disobedience between the servant and his Lord, and it is noteworthy that if the sin is not shirk [polytheism], then it is easier [to repent] than the following sin that will be discussed. That is because the servant finds forgiveness for the aforementioned sins nearer and can be more hopeful of attaining it. In a narration attributed to Amīr al-Mu'minīn عليه السلام:

> ...Sins are of three kinds: a sin that is forgiven, a sin that is not forgiven, and a sin for whose owner we have hopes and fears.[36]

The Imām عليه السلام was then asked,

> O Amīr al-Mu'minīn, explain them for us.

The Imām عليه السلام said,

> Yes, the sin that is forgiven is one for which God has punished the sinner in this world, and He is by far much Forbearing and Honorable to punish His servant

[36] Kulaynī, Shaykh Muḥammad b. Ya'qūb, *al-Kāfī*.

> twice. The sin that is not forgiven is people's injustice to each other (in matters of property and so forth). When God, the Most Blessed, the Highest, will manifest himself to His creatures, He will swear by His Ownself saying,
>
> > By My Majesty and Glory that the injustice of the unjust cannot bypass Me, even though it is in the form of a slap for a slap, a nibbling for a slap, or blow by those having horns to those without horns.
>
> He will retaliate for His servants from the others until no one is left without receiving justice, and they are sent for reckoning. The third kind of sin is the sin that God has covered up for His servants and has granted them repentance. He lives in fear because of his sin with hopes in his Lord. We are toward him just as he is to himself. We wish he will be granted mercy and fear for his suffering punishment.[37]

The second type of sin includes sins related to other people and their rights, such as withholding Zakāt [almsgiving], killing a person, usurping unlawful money, cursing people's honors, and usurping the rights of others. In addition to this, other such sins include manipulating people against religion by temptation and heresy, enticing them toward sin, and encouraging boldness against God, as

[37] Kulaynī, Shaykh Muḥammad b. Ya'qūb, *al-Kāfī*, Vol. 2, p. 443.

some preachers may do. In this way, hope [in God's mercy] overpowers and eliminates the fear [of God] in people, facilitating their disobedience and causing the loss of people's rights to guidance to the path of salvation. The preacher has thus led them astray, and it is narrated that whoever is the reason for someone going astray will not be forgiven unless he guides whom he led astray to the right path again.

These are the sins that are related to other people; it is prudent that one rectify any such act of transgression against others, for repentance from such sins can only be achieved by remedying this transgression of rights, as evidenced by the aforementioned narration and other narrations such as one reported on the authority of Imām Muḥammad al-Bāqir ﷺ:

> There are three types of injustice: an injustice that God will forgive, an injustice that He will not forgive, and an injustice that He will not neglect. As for the injustice that God will not forgive, it is associating partners with God. As for the injustice that He will forgive, it is when one commits an injustice towards himself in a matter that is between him and God. As for that which He will not neglect, it is the [ill] treatment of others.[38]

---

[38] al-Ḥurr al-ʿĀmilī, Shaykh Muḥammad, *Wasāʾil al-Shīʿah*, Chapter 52; Kulaynī, Shaykh Muḥammad b. Yaʿqūb, *al-Kāfī*.

Shaykh Ṣadūq ﵀ also reported on the authority of Imām Ja'far aṣ-Ṣādiq ﵇ in the same narration, adding the following,

> What the oppressed takes from the religion of the oppressor is more than what the oppressor takes from the world of the oppressed.[39]

Furthermore, 'Alī b. Ibrāhīm narrated on the authority of a Shaykh from Nakhā' who said,

> I once asked Abī Ja'far ﵇,
>
> > I have been working as a governor from the time of al-Ḥajjāj to this time, can my repentance be accepted?
>
> The Imām remained quiet. I repeated my question, and then he said,
>
> > No, not until you pay back everything that you owe to the people.[40]

Similarly, it is narrated that Imām Ja'far aṣ-Ṣādiq ﵇ said,

> The Messenger of God ﷺ said,

[39] Ibid.

[40] Ibid.

> One who usurps the wealth of a believer unlawfully, God will have hatred and enmity with him and his good deeds will not be accepted till he repents and returns the wealth to its owner.[41]

Attention

Know, dear reader, that no one in existence deserves, and it is more important for you to seek to fulfill his right than God ﷻ. For He bestowed upon you the blessing of existence and gave you uncountable, hidden, and apparent blessings. He invited you to thankfulness and promised you even more if you tread the path of those who are thankful to Him, as He said,

﴿لَئِن شَكَرْتُمْ لَأَزِيدَنَّكُمْ﴾

﴿la-'in shakartum la-'azīdannakum﴾

﴿If you are grateful, I will surely enhance you [in blessing]﴾[42]

If you were to contemplate His blessings and realize that you cannot give thanks for anything except with His approval and guidance and the strength He gave you, you would know that this makes Him even more deserving of your thanks. That is why the prophets, the Imāms, and the righteous always confessed that it is impossible to give

[41] Ibid.

[42] Sūrat Ibrāhīm, Verse 7.

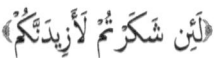

sufficient thanks, and that is why it is said that one can give thanks for every blessing except the blessing of God. Man must thank God for the blessing and then for [the opportunity of] endlessly giving thanks—no end. Rather, its end is in its beginning. Therefore, from the start, one must express his inability to provide sufficient thanks to God and admit to falling short. In this way, the knowledge of falling short in thankfulness also becomes a form of thankfulness. Otherwise, how else would the servants thank their Lord, the Most Magnanimous? How incomparable is the finite, mortal being compared to the Immortal One, who diminishes compared to the One Who does not perish? As such, we become aware that we cannot fulfill His right of worship as He deserves. And as we cannot fulfill God's rights in thankfulness, worship, obedience, and inclination to His divine sanctuary and the warmth of His kindness, we cannot meet the rights of the prophets and infallible Imāms عليهم السلام.

As for the rights of the people, we have highlighted their material rights. Regarding their non-material rights, if one misleads and misguides another, then he must guide him back again [as a way to repent from this action]. Suppose a case would require Qiṣāṣ [i.e., retaliation in kind (eye for eye), retribution]. In that case, the transgressor must confess to the person against whom the transgression was done and make it possible for the deserving party to fulfill the Qiṣāṣ and retaliate. For instance, he would say,

> I am the one who killed your father, so if you seek retaliation, then take it from me. If you choose forgiveness, then pardon me.

Furthermore, regarding punishment in the case of slander [such as accusation of adultery], if the person is made aware of the slander against him, he must be capable of punishment.[43] But what about if he was not aware of the slander? Should he be informed or not? There are two aspects to this matter: First, as it is a human right, it does not expire except through the pardon of the offended party. On the other hand, informing the offended party serves as a renewal of harm and alerts them to what may foster animosity. Similarly, this principle applies to cases of backbiting.[44]

A man should ask God, the Creator and the Most Capable, for assistance in fulfilling the rights of people owed by him, and that is why the following is recited in the supplication of Imām Zayn al-ʿĀbidīn عليه السلام,

> O God if there is a servant from among Your servants whom an ill visits on my account, harm touches from my direction, or a wrong overtakes through me or because of me, and should I fail to take care of his right or go before him [in death] with his complaint, bless

[43] Al-Ḥusaynī, Sayyid ʿAlī Khān, *Riyāḍ al-Sālikīn*, Vol. 3, p. 234.

[44] According to al-Ṭūsī and his study al-ʿAllāmah, it is not obligatory to inform the person.

> Muḥammad and his Household, satisfy him toward me through Your wealth, and give him his full right from Yourself! Then protect me from what Your decision mandates and save me from what Your justice decides, for my strength, cannot bear Your vengeance, and my power cannot stand up to Your displeasure! If You recompense me with the right, You will destroy me, and if You do not shield me in Your mercy, You will lay me waste.[45]

The rights of the believer are those that are made obligatory by the brotherhood of faith, as highlighted by Imām Jaʿfar aṣ-Ṣādiq ﷺ,

> God has never been worshiped with anything better than fulfilling the right of a believer.[46]

Furthermore, Shaykh Kulaynī ؒ dedicated a chapter in *al-Kāfī* on the rights of the believer upon his brother in faith and the fulfillment of these rights. Below are some narrations from this chapter:

The following narration reports the authority of al-Muʿallā b. Khānis regarding Imām Jaʿfar aṣ-Ṣādiq ﷺ:

> Once I asked the Imām,

---

[45] Imām Zayn al-ʿĀbidīn ﷺ, *al-Ṣaḥīfah al-Sajjādīyyah*, supplication 39.

[46] Kulaynī, Shaykh Muḥammad b. Yaʿqūb, *al-Kāfī*, Vol. 2, p. 170.

What are the rights of the Muslim on the Muslim?

The Imām said,

> He has seven categories of obligatory rights, each of which is compulsory. If he jeopardizes one of them, he is out of the domain of guardianship (Wilāyah) of God and obedience to Him. There will be no share for God in him.

I said,

> May God keep my soul in service for your cause; what are these rights?

The Imām said,

> O Muʿallā, I am afraid you may jeopardize them and may not protect them. You learn them but do not act upon them.

I (the narrator) said,

> There is no power without the power of God.

The Imām said,

> Of those rights, the easiest to fulfill is to love for him what you love for yourself and dislike for him what you dislike for yourself. The second right is to avoid (stirring) his anger, follow his wishes, and

> obey his commands. The third right is to support him with your soul, property, tongue, hands, and legs. The fourth right is to be his eyes, guide, and mirror. The fifth right is that you must not be satisfied with food while he is hungry, with drinks while he is thirsty and that you dress up in finery while he has no clothes. The sixth right is not to allow yourself to have a servant while your brother does not. It then is necessary to send your servant to wash his clothes and prepare food and his bed for him. The seventh right is to keep his share handsomely, accept his invitations, visit him when he is ill, attend his funeral, and, if he needs something, take the initiative to fulfill it. Do not delay until he asks you for help. You must hurry quickly, and when you do so, you have connected your guardianship with his guardianship and vice versa.[47]

One narration reports that Imām Ja'far aṣ-Ṣādiq ﷺ said,

> Of the rights of the believer on his brother [in faith] is to satisfy his hunger, provide cover for his privacy, facilitate his hardships, pay off his debts, and, when he dies, look after his family and children.[48]

---

[47] Ibid., p. 169.

[48] Ibid.

Another narration reports that Imām Ja'far aṣ-Ṣādiq ﷺ said,

> Of the rights of the believer on the believer is to have compassion for him in his heart, assist him with his property, protect his interests in his absence in the matters of his family and support him against those who do injustice to him. If a benefit is distributed among the Muslims in his absence, his believing brother should secure his share. When he dies, he should visit his grave, and he must not do injustice to him, must not deceive him, must not violate his trust, must not betray him, must not call him a liar. He must not say to him, 'Fie upon you [expression of anger or disapproval],' if he does so, then no guardianship (Wilāyah) relations will remain between them. If he says, 'You are my enemy,' one of them becomes an unbeliever, and if he accuses him, belief in his heart will melt as salt melts in water.[49]

Furthermore, Muḥammad b. 'Ajlān narrated the following:

> Once, I was in the presence of Imām Ja'far aṣ-Ṣādiq ﷺ when a man came and offered the greeting of peace.
>
> The Imām asked,

[49] Ibid., p. 171.

> How are your brothers [in faith] whom you have left behind?

He praised, admired, and extolled them.

The Imām asked,

> Do their wealthy ones visit their poor ones?

He said,

> It is very rare.

The Imām asked,

> Do their rich ones reach out to the poor ones?

He said,

> It is very rare.

The Imām asked,

> Do their rich ones maintain good relations with their poor ones financially?

He said,

> You are speaking of moral behavior practiced rarely in our people.

The Imām then asked,

> Why do you then claim that they are Shī'ah [Muslims]?[50]

Shahīd Thānī ﵀ reported with a chain of narrators [sanad] that Amīr al-Mu'minīn ﵇ said,

> The Messenger of God ﷺ said:
>
> > There are thirty rights for each Muslim incumbent upon his believing brother. He cannot be relieved from them unless he honors them or is forgiven by his brother. They are as follows:

1. He must forgive his brother's faults.
2. He must be kind to his brother during hard times.
3. He must hide his brother's secrets.
4. He must compensate for his brother's faults.
5. He must accept his brother's apologies.
6. He must defend his brother against those who gossip behind his back.

---

[50] Ibid., p. 173.

7. He must always advise his brother.
8. He must safeguard his brother's friendship.
9. He must honor his brother's covenant.
10. He must visit him when his brother gets ill.
11. He must attend his brother's funeral procession.
12. He must accept his brother's invitations.
13. He must accept his brother's gifts.
14. He must return his brother's favors.
15. He must be grateful for his brother's blessings.
16. He must try to help his brother.
17. He must guard his brother's honor.
18. He must fulfill his brother's needs.
19. He must intercede on behalf of his brother.
20. He must say "God bless you" when his brother sneezes.
21. He must guide his brother in case he loses his way.
22. He must respond to his brother's greetings.

23. He must welcome his brother's words.

24. He must welcome his brother's kindness.

25. He must accept and believe his brother's swearing.

26. He must stand by his brother.

27. He must not treat his brother with animosity.

28. He must help his brother whether he is an oppressor or an oppressed one; if he is an oppressor, he must prevent and turn him away from his oppression; if he is oppressed, he must help him take his right.

29. He should not leave his brother alone in the face of calamities.

30. He must like for his brother whatever he likes for himself and dislike for him whatever he dislikes for himself.

Then Imām ʿAlī ﷺ said,

> Verily, one of you may relinquish a right owed to his brother in this world, but on the Day of Resurrection, that right will be demanded from him, and it will be settled between them.[51]

---

[51] Shahīd Thānī, Zayn al-Dīn al-ʿAmilī al-Jubaʿī, *Kashf al-Rībah ʿan Aḥkām al-Ghībah*, p. 115.

Another narration reports that Imām Ja'far aṣ-Ṣādiq ﷺ said,

> My father told me from his fathers from Imām 'Alī ﷺ about Prophet Muḥammad ﷺ that he said:
>
> > A lower degree of kufr is for a man to hear something from his brother and to commit it to his memory intending thereby to cause him humiliation. Such persons shall have no share [in the Hereafter].[52]

The same implications are also prominent in the supplication of Imām Zayn al-'Ābidīn ﷺ, where he said,

> O God, I ask pardon from You for the person wronged in my presence whom I did not help, the favor conferred upon me for which I returned no thanks, the evildoer who asked pardon from me and whom I did not pardon, the needy person who asked from me and whom I preferred not over myself, the right of a believer who possesses a right incumbent upon me which I did not fulfill, the fault of a believer which became evident to me and which I did not conceal, and every sin which presented itself to me and which I failed to avoid.[53]

---

[52] Ibid., p. 130.

[53] Imām Zayn al-'Ābidīn ﷺ, *al-Ṣaḥīfah al-Sajjādīyyah*, Supplication no. 38.

Third Condition

It is for man not to forget his sins and, instead, to always recall them so that he remains in fear and awe of God's judgment if He does not accept his repentance due to shortcomings or deficiencies in his sincerity. Thus, remorse continues to squeeze his heart and motivates him to stay away from the clutches of Shayṭān and the inclinations of their souls, which have the potential for evil. In this regard, Shaykh Kulaynī 🕮 narrated the following on the authority of some of the companions of Imām Jaʿfar aṣ-Ṣādiq 🕮:

> I heard him [Imām Jaʿfar aṣ-Ṣādiq] saying,
>
>> A man commits a sin and because of it, God will admit him into Paradise.
>
> I asked,
>
>> Will God admit him into Paradise because of his sin?
>
> The Imām said,
>
>> Yes, he commits a sin and continues living in fear and anger at himself. God then grants him mercy and admits him into Paradise.[54]

---

[54] Kulaynī, Shaykh Muḥammad b. Yaʿqūb, al-Kāfī, Vol. 2, p. 426.

Furthermore, we infer from some narrations that God ﷻ does not leave His believing servants to be heedless of their sins and disobedience, so they continue to feel remorse for what they have committed and hope for His forgiveness. Thus, in repentance, it is appropriate for the servants to remember their sins, acknowledge them, and confess their shortcomings before their Lord. In this regard, it has been narrated that confessing sins with remorse and seeking forgiveness and pardon brings God's forgiveness and draws His mercy upon the repentant soul. One such narration reports that Imām Muḥammad al-Bāqir ؑ said,

> By God! No one can be saved from sin unless he confesses to [committing] it.[55]

Moreover, it is also narrated that Imām Muḥammad al-Bāqir ؑ said,

> I swear by God that God has only asked from the people to do the following two: to acknowledge [and thank for] His blessings so that He may increase them and to confess to their sins so that He may forgive them.[56]

It is also reported that Imām Jaʿfar aṣ-Ṣādiq ؑ said,

---

[55] Ibid.

[56] Ibid.

> God loves it when a servant asks it when a servant asks Him for help in major sins, and He hates it when a servant considers it when a servant considers trivial sins insignificant.[57]

Similarly, it is also reported that Imām Ja'far aṣ-Ṣādiq ﷺ said,

> By God! A servant cannot escape a sin escape, a sin while persisting in it nor without confessing to it.[58]

As for the one who indulges in disobedience and the darkness of sins engulfs the light of his intellect, his inner self darkening. At the same time, he persistently ventures deeper into corruption; he becomes heedless of the immoral acts he has committed. As such, he does not recognize those to whom he has caused financial harm, violated their dignity, shed their blood, or those he has been involved in killing. Likewise, he forgets all about the believers he backbites or committed shameful acts against and the sins he committed between himself and his Lord. Thus, you may find such a person enjoying abundant blessings all day and all night, seemingly prosperous and content yet unaware that he is being lured into a trap. God refers to such people in the following verses:

---

[57] Ibid., p. 427.

[58] Ibid., pp. 426–427.

﴿فَلَمَّا نَسُوا۟ مَا ذُكِّرُوا۟ بِهِۦ فَتَحْنَا عَلَيْهِمْ أَبْوَٰبَ كُلِّ شَىْءٍ حَتَّىٰٓ إِذَا فَرِحُوا۟ بِمَآ أُوتُوٓا۟ أَخَذْنَٰهُم بَغْتَةً فَإِذَا هُم مُّبْلِسُونَ﴾

﴾fa-lammā nasū mā dhukkirū bihī fataḥnā ʿalayhim ʾabwāba kulli shayʾin ḥattā ʾidhā fariḥū bi-mā ʾūtū ʾakhadhnāhum baghtatan fa-ʾidhā hum mublisūna﴿

﴾So when they forgot what they had been admonished of, We opened for them the gates of all [good] things. When they became proud of what they were given, We seized them suddenly, whereat, behold, they were despondent﴿[59]

and

﴿وَٱلَّذِينَ كَذَّبُوا۟ بِـَٔايَٰتِنَا سَنَسْتَدْرِجُهُم مِّنْ حَيْثُ لَا يَعْلَمُونَ﴾

﴾wa-lladhīna kadhdhabū bi-ʾāyātinā sa-nastadrijuhum min ḥaythu lā yaʿlamūna﴿

﴾As for those who deny Our signs, We will draw them imperceptibly [into ruin], whence they do not know﴿[60]

Yet, this does not mean that the door of repentance has been closed for him. Rather, it signifies that due to his poor choices and the ugliness of his inner self and intentions, he

59 Sūrat al-Anʿām, Verse 44.

60 Sūrat al-Aʿrāf, Verse 182.

has turned his face away from the mercy of God, and his soul has become receptive to the influence of Shayṭān. Misery has overtaken him as a consequence of his own willful decisions. However, God ﷻ does not completely deprive him of His mercy. He occasionally puts him through situations that may guide him towards the right path, such as God having a full argument against him, while the servant does not argue against his Lord.

Fourth Condition

It is for man to distance himself from the conditions and circumstances surrounding him when he committed his disobedience, which encouraged and facilitated the means of transgression. He must also abandon the people he was with during his disobedience, and perhaps that is what God ﷻ refers to in this verse,

﴿رَبَّنَآ أَخْرِجْنَا مِنْ هَـٰذِهِ ٱلْقَرْيَةِ ٱلظَّالِمِ أَهْلُهَا﴾

﴿rabbanā ʾakhrijnā min hādhihi l-qaryati ẓ-ẓālimi ʾahluhā﴾

﴿Our Lord, bring us out of this town whose people are oppressors﴾[61]

Yes, if that group of people repented and returned to God's path, then staying with them thereafter would perhaps

[61] Sūrat an-Nisā', Verse 75.

help him continue in his repentance and pursuit of forgiveness, but that would be another matter altogether.

Fifth Condition

It is for man to make up for the acts of worship he missed during his days of heedlessness and sins, such as missed prayers, fasting, and other acts of worship, and to strive to repeat what he has performed of those acts as an extra precaution [to protect] his religion. This is because he does not know if those deeds were accepted, and [if] an ordinary servant who is not infallible suspects that his deeds are not valid, he repeats them. Indeed, several of our great scholars have done this. It is narrated that al-ʿAllāmah al-Ḥillī قدس سره repeated all his prayers three times. He advised his son, Khaṭīb al-Muhajjat قدس سره, to repeat his prayers and fasts as an extra precaution. Likewise, our great master, Sayyid Abū al-Qāsim al-Khū'ī, advised his son, the scholar Sayyid Muḥammad Taqī al-Khū'ī قدس سره with the same. Moreover, even if a servant knows that his prayers, for example, were valid, he may also repeat them out of precaution, considering that they might not have been performed in the manner expected from him, with the proper focus, attention, and devotion to God, as it is known that the only prayers accepted by God are those that are performed with sincerity and devotion to Him.

Moving on, among these sins, some are related to other people's rights, and some are related to other people's rights but may not involve financial matters. Instead, they pertain to personal dignity and reputation, such as backbiting someone, making false accusations against them, or belittling their status in any context. There is no excuse for such sins, and the person does not deserve forgiveness from God unless they seek forgiveness from the person they wronged—if possible—even if it requires him to humble himself and admit the wrongdoing before the offended party. He should not hesitate to do so, as humbling oneself momentarily in front of some of God's servants is lighter and easier than the shame on the Day of Judgment. Indeed, some ignorant individuals might consider such an act demeaning, but the Master of the Martyrs, Imām Husayn ﷺ, said:

> Death is better than embarking on [a life of] indignity
>
> And indignity is preferable over plunging into Hellfire

No disgrace or shame exceeds the shame of entering Hellfire. In light of this, the following verse conveys supplication of sincere believers,

﴿رَبَّنَآ إِنَّكَ مَن تُدۡخِلِ ٱلنَّارَ فَقَدۡ أَخۡزَيۡتَهُۥۖ وَمَا لِلظَّٰلِمِينَ مِنۡ أَنصَارٖ﴾

﴾rabbanā ʾinnaka man tudkhili n-nāra fa-qad ʾakhzaytahū wa-mā li-ẓ-ẓālimīna min ʾanṣārin﴿

﴾Our Lord, whoever that You make enter the Fire will surely have been disgraced by You, and the wrongdoers will have no helpers﴿[62]

Sixth Condition

It is for man to ask God for forgiveness and pardon and simultaneously admit to his shortcomings and persist in this.

Know, dear reader, that seeking forgiveness [Istighfār] is an act of worship, and the ordinary servant is not exempt from this obligation as he is not free of sin and slip-ups. Although hope in God's mercy is essential, we must also realize that an individual's time in disobedience cannot be reclaimed. The act of seeking forgiveness during repentance occurs at a different time than when those sins were committed. If the servant reflects on the loss of the time spent away from the mercy of God and closeness to Him, it would be enough to make him weep for his entire life. Even if he were to weep, recovering that lost time would not be possible.

Indeed, it is mentioned that a repentant person is one without sin, especially when their repentance is accepted and their pursuit of forgiveness is answered. How could one know for sure? However, the most that can be achieved through repentance is removing that particular

[62] Sūrat Āl 'Imrān, Verse 192.

sin from one's record of deeds. But the time spent in disobedience yielded no good; it was undoubtedly a loss that cannot be compensated.

Furthermore, forgiveness can only be achieved after going through six stages that Imām ʿAlī ؑ clarified when someone said Astaghfiru-llāh [I ask God's forgiveness] in his presence. In response, Amīr al-Muʾminīn ؑ said,

> Your mother may lose you! Do you know what istighfār [asking God's forgiveness] is? Istighfār is meant for people of a high position. It is a word that stands on six supports. The first is to repent over the past; the second is to be firmly determined never to return to it; the third is to discharge all the rights of people so that you may meet God cleansed and with nothing to account for; the fourth is to fulfill every obligation which you ignored [in the past] so that you may now do it justice; the fifth is to aim at the flesh grown as a result of unlawful earning so that you may melt it by grief [of repentance] till the skin touches the bone and a new flesh grows between them. The sixth is to make the body taste the pain of obedience as you [previously] made it taste the sweetness of disobedience. Only then can you say 'Astaghfiru-llāh.'[63]

---

[63] Sharīf Raḍī, Muḥammad b. al-Ḥusayn, *Nahj al-Balāghah*, Saying 417.

And know, dear reader, that we have discussed some points regarding the first three meanings: remorse for the past, determination to abandon sin, and fulfilling the rights owed to others. It is necessary to refer to some of what the Imām's ﷺ words indicate in the last three points of the passage above.

Regarding "to fulfill every obligation which you ignored [in the past] so that you may now perform it and do it justice," he does not mean merely failing to fulfill the obligation. Just as missing the obligation can occur by not performing it at all or by not fulfilling its requirements and conditions correctly, this can also happen when the obligatory act is performed while lacking its essence, sincerity, and devotion. If the prayer, for example, does not achieve the essence of spiritual ascension [miʿrāj] and does not achieve for the person the desired closeness to God behind the obligation, and if it does not function as it should, preventing him from indecency, evil, and transgression, then it is lost or invalid.

As for when the Imām ﷺ said "to aim at the flesh grown as a result of unlawful earning," it is possible that infer two implications:

First meaning: This is the apparent meaning, which is seen from a Bedouin perspective, where a person has consumed something unlawful, and his flesh grows from that forbidden consumption.

Second meaning: Just like it requires nourishment from food and drink, the growth of flesh also needs spiritual and psychological refreshment. No matter how nutritious the food is for the body, if it is not accompanied by spiritual vitality, it will not benefit the body. Doctors have evidenced this, stating that eating food while suffering from spiritual torment, sadness, or fear does not benefit the body, and experiences in this regard and stories illustrate this point. As such, if a person is preoccupied with sins and is driven towards them, his soul's nourishment comes from disobeying God, and this soul activity becomes an essential and potent factor in his benefiting from the food that is in itself lawful, leading to the growth of his flesh based on disobedience [even if what he eats is lawful]. Hence, unlawful or filthy activity [Suḥt; can also be unlawful earning] refers to that spiritual activity that was the basis for the effect of the food in the growth of flesh. In this second meaning, it is valid and essential to consider all these meanings for each sinner, even if they have not consumed what God has prohibited.

As for his ﷺ statement, "to make the body taste the pain of obedience as you [previously] made it taste the sweetness of disobedience," one can interpret the pain of obedience in several ways:

At first glance, religious obligations entail certain costs and burdens. They involve the pain of physical exertion and the pain of restraining oneself from permissible things that one must abstain from during these obligations, such as the prohibitions imposed on a person during prayer, fasting, and the acts of Ḥajj and Umrah [pilgrimage]. The pain arises from physical fatigue and hardship and the pain of refraining from the permissible things that human nature naturally inclines towards.

Second, "pain" could also refer to the pain of shame and remorse that every sensible person feels when standing before their Lord, having rebelled against Him, disobeyed Him, and transgressed His boundaries. This spiritual pain is much stronger than the physical pain mentioned in the first context. Some wise men have even expressed that the discomfort felt in the company of certain individuals is heavier on the soul than the burden of lifting heavy physical weight, and the latter is burdensome on the body. Many people endure physical pain and bodily exertion with ease, seeking to get rid of spiritual and psychological pain.

Third, when observed by obedient and sincere believers, prayer and other acts of worship bring about immense spiritual pleasure and a sense of tranquility that surpasses any other comfort. It is narrated that the Messenger of God ﷺ would be engaged in conversation with his companions, and when the time for prayer arrives, he would say to Bilāl, the one who calls to prayer,

> Give us some rest, O Bilāl.

It was as if the Prophet's ﷺ comfort during prayer was due to his delight in it, as it was a source of great comfort and solace to him. However, compared to sinners and ordinary people like us, we find that prayer and other acts of worship come with difficulty because of our deep entanglement in disobedience and our distance from God, which resulted from the sins we have committed. Our souls have been imprinted with corruption contrary to what they should have been—our souls and lives should have been upright, but they have become crooked; what was once clean has been tainted with filth, what was once unified has been scattered, and what was once illuminated has been darkened. Therefore, prayer serves as a remedy for these impurities, a correction for our deviations, and a purification for the darkness. It is like the medicine that combats the illness and the chemical agent that scrubs away these corruptions that have deeply embedded themselves in our souls, thus causing us to feel pain while performing these acts of worship.

Moving on and on another note, there are two crucial times for seeking forgiveness:

The first is after committing any sin or whenever a person reflects upon themselves and their deeds. It has been reported that whoever seeks forgiveness after every sin in their record of deeds will be forgiven by God.

The second time is in the early morning [before dawn], as God has praised those who seek forgiveness during these hours. Perhaps the intended meaning here is the Witr prayer after Tahajjud [night prayer].

Furthermore, it is prudent to know that seeking forgiveness is a form of supplication [Duʿāʾ]. Therefore, those seeking forgiveness should be mindful of the preferred times for supplication. Also, one should not overlook that the true essence of seeking forgiveness is only realized when the seeker turns to themselves as a sinner in need of the mercy of their Lord. They should reflect upon the sins they have committed, even if it is in a general sense. At the same time, they should direct themselves sincerely to their Master, acknowledging their disobedience and rebellion against Him while firmly believing in His kindness, mercy, and promise of forgiveness. They must also be diligent in following His urgent commands to seek forgiveness.

Ultimately, the essence of seeking forgiveness cannot be fully realized without incorporating these aforementioned meanings.

Repentance: A Rational and an Islāmic Obligation

It has been established that a sound intellect recognizes the necessity of obedience to the Lord and the essentiality of submission to Him and acknowledges the ugliness of rebelling against Him and deviating from the path of servitude, especially when the Lord is the One Who bestowed existence upon him and has generously granted him the gift of life and the ability to enjoy the various blessings He endowed him with.

Returning to the embrace of His mercy and compassion is one of the foremost rational obligations, especially when one knows that if they repent and return to God, knocking on the door of His mercy, He will forgive them, overlook their sins, and include them in His compassion. Thus, persisting in rebellion, striving to distance oneself from Him, and continuing to disobey are among the most heinous and abhorrent actions. It should be noted that He has warned His servants about His severe punishment and intense wrath. If He seeks retribution, there will be no escape, refuge, or sanctuary from Him except unto Him. He has granted His servants time as long as they possess reason, speaking to them with the language of their conscience, calling them to Him with the voice of their intellect, presenting them with evidence and displaying for them signs, and providing ample reminders whichever way they turn. Hence, man should be ashamed of continuing to stray from the right path.

In the divine law, some exhortations encourage the servant to repent and obligate them to do so. God ﷻ has said much in this regard, evidenced in the following verses:

﴿وَتُوبُوٓاْ إِلَى ٱللَّهِ جَمِيعًا أَيُّهَ ٱلۡمُؤۡمِنُونَ لَعَلَّكُمۡ تُفۡلِحُونَ﴾

﴿*wa-tūbū 'ilā llāhi jamī'an 'ayyuha l-mu'minūna la'allakum tufliḥūna*﴾

﴿*Rally to God in repentance, O faithful, so that you may be felicitous*﴾[64]

﴿يَٰٓأَيُّهَا ٱلَّذِينَ ءَامَنُواْ تُوبُوٓاْ إِلَى ٱللَّهِ تَوۡبَةً نَّصُوحًا عَسَىٰ رَبُّكُمۡ أَن يُكَفِّرَ عَنكُمۡ سَيِّـَٔاتِكُمۡ وَيُدۡخِلَكُمۡ جَنَّٰتٖ تَجۡرِي مِن تَحۡتِهَا ٱلۡأَنۡهَٰرُ﴾

﴿*yā-'ayyuhā lladhīna 'āmanū tūbū 'ilā llāhi tawbatan naṣūḥan 'asā rabbukum 'an yukaffira 'ankum sayyi'ātikum wa-yudkhilakum jannātin tajrī min taḥtihā l-'anhāru*﴾

﴿*O you who have faith! Repent to God with sincere repentance! Maybe your Lord will absolve you of your misdeeds and admit you into gardens with streams running in them*﴾[65]

---

[64] Sūrat an-Nūr, Verse 31.

[65] Sūrat at-Taḥrīm, Verse 8.

﴿وَأَنِ ٱسْتَغْفِرُوا۟ رَبَّكُمْ ثُمَّ تُوبُوٓا۟ إِلَيْهِ يُمَتِّعْكُم مَّتَٰعًا حَسَنًا إِلَىٰٓ أَجَلٍ مُّسَمًّى وَيُؤْتِ كُلَّ ذِى فَضْلٍ فَضْلَهُۥ﴾

﴿*wa-'ani staghfirū rabbakum thumma tūbū 'ilayhi yumatti'kum matā'an ḥasanan 'ilā 'ajalin musamman wa-yu'ti kulla dhī faḍlin faḍlahū*﴾

﴿*Plead with your Lord for forgiveness, then turn to Him penitently. He will provide you with a good provision for a specified term and grant His grace to every meritorious person*﴾[66]

﴿فَقُلْتُ ٱسْتَغْفِرُوا۟ رَبَّكُمْ إِنَّهُۥ كَانَ غَفَّارًا﴾

﴿*fa-qultu staghfirū rabbakum 'innahū kāna ghaffāra*^{n}﴾

﴿يُرْسِلِ ٱلسَّمَآءَ عَلَيْكُم مِّدْرَارًا﴾

﴿*yursili s-samā'a 'alaykum midrāra*^{n}﴾

﴿وَيُمْدِدْكُم بِأَمْوَٰلٍ وَبَنِينَ وَيَجْعَل لَّكُمْ جَنَّٰتٍ وَيَجْعَل لَّكُمْ أَنْهَٰرًا﴾

﴿*wa-yumdidkum bi-'amwālin wa-banīna wa-yaj'al lakum jannātin wa-yaj'al lakum 'anhāra*^{n}﴾

---

[66] Sūrat Hūd, Verse 3.

﴿*telling [them]: 'Plead to your Lord for forgiveness. Indeed, He is Forgiving. He will send for you abundant rains from the sky, and aid you with wealth and sons, and provide you with gardens and provide you with streams'*﴾[67]

﴿وَٱلَّذِينَ لَا يَدۡعُونَ مَعَ ٱللَّهِ إِلَٰهًا ءَاخَرَ وَلَا يَقۡتُلُونَ ٱلنَّفۡسَ ٱلَّتِي حَرَّمَ ٱللَّهُ إِلَّا بِٱلۡحَقِّ وَلَا يَزۡنُونَۚ وَمَن يَفۡعَلۡ ذَٰلِكَ يَلۡقَ أَثَامًا﴾

﴿*wa-lladhīna lā yad'ūna ma'a llāhi 'ilāhan 'ākhara wa-lā yaqtulūna n-nafsa llatī ḥarrama llāhu 'illā bi-l-ḥaqqi wa-lā yaznūna wa-man yaf'al dhālika yalqa 'athāman*﴾

﴿يُضَٰعَفۡ لَهُ ٱلۡعَذَابُ يَوۡمَ ٱلۡقِيَٰمَةِ وَيَخۡلُدۡ فِيهِۦ مُهَانًا﴾

﴿*yuḍā'af lahu l-'adhābu yawma l-qiyāmati wa-yakhlud fīhi muhānan*﴾

﴿إِلَّا مَن تَابَ وَءَامَنَ وَعَمِلَ عَمَلًا صَٰلِحًا فَأُوْلَٰٓئِكَ يُبَدِّلُ ٱللَّهُ سَيِّـَٔاتِهِمۡ حَسَنَٰتٖۗ وَكَانَ ٱللَّهُ غَفُورًا رَّحِيمًا﴾

﴿*illā man tāba wa-'āmana wa-'amila 'amalan ṣāliḥan fa-'ulā'ika yubaddilu llāhu sayyi'ātihim ḥasanātin wa-kāna llāhu ghafūran raḥīman*﴾

﴿*Those who do not invoke another deity besides God, and do not kill a soul [whose life] God has made inviolable, except*

[67] Sūrat Nūḥ, Verses 10–12.

*with due cause, and do not commit fornication. (Whoever
does that shall encounter its retribution, the punishment
being doubled for him on the Day of Resurrection. In it he
will abide in humiliation forever, except those who repent,
attain faith, and act righteously. For such, God will replace
their misdeeds with good deeds, and God is Forgiving,
Merciful)*[68]

﴿ٱلَّذِينَ يَحْمِلُونَ ٱلْعَرْشَ وَمَنْ حَوْلَهُ يُسَبِّحُونَ بِحَمْدِ رَبِّهِمْ وَيُؤْمِنُونَ بِهِۦ
وَيَسْتَغْفِرُونَ لِلَّذِينَ ءَامَنُواْ رَبَّنَا وَسِعْتَ كُلَّ شَيْءٍ رَّحْمَةً وَعِلْمًا فَٱغْفِرْ لِلَّذِينَ
تَابُواْ وَٱتَّبَعُواْ سَبِيلَكَ وَقِهِمْ عَذَابَ ٱلْجَحِيمِ﴾

*(alladhīna yaḥmilūna l-ʿarsha wa-man ḥawlahū
yusabbiḥūna bi-ḥamdi rabbihim wa-yuʾminūna bihī wa-
yastaghfirūna li-lladhīna ʾāmanū rabbanā wasiʿta kulla
shayʾin raḥmatan wa-ʿilman fa-ghfir li-lladhīna tābū wa-
ttabaʿū sabīlaka wa-qihim ʿadhāba l-jaḥīmⁱ)*

﴿رَبَّنَا وَأَدْخِلْهُمْ جَنَّٰتِ عَدْنٍ ٱلَّتِي وَعَدْتَّهُمْ وَمَن صَلَحَ مِنْ ءَابَآئِهِمْ وَأَزْوَٰجِهِمْ
وَذُرِّيَّٰتِهِمْ إِنَّكَ أَنتَ ٱلْعَزِيزُ ٱلْحَكِيمُ﴾

*(rabbanā wa-ʾadkhilhum jannāti ʿadnin-i llatī
waʿadtahum wa-man ṣalaḥa min ʾābāʾihim wa-ʾazwājihim
wa-dhurriyyātihim ʾinnaka ʾanta l-ʿazīzu l-ḥakīmᵘ)*

---

[68] Sūrat al-Furqān, Verses 68–70.

﴿وَقِهِمُ ٱلسَّيِّـَٔاتِۚ وَمَن تَقِ ٱلسَّيِّـَٔاتِ يَوْمَئِذٍ فَقَدْ رَحِمْتَهُۥۚ وَذَٰلِكَ هُوَ ٱلْفَوْزُ ٱلْعَظِيمُ﴾

﴿*wa-qihimu s-sayyi'āti wa-man taqi s-sayyi'āti yawma'idhin fa-qad raḥimtahū wa-dhālika huwa l-fawzu l-'aẓīm*[u]﴾

﴿*Those who bear the Throne, and those who are around it, celebrate the praise of their Lord and have faith in Him, and they plead for forgiveness for the faithful: 'Our Lord! You embrace all things in mercy and knowledge. So forgive those who repent and follow Your way and save them from the punishment of hell. Our Lord! Admit them into the Gardens of Eden, which You have promised them, along with whoever is righteous among their forebears, their spouses and their descendants. Indeed You are the Mighty, the Wise. Save them from the ills [of the Day of Retribution]; and whomever You save from the ills that day, You will have had mercy upon him, and that is the great triumph'*﴾[69]

﴿وَٱلَّذِينَ إِذَا فَعَلُواْ فَٰحِشَةً أَوْ ظَلَمُوٓاْ أَنفُسَهُمْ ذَكَرُواْ ٱللَّهَ فَٱسْتَغْفَرُواْ لِذُنُوبِهِمْ وَمَن يَغْفِرُ ٱلذُّنُوبَ إِلَّا ٱللَّهُ وَلَمْ يُصِرُّواْ عَلَىٰ مَا فَعَلُواْ وَهُمْ يَعْلَمُونَ﴾

﴿*wa-lladhīna 'idhā fa'alū fāḥishatan 'aw ẓalamū 'anfusahum dhakarū llāha fa-staghfarū li-dhunūbihim wa-*

[69] Sūrat Ghāfir, Verses 7–9.

man yaghfiru dh-dhunūba ʾillā llāhu wa-lam yuṣirrū ʿalā mā faʿalū wa-hum yaʿlamūn[a]﴾

﴿أُو۟لَـٰٓئِكَ جَزَآؤُهُم مَّغْفِرَةٌ مِّن رَّبِّهِمْ وَجَنَّـٰتٌ تَجْرِى مِن تَحْتِهَا ٱلْأَنْهَـٰرُ خَـٰلِدِينَ فِيهَا ۚ وَنِعْمَ أَجْرُ ٱلْعَـٰمِلِينَ﴾

﴿*ulāʾika jazāʾuhum maghfiratun min rabbihim wa-jannātun tajrī min taḥtihā l-ʾanhāru khālidīna fīhā wa-niʿma ʾajru l-ʿāmilīn*[a]﴾

﴿*and those who, when they commit an indecent act or wrong themselves, remember God, and plead [to God seeking His] forgiveness for their sins—and who forgives sins except God? —and who knowingly do not persist in what [sins] they have committed. Their reward is forgiveness from their Lord, and gardens with streams running in them, to remain in them [forever]. How excellent is the reward of the workers!*﴾[70]

﴿إِنَّ ٱلَّذِينَ فَتَنُوا۟ ٱلْمُؤْمِنِينَ وَٱلْمُؤْمِنَـٰتِ ثُمَّ لَمْ يَتُوبُوا۟ فَلَهُمْ عَذَابُ جَهَنَّمَ﴾

﴿*inna lladhīna fatanū l-muʾminīna wa-l-muʾmināti thumma lam yatūbū fa-lahum ʿadhābu jahannama*﴾

[70] Sūrat Āl ʿImrān, Verses 135–136.

﴿*Indeed those who persecute the faithful, men and women, and do not repent thereafter, there is the punishment of hell for them*﴾[71]

﴿فَسَبِّحْ بِحَمْدِ رَبِّكَ وَٱسْتَغْفِرْهُ إِنَّهُۥ كَانَ تَوَّابًا﴾

﴿*fa-sabbiḥ bi-ḥamdi rabbika wa-staghfirhu ʾinnahū kāna tawwāba*[n]﴾

﴿*celebrate the praise of your Lord, and plead to Him for forgiveness. Indeed, He is Clement*﴾[72]

﴿وَإِذَا جَآءَكَ ٱلَّذِينَ يُؤْمِنُونَ بِـَٔايَـٰتِنَا فَقُلْ سَلَـٰمٌ عَلَيْكُمْ كَتَبَ رَبُّكُمْ عَلَىٰ نَفْسِهِ ٱلرَّحْمَةَ أَنَّهُۥ مَنْ عَمِلَ مِنكُمْ سُوٓءًۢا بِجَهَـٰلَةٍ ثُمَّ تَابَ مِنۢ بَعْدِهِۦ وَأَصْلَحَ فَأَنَّهُۥ غَفُورٌ رَّحِيمٌ﴾

﴿*wa-ʾidhā jāʾaka lladhīna yuʾminūna bi-ʾāyātinā fa-qul salāmun ʿalaykum kataba rabbukum ʿalā nafsihi r-raḥmata ʾannahū man ʿamila minkum sūʾan bi-jahālatin thumma tāba min baʿdihī wa-ʾaṣlaḥ fa-ʾannahū ghafūrun raḥīm*[un]﴾

﴿*When those who have faith in Our signs come to you, say, 'Peace to you! Your Lord has made mercy incumbent upon Himself: whoever of you commits an evil [deed] out of*

---

[71] Sūrat al-Burūj, Verse 10.

[72] Sūrat an-Naṣr, Verse 3.

ignorance and then repents after that and reforms, then He is indeed Forgiving, Merciful'﴿[73]

﴿فَإِن تُبْتُمْ فَهُوَ خَيْرٌ لَّكُمْ﴾

﴾*fa-'in tubtum fa-huwa khayrun lakum*﴿

﴾*If you repent that is better for you*﴿[74]

﴿فَإِن تَابُوا۟ وَأَقَامُوا۟ ٱلصَّلَوٰةَ وَءَاتَوُا۟ ٱلزَّكَوٰةَ فَخَلُّوا۟ سَبِيلَهُمْ
إِنَّ ٱللَّهَ غَفُورٌ رَّحِيمٌ﴾

﴾*fa-'in tābū wa-'aqāmū ṣ-ṣalāta wa-'ātawu z-zakāta fa-khallū sabīlahum 'inna llāha ghafūrun raḥīm*[un]﴿

﴾*But if they repent, and maintain the prayer and give the zakat, then let them alone. Indeed God is Forgiving, Merciful*﴿[75]

﴿فَإِن تَابُوا۟ وَأَقَامُوا۟ ٱلصَّلَوٰةَ وَءَاتَوُا۟ ٱلزَّكَوٰةَ فَإِخْوَٰنُكُمْ فِى ٱلدِّينِ﴾

﴾*fa-'in tābū wa-'aqāmū ṣ-ṣalāta wa-'ātawu z-zakāta fa-'ikhwānukum fī d-dīni*﴿

---

[73] Sūrat al-An'ām, Verse 54.

[74] Sūrat at-Tawbah, Verse 3.

[75] Sūrat at-Tawbah, Verse 5.

﴾*Yet if they repent and maintain the prayer and give the zakat, then they are your brethren in faith*﴿[76]

Furthermore, some narrations indicate the necessity of repentance and highlight how the infallibles encouraged people toward it. Among them is what al-Rawandī narrated in the book of supplications:

Prophet Muḥammad ﷺ said,

> Turn to your Lord [in repentance] before you die and hasten to do good deeds before you become busy [with other things] and keep what is between you and your Lord by mentioning Him abundantly.[77]

It is also narrated that Amīr al-Mu'minīn ؑ said,

> There is no intercessor more successful than repentance.[78]

Shaykh Ṣadūq reported on the authority of ʿAbdullāh b. Sanan that Imām Jaʿfar aṣ-Ṣādiq ؑ said,

---

[76] Sūrat at-Tawbah, Verse 11.

[77] Majlisī, ʿAllāmah Muḥammad Bāqir, *Biḥār al-Anwār*, Vol. 6, p. 19.

[78] al-Ḥarrānī, Ibn Shuʿba, *Tuḥaf al-ʿUqūl*; Ṣadūq, Shaykh Muḥammad b. ʿAlī, *al-Amālī*.

The Prophet ﷺ said:

> My nation should always do the following four: They should love those who repent. They should be sympathetic to the weak. They should help the good-doers. They should pray [for repentance] for all sinners [for their sins].[79]

Similarly, it has also been reported in the same book that Imām Ja'far aṣ-Ṣādiq ؑ said,

> Whoever is granted [these] four things would not be deprived of four other things: The one who is given [these] four will not be prevented from [these] other four: the one who is given prayer will not be denied a response to it; the one who is given the means to seek forgiveness will not be denied repentance; the one who is given the means to thankfulness will not be denied increasement [of blessing and sustenance]; and the one who is given patience will not be denied its reward.[80]

Moreover, it has also been reported with a chain of narrators on the authority of Abī Miqdād that Imām Ja'far aṣ-Ṣādiq ؑ narrated from his father ؑ,

---

[79] Ṣadūq, Shaykh Muḥammad b. 'Alī, *al-Khiṣāl.*, p. 20.

[80] Ibid.

The Messenger of God ﷺ said:

> The one who has [these] four [qualities] in him would be in the Magnificent Light of God: the one who adheres to the testimony that there is no god except for God and that I am the Messenger of God; the one who says 'To God we belong, and to Him we return' when he is afflicted with a calamity; the one who says 'praise be to God' when good befalls him; and the one who says 'I seek the forgiveness of God and I repent to Him' when he sins.[81]

And it is narrated from him ﵇ from his fathers ﵈,

The Messenger of God ﷺ said:

> The one who repents from a sin is like the one who has no sin at all.[82]

Shaykh al-Ṭūsī ؒ narrated from Shaykh Mufīd ؒ with his chain of narrators from al-Shaʿbī the following:

I heard Imām ʿAlī ﵇ say,

---

[81] Ibid.

[82] Ṣadūq, Shaykh Muḥammad b. ʿAlī, *ʿUyūn Akhbār al-Riḍā* ﵇.

> I wonder about the man who loses hope despite the possibility of seeking forgiveness.[83]

The Shaykh also narrated from Imām ʿAlī ar-Riḍā ﷺ from his fathers ﷺ the following:

> Amīr al-Mu'minīn ﷺ said,
>
> > Perfume yourselves with seeking forgiveness [istighfar] so that the scents of sins do not expose you.[84]

Ibn Fahd narrated that the most knowledgeable Imām Jaʿfar aṣ-Ṣādiq ﷺ said,

> By God! A believer never receives any good in this life and the Hereafter except because of his hope and confidence in God, good moral behavior, and abstaining from backbiting believers. God does not punish a believer after he has repented and asked for forgiveness except because of his despair toward God, his shortcoming in his hope in God, his bad moral behavior, and his backbiting of believers.[85]

---

[83] Ṣadūq, Shaykh Muḥammad b. ʿAlī, *al-Amālī*, pp. 21–22.

[84] Ibid., p. 22.

[85] al-Ḥillī, Aḥmad b. Fahd, *'Uddat al-Dāʿī wa Najāḥ al-Sāʿī.*, p. 28.

Shaykh Ṣadūq ﵀ narrated with his chain of narrators from Abū Baṣīr that Imām Ja'far aṣ-Ṣādiq ﵇ said,

> God revealed onto Prophet Dāwūd,
>
> > O Dāwūd! If a believer commits sins, repents for them, and feels ashamed in front of Me while repenting, I forgive him. I will make the angel forget this sin and convert this sin into a good deed. I do not care [it is not difficult for me] for I am the Most Merciful.[86]

Shaykh Ṣadūq also narrated in the same book with his chain of narrators from Mu'āwīyah b. Wahab the following narration:

> I heard Imām Ja'far aṣ-Ṣādiq ﵇ say,
>
> > If one truly repents, God likes to cover up his sins in the world and the Hereafter.
>
> I asked him,
>
> > How does God cover up the sins?

---

[86] Ṣadūq, Shaykh Muḥammad b. 'Alī, *Thawāb al-A'māl*.

The Imām said,

> He makes both guardian angels forget whatever they have recorded in the letter of deeds regarding his sins, He reveals to his body parts to cover up whatever sins he has done with them, and He reveals to the places on Earth where the sins were committed to cover up the sins. Thus when he goes to meet his Lord in the Hereafter, nothing of his sins is left to bear witness against him.[87]

The Shaykh also reported with his chain of narrators from al-Masʿūdī that he said,

Amīr al-Muʾminīn 🕮 said:

> Whoever repents, God will accept his repentance, and his body parts are commanded to conceal his sins, and the far corners of the earth are ordered to keep his sins hidden, and the recording angels forget what they were writing down against him.[88]

---

[87] Ibid.

[88] Ibid.

Al-Rawandī narrated in *al-Kharā'ij* that Imām Muḥammad al-Bāqir ؑ was performing Ḥajj, and his son Jaʿfar ؑ was with him. A man came to him, greeted him, and sat before him. Then, he said,

> I want to ask you something.

He ؑ said,

> Ask my son Jaʿfar.

Then, the man turned to Jaʿfar, sat beside him, and said,

> May I ask you?

Jaʿfar ؑ replied,

> Ask about whatever comes to your mind.

The man asked,

> I want to ask you about a man who committed a major sin.

Jaʿfar ؑ asked,

> Did he deliberately break fast on a day during Ramaḍān?

The man replied,

> It is greater than that.

Ja'far 🕮 asked,

> Did he commit adultery during the month of Ramaḍān?

The man replied,

> It is greater than that.

Ja'far 🕮 asked,

> Did he kill a soul?

The man replied,

> It is greater than that.

Ja'far 🕮 said,

> If the murdered person was one of the Shī'ah of 'Alī, then he (the murdered person) went to the Ka'bah and swore not to return. But if he (the murdered person) was not one of his ['Alī's] Shī'ah, then there is no problem.

The man said to him,

> May God have mercy on you, O son of Fāṭimah [three times]. I heard this from the Messenger of God ﷺ.

Then the man departed, and Imām Muḥammad al-Bāqir ﷷ turned and said,

> Did you recognize the man?

He (Jaʿfar) replied,

> No.

Imām Muḥammad al-Bāqir ﷷ said,

> That was Khiḍr. I only wanted to introduce him to you.[89]

I say: The intended meaning of Shīʿah here is every sincere and devoted believer who adheres to the religion of God, adorns himself with God-consciousness [taqwā], and abstains from what God has prohibited. This is how Shīʿah has been interpreted in the narrations of the Imāms ﷷ.

Overall, these are selected narrations among many that highlight the virtue of repentance and its consequences of forgiveness of sins and liberation from them. It is known

---

[89] Ibid., pp. 30–31.

that liberation from sins is required by reason. What is mentioned in these narrations and others is evidence and guidance on how a person can liberate themselves from sins. Additionally, the clear Qur'ānic verses we mentioned earlier establish the obligation of repentance. As we pointed out earlier, repentance is obligatory based on rational judgment, and all mentioned in the religious texts serve as guidance to that clear rational judgment.

Repentance is an Immediate Obligation

Our righteous scholars and wise jurists unanimously agree that repentance is immediate and obligatory. Shaykh Bahāʾī ﷺ even likened sins to harmful poisons for the body. Just as a person who ingests poison must promptly induce vomiting to rid their body of the substance that leads to destruction, similarly, a person burdened with sins must promptly initiate repentance and seek forgiveness to avoid the perishing and decay of their soul. Whoever neglects to repent promptly and continuously postpones it is faced with two great dangers, and if they manage to avoid one, they might not be able to escape the other:

The first danger is that death may suddenly strike. The person remains heedless in their negligence, unaware of their slumber, and so, when death approaches and confronts them, there will be no chance for remedy. The doors of recovery will be closed to them, as indicated by the saying of God ﷻ:

﴿وَحِيلَ بَيْنَهُمْ وَبَيْنَ مَا يَشْتَهُونَ﴾

﴿*wa-ḥīla baynahum wa-bayna mā yashtahūna*﴾

﴿*and a barrier is set between them and what they desire*﴾[90]

---

[90] Sūrat Sabaʾ, Verse 54.

So, the person attempts to repent but is unable to; perhaps the death rattle choked them, or they asked for time but could not get it. God ﷻ said,

﴿وَأَنفِقُواْ مِن مَّا رَزَقْنَٰكُم مِّن قَبْلِ أَن يَأْتِيَ أَحَدَكُمُ ٱلْمَوْتُ فَيَقُولَ رَبِّ لَوْلَآ أَخَّرْتَنِيٓ إِلَىٰٓ أَجَلٍ قَرِيبٍ فَأَصَّدَّقَ وَأَكُن مِّنَ ٱلصَّٰلِحِينَ﴾

﴾*wa-ʾanfiqū min mā razaqnākum min qabli ʾan yaʾtiya ʾaḥadakumu l-mawtu fa-yaqūla rabbi law-lā ʾakhkhartanī ʾilā ʾajalin qarībin fa-ʾaṣṣaddaqa wa-ʾakun mina ṣ-ṣāliḥīn*[a]﴿

﴾*Spend out of what We have provided you before death comes to any of you, whereat he might say, 'My Lord, why did You not respite me for a short time so that I could give charity and become one of the righteous!'*﴿[91]

Shaykh Bahāʾī ﵀ narrated from some of the interpreters the explanation of this verse that the dying person says, when he senses death and the veil of death is lifted by the Angel of Death,

> Give me one more day to apologize to my Lord, to repent to Him, and to prepare good deeds.

The Angel of Death says,

> The days have come to an end.

---

[91] Sūrat al-Munāfiqūn, Verse 10.

So the dying person says,

> Give me one more hour.

He replies,

> The hours have come to an end.

Then, the door of repentance is closed for him, and he is overwhelmed with despair, regretting the wasted time, and his state may disturb the core of his faith. We seek refuge in God from the shock of these horrors.

The second scenario is when the darkness of sins accumulates in his heart, the state of sins becomes a fixed stain, and he becomes accustomed to committing sins, losing the capacity to erase them. Every sin a person commits causes darkness in his heart and a dark veil over his soul. When these stains accumulate, they leave an imprint on his heart from their corruption. As the darkness piles up, he becomes lost and immersed in it, corrupting his soul to the point where he becomes unwilling to return to God. This is described as a tarnished and blackened heart.

Upon reflection, it becomes apparent that sins cause the heart to become crooked, just like when you place a green stick in a bent mold and leave it there until it dries, making it very difficult to straighten. Similarly, suppose the soul indulges in sins and remains immersed in them for a long time. In that case, it becomes a reason that the servant voluntarily engaged, leading to him finding it extremely difficult to return to the right path. Perhaps this is indicated by the verse:

﴿خَتَمَ ٱللَّهُ عَلَىٰ قُلُوبِهِمْ وَعَلَىٰ سَمْعِهِمْ وَعَلَىٰٓ أَبْصَـٰرِهِمْ غِشَـٰوَةٌ﴾

﴿khatama llāhu ʿalā qulūbihim wa-ʿalā samʿihim wa-ʿalā ʾabṣārihim ghishāwatun﴾

﴿God has set a seal on their hearts and their hearing, and there is a blindfold on their sight﴾[92]

Imām Jaʿfar aṣ-Ṣādiq ﷺ said,

> My father used to say:
>
> > There is nothing that corrupts the heart like sin. The heart will be entangled in sin, and it will not be free from it until the sin overcomes the heart and turns it upside down.[93]

It is also narrated by Imām Muḥammad al-Bāqir ﷺ,

> In the heart of every servant [of God] there is a white dot. When he sins, a black dot appears in the white one. If he repents, the black dot goes away,

---

[92] Sūrat al-Baqarah, Verse 7.

[93] Kulaynī, Shaykh Muḥammad b. Yaʿqūb, *al-Kāfī*.

but if he continues committing sins, it enlarges until it covers the white dot. When the white dot is covered, the person thereafter does not return to goodness, as God ﷻ has said,

﴿كَلَّا ۖ بَلْ ۜ رَانَ عَلَىٰ قُلُوبِهِم مَّا كَانُوا يَكْسِبُونَ﴾

﴾*kallā bal rāna ʿalā qulūbihim mā kānū yaksibūn*[a]﴿

﴾*No, that is not the case! Rather, their hearts have been sullied by what they have been earning*﴿[94]

The meaning of his ﷺ saying, "the person thereafter does not return to goodness," is that, by his own choice, the person has put himself in this predicament and pushed himself into a narrow and wasted alley, depriving himself of opportunities to escape and cutting off the path of return, just like someone who throws himself from a precipice and becomes unable to prevent himself from falling. We seek God's forgiveness and pardon.

It has been narrated that procrastination in repentance is a delusion.[95]

---

[94] Sūrat al-Muṭaffifīn, Verse 14.

[95] See Majlisī, ʿAllāmah Muḥammad Bāqir, *Biḥār al-Anwār*, Vol. 6, p. 30. Ṭabrisī, Mīrzā Ḥusayn Nūrī, *Mustadrak al-Wasāʾil wa-Mustanbaṭ al-Masāʾil*, Vol. 12, p. 124.

Several blessed verses indicate that the repentance that benefits the servant is followed by self-reformation and righteous deeds. This means that mere regret alone is not sufficient as repentance. It is well-established that repentance, along with self-reformation and righteous deeds, can only be achieved by taking the first step toward repentance and initiating it—with no delay or postponement. Without this initiative and with procrastination, the person may miss the opportunity to reform themselves and their deeds, so they may not be able to rectify what has passed.

Upon contemplating the noble verses regarding repentance and its acceptance, we find that they can be divided into two categories:

The first category indicates that repentance is, in essence, accepted when its conditions and prerequisites are fulfilled.

The second category points to what we previously mentioned: forgiveness and pardon combine repentance with the meaning we highlighted earlier, self-reformation and righteous deeds. Thus, the first category must be linked to the second; otherwise, restricting acceptance of repentance to self-reformation and righteous deeds alone would be futile.

Among the verses of the first category, there are the following:

﴿ثُمَّ تَابَ عَلَيْهِمْ لِيَتُوبُوٓاْ إِنَّ ٱللَّهَ هُوَ ٱلتَّوَّابُ ٱلرَّحِيمُ﴾

﴿*thumma tāba ʿalayhim li-yatūbū ʾinna llāha huwa t-tawwābu r-raḥīmu*﴾

﴿*then He turned clemently toward them so that they might be penitent. Indeed God is the Clement, the Merciful*﴾[96]

﴿فَٱسْتَقِمْ كَمَآ أُمِرْتَ وَمَن تَابَ مَعَكَ وَلَا تَطْغَوْاْ﴾

﴿*fa-staqim ka-mā ʾumirta wa-man tāba maʿaka wa-lā taṭghaw*﴾

﴿*So be steadfast, just as you have been commanded—[you] and whoever has turned [to God] with you—and do not overstep the bounds*﴾[97]

﴿وَإِن تُبْتُمْ فَلَكُمْ رُءُوسُ أَمْوَٰلِكُمْ لَا تَظْلِمُونَ وَلَا تُظْلَمُونَ﴾

﴿*wa-ʾin tubtum fa-lakum ruʾūsu ʾamwālikum lā taẓlimūna wa-lā tuẓlamūna*﴾

﴿*And if you repent, then you will have your principal, neither harming others, nor suffering harm*﴾[98]

---

96 Sūrat at-Tawbah, Verse 118.

97 Sūrat Hūd, Verse 112.

98 Sūrat al-Baqarah, Verse 279.

﴿فَإِن تُبْتُمْ فَهُوَ خَيْرٌ لَّكُمْ﴾

﴿*fa-'in tubtum fa-huwa khayrun lakum*﴾

﴿*If you repent that is better for you*﴾[99]

﴿فَإِن يَتُوبُوا۟ يَكُ خَيْرًا لَّهُمْ﴾

﴿*fa-'in yatūbū yaku khayran lahum*﴾

﴿*Yet if they repent, it will be better for them*﴾[100]

﴿وَهُوَ ٱلَّذِي يَقْبَلُ ٱلتَّوْبَةَ عَنْ عِبَادِهِۦ وَيَعْفُوا۟ عَنِ ٱلسَّيِّـَٔاتِ﴾

﴿*wa-huwa lladhī yaqbalu t-tawbata ʿan ʿibādihī wa-yaʿfū ʿani s-sayyi'āti*﴾

﴿*It is He who accepts the repentance of His servants, and excuses their misdeeds*﴾[101]

﴿وَيَتُوبَ ٱللَّهُ عَلَى ٱلْمُؤْمِنِينَ وَٱلْمُؤْمِنَـٰتِ﴾

﴿*wa-yatūba llāhu ʿalā l-mu'minīna wa-l-mu'mināti*﴾

---

[99] Sūrat at-Tawbah, Verse 2.

[100] Sūrat at-Tawbah, Verse 74.

[101] Sūrat ash-Shūrā, Verse 25.

﴾*and God will turn clemently to the faithful, men and women*﴿[102]

﴿وَٱسْتَغْفِرُواْ رَبَّكُمْ ثُمَّ تُوبُوٓاْ إِلَيْهِ إِنَّ رَبِّي رَحِيمٌ وَدُودٌ﴾

﴾*wa-staghfirū rabbakum thumma tūbū ʾilāyhi ʾinna rabbī raḥīmun wadūd*[un]﴿

﴾*Plead with your Lord for forgiveness, then turn to Him penitently. My Lord is indeed Merciful, Affectionate*﴿[103]

Among the verses of the second category are the following:

﴿فَمَن تَابَ مِنۢ بَعْدِ ظُلْمِهِۦ وَأَصْلَحَ فَإِنَّ ٱللَّهَ يَتُوبُ عَلَيْهِ﴾

﴾*fa-man tāba min baʿdi ẓulmihī wa-ʾaṣlaḥa fa-ʾinna llāha yatūbu ʿalayhi*﴿

﴾*But whoever repents after his wrongdoing, and reforms, then God shall accept his repentance*﴿[104]

﴿مَنْ عَمِلَ مِنكُمْ سُوٓءًۢا بِجَهَٰلَةٍ ثُمَّ تَابَ مِنۢ بَعْدِهِۦ وَأَصْلَحَ فَأَنَّهُۥ غَفُورٌ رَّحِيمٌ﴾

---

[102] Sūrat al-Aḥzāb, Verse 73.

[103] Sūrat Hūd, Verse 90.

[104] Sūrat al-Māʾidah, Verse 39.

﴿*man ʿamila minkum sū'an bi-jahālatin thumma tāba min baʿdihī wa-'aṣlaḥa fa-'annahū ghafūrun raḥīm*[un]﴾

﴿*whoever of you commits an evil [deed] out of ignorance and then repents after that and reforms, then He is indeed Forgiving, Merciful*﴾[105]

﴿إِلَّا مَن تَابَ وَءَامَنَ وَعَمِلَ صَٰلِحًا فَأُوْلَٰٓئِكَ يَدْخُلُونَ ٱلْجَنَّةَ وَلَا يُظْلَمُونَ شَيْـًٔا﴾

﴿*illā man tāba wa-'āmana wa-ʿamila ṣāliḥan fa-'ulā'ika yadkhulūna l-jannata wa-lā yuẓlamūna shay'a*[n]﴾

﴿*barring those who repent, believe, and act righteously. Such will enter paradise, and they will not be wronged in the least*﴾[106]

﴿إِلَّا مَن تَابَ وَءَامَنَ وَعَمِلَ عَمَلًا صَٰلِحًا فَأُوْلَٰٓئِكَ يُبَدِّلُ ٱللَّهُ سَيِّـَٔاتِهِمْ حَسَنَٰتٍ ۗ وَكَانَ ٱللَّهُ غَفُورًا رَّحِيمًا﴾

﴿*illā man tāba wa-'āmana wa-ʿamila ʿamalan ṣāliḥan fa-'ulā'ika yubaddilu llāhu sayyi'ātihim ḥasanātin wa-kāna llāhu ghafūran raḥīma*[n]﴾

---

[105] Sūrat al-Anʿām, Verse 54.

[106] Sūrat Maryam, Verse 60.

﴾*except those who repent, attain faith, and act righteously. For such, God will replace their misdeeds with good deeds, and God is Forgiving, Merciful*﴿[107]

﴿فَأَمَّا مَن تَابَ وَءَامَنَ وَعَمِلَ صَٰلِحًا فَعَسَىٰٓ أَن يَكُونَ مِنَ ٱلْمُفْلِحِينَ﴾

﴾*fa-ʾammā man tāba wa-ʾāmana wa-ʿamila ṣāliḥan fa-ʿasā ʾan yakūna mina l-mufliḥīn*[a]﴿

﴾*As for him who repents, has faith and acts righteously, maybe he will be among the felicitous*﴿[108]

﴿فَإِن تَابَا وَأَصْلَحَا فَأَعْرِضُوا۟ عَنْهُمَآ ۗ إِنَّ ٱللَّهَ كَانَ تَوَّابًا رَّحِيمًا﴾

﴾*fa-ʾin tābā wa-ʾaṣlaḥā fa-ʾaʿriḍū ʿanhumā ʾinna llāha kāna tawwāban raḥīma*[n]﴿

﴾*but if they repent and reform, let them alone. Indeed God is Clement, Merciful*﴿[109]

﴿إِلَّا ٱلَّذِينَ تَابُوا۟ وَأَصْلَحُوا۟ وَبَيَّنُوا۟ فَأُو۟لَٰٓئِكَ أَتُوبُ عَلَيْهِمْ ۚ وَأَنَا ٱلتَّوَّابُ ٱلرَّحِيمُ﴾

﴾*illā lladhīna tābū wa-ʾaṣlaḥū wa-bayyanū fa-ʾulāʾika ʾatūbu ʿalayhim wa-ʾana t-tawwābu r-raḥīm*[u]﴿

---

[107] Sūrat al-Furqān, Verse 70.

[108] Sūrat al-Qaṣaṣ, Verse 67.

[109] Sūrat an-Nisāʾ, Verse 16.

﴾except such as repent, make amends, and clarify—those I shall pardon, and I am the Clement, the Merciful﴿[110]

﴿إِلَّا ٱلَّذِينَ تَابُواْ وَأَصۡلَحُواْ وَٱعۡتَصَمُواْ بِٱللَّهِ وَأَخۡلَصُواْ دِينَهُمۡ لِلَّهِ
فَأُوْلَٰٓئِكَ مَعَ ٱلۡمُؤۡمِنِينَ﴾

﴾illā lladhīna tābū wa-ʾaṣlaḥū wa-ʿtaṣamū bi-llāhi wa-ʾakhlaṣū dīnahum li-llāhi fa-ʾulāʾika maʿa l-muʾminīna﴿

﴾except for those who repent and reform, and hold fast to God and dedicate their religion [exclusively] to God. Those are with the faithful﴿[111]

﴿إِلَّا ٱلَّذِينَ تَابُواْ مِنۢ بَعۡدِ ذَٰلِكَ وَأَصۡلَحُواْ فَإِنَّ ٱللَّهَ غَفُورٞ رَّحِيمٌ﴾

﴾illā lladhīna tābū min baʿdi dhālika wa-ʾaṣlaḥū fa-ʾinna llāha ghafūrun raḥīm^{un}﴿

﴾except such as repent after that and make amends, for God is Forgiving, Merciful﴿[112]

﴿وَٱلَّذِينَ عَمِلُواْ ٱلسَّيِّـَٔاتِ ثُمَّ تَابُواْ مِنۢ بَعۡدِهَا وَءَامَنُوٓاْ
إِنَّ رَبَّكَ مِنۢ بَعۡدِهَا لَغَفُورٞ رَّحِيمٞ﴾

---

[110] Sūrat al-Baqarah, Verse 160.

[111] Sūrat an-Nisāʾ, Verse 146.

[112] Sūrat Āl ʿImrān, Verse 89.

﴿*wa-lladhīna ʿamilū s-sayyiʾāti thumma tābū min baʿdihā wa-ʾāmanū ʾinna rabbaka min baʿdihā la-ghafūrun raḥīmun*﴾

﴿*Yet [to] those who commit misdeeds but repent after that, and believe—indeed, after that, your Lord shall surely be Forgiving, Merciful*﴾[113]

﴿فَإِن تَابُوا۟ وَأَقَامُوا۟ ٱلصَّلَوٰةَ وَءَاتَوُا۟ ٱلزَّكَوٰةَ فَخَلُّوا۟ سَبِيلَهُمْ ۚ إِنَّ ٱللَّهَ غَفُورٌ رَّحِيمٌ﴾

﴿*fa-ʾin tābū wa-ʾaqāmū ṣ-ṣalāta wa-ʾātawu z-zakāta fa-khallū sabīlahum ʾinna llāha ghafūrun raḥīmun*﴾

﴿*But if they repent, and maintain the prayer and give the zakat, then let them alone. Indeed God is Forgiving, Merciful*﴾[114]

﴿فَإِن تَابُوا۟ وَأَقَامُوا۟ ٱلصَّلَوٰةَ وَءَاتَوُا۟ ٱلزَّكَوٰةَ فَإِخْوَٰنُكُمْ فِى ٱلدِّينِ﴾

﴿*fa-ʾin tābū wa-ʾaqāmū ṣ-ṣalāta wa-ʾātawu z-zakāta fa-ʾikhwānukum fī d-dīni*﴾

---

113 Sūrat al-Aʿrāf, Verse 153.

114 Sūrat at-Tawbah, Verse 5.

﴿*Yet if they repent and maintain the prayer and give the zakat, then they are your brethren in faith*﴾[115]

﴿ثُمَّ إِنَّ رَبَّكَ لِلَّذِينَ عَمِلُوا۟ ٱلسُّوٓءَ بِجَهَـٰلَةٍ ثُمَّ تَابُوا۟ مِنۢ بَعْدِ ذَٰلِكَ وَأَصْلَحُوٓا۟ إِنَّ رَبَّكَ مِنۢ بَعْدِهَا لَغَفُورٌ رَّحِيمٌ﴾

﴿*thumma 'inna rabbaka li-lladhīna 'amilū s-sū'a bi-jahālatin thumma tābū min ba'di dhālika wa-'aṣlaḥū 'inna rabbaka min ba'dihā la-ghafūrun raḥīmun*﴾

﴿*Moreover, your Lord will indeed be forgiving and merciful to those who repent after they having committed evil out of ignorance and reform themselves*﴾[116]

﴿فَٱغْفِرْ لِلَّذِينَ تَابُوا۟ وَٱتَّبَعُوا۟ سَبِيلَكَ وَقِهِمْ عَذَابَ ٱلْجَحِيمِ﴾

﴿*fa-ghfir li-lladhīna tābū wa-ttaba'ū sabīlaka wa-qihim 'adhāba l-jaḥīmi*﴾

﴿*So forgive those who repent and follow Your way and save them from the punishment of hell*﴾[117]

Moreover, it can be inferred from some verses that repentance is not realized unless accompanied by initiative,

---

115 Sūrat at-Tawbah, Verse 11.

116 Sūrat an-Naḥl, Verse 119.

117 Sūrat Ghāfir, Verse 7.

self-reformation, and righteous deeds. Among these verses are the following:

﴿وَمَن تَابَ وَعَمِلَ صَٰلِحًا فَإِنَّهُۥ يَتُوبُ إِلَى ٱللَّهِ مَتَابًا﴾

﴿*wa-man tāba wa-ʿamila ṣāliḥan fa-ʾinnahū yatūbu ʾilā llāhi matāba*^{n}﴾

﴿*And whoever repents and acts righteously indeed turns to God with due penitence*﴾[118]

﴿إِنَّمَا ٱلتَّوْبَةُ عَلَى ٱللَّهِ لِلَّذِينَ يَعْمَلُونَ ٱلسُّوٓءَ بِجَهَٰلَةٍ ثُمَّ يَتُوبُونَ مِن قَرِيبٍ
فَأُوْلَٰٓئِكَ يَتُوبُ ٱللَّهُ عَلَيْهِمْ﴾

﴿*innamā t-tawbatu ʿalā llāhi li-lladhīna yaʿmalūna s-sūʾa bi-jahālatin thumma yatūbūna min qarībin fa-ʾulāʾika yatūbu llāhu ʿalayhim*﴾

﴿*[Acceptance of] repentance by God is only for those who commit evil out of ignorance and then repent promptly. It is such whose repentance God will accept*﴾[119]

﴿وَلَيْسَتِ ٱلتَّوْبَةُ لِلَّذِينَ يَعْمَلُونَ ٱلسَّيِّـَٔاتِ حَتَّىٰٓ إِذَا حَضَرَ أَحَدَهُمُ ٱلْمَوْتُ
قَالَ إِنِّى تُبْتُ ٱلْـَٰٔنَ﴾

118 Sūrat al-Furqān, Verse 71.

119 Sūrat an-Nisāʾ, Verse 17.

﴾wa-laysati t-tawbatu li-lladhīna yaʿmalūna s-sayyiʾāti ḥattā ʾidhā ḥaḍara ʾaḥadahumu l-mawtu qāla ʾinnī tubtu l-ʾāna﴿

﴾But [acceptance of] repentance is not for those who go on committing misdeeds: when death approaches any of them, he says, 'I repent now'﴿[120]

﴿فَلَمَّا رَأَوْا بَأْسَنَا قَالُوٓا۟ ءَامَنَّا بِٱللَّهِ وَحْدَهُۥ﴾

﴾fa-lammā raʾaw baʾsanā qālū ʾāmannā bi-llāhi waḥdahū﴿

﴾Then, when they sighted Our punishment, they said, 'We believe in God alone﴿[121]

﴿فَلَمْ يَكُ يَنفَعُهُمْ إِيمَٰنُهُمْ لَمَّا رَأَوْا۟ بَأْسَنَا ۖ سُنَّتَ ٱللَّهِ ٱلَّتِى قَدْ خَلَتْ فِى عِبَادِهِۦ ۖ وَخَسِرَ هُنَالِكَ ٱلْكَٰفِرُونَ﴾

﴾fa-lam yaku yanfaʿuhum ʾīmānuhum lammā raʾaw baʾsanā sunnata llāhi llatī qad khalat fī ʿibādihī wa-khasira hunālika l-kāfirūn[a]*﴿*

﴾But their faith was of no benefit to them when they sighted Our punishment—God's precedent, which has passed among

[120] Sūrat an-Nisāʾ, Verse 18.

[121] Sūrat Ghāfir, Verse 84.

His servants, and it is thence that the faithless will be losers﴿[122]

As for the narrations that mention that God accepts repentance even if it is just before death, they either imply —if the chain of narration is authentic—those who did not have the opportunity to repent, or were unaware of it, or received guidance only at that time of distress and at the door of death. However, it could also indicate situations where other factors lead to the acceptance of repentance and forgiveness, such as intercession from someone whose intercession is accepted or special circumstances like God forgiving someone out of respect for their parents or because they were destined to perform a significant act, like being martyred in the way of God or in the way of Imām al-Ḥusayn ﷺ.

It should be known that delaying repentance is connected to prolonged hope, just as it is connected to love for the worldly life and attachment to it. The Islāmic law [sharīʿah] considers these acts as crimes in themselves.

The righteous servants of God have been warned against prolonged hope and have taken precautions against it. In a supplication attributed to him, Imām ʿAlī ﷺ says,

---

[122] Sūrat Ghāfir, Verse 85.

> My God, do You see that I have only come to You from the direction of hopes.[123]

In the same vein, Imām Zayn al-ʿĀbidīn ﷺ said in one of his supplications,

> O God, bless Muḥammad and his Household, spare us from drawn-out expectations and cut them short in us through sincerity of works, so that we may not hope expectantly for completing an hour after an hour, closing day after day, joining a breath to a breath, or overtaking a step with a step! Keep us safe from the delusions of expectations; make us secure from their evils.[124]

The Imām ﷺ only sought sufficiency in God and refrained from prolonged hope, warning against excessive expectations and prolonging hope because of the religious harms and the negative consequences in the Hereafter that result from it. Numerous narrations and reports have come warning and cautioning against prolonged hope. Sufficient evidence for this is the saying of God:

﴿رُّبَمَا يَوَدُّ ٱلَّذِينَ كَفَرُواْ لَوْ كَانُواْ مُسْلِمِينَ﴾

﴾*rubamā yawaddu lladhīna kafarū law kānū muslimīn*﴿

---

[123] From Du'ā' al-Ṣabāḥ [the morning supplication].

[124] Imām Zayn al-ʿĀbidīn ﷺ, *al-Ṣaḥīfah al-Sajjādīyyah*, supplication no. 40.

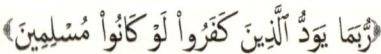

﴿ذَرْهُمْ يَأْكُلُوا۟ وَيَتَمَتَّعُوا۟ وَيُلْهِهِمُ ٱلْأَمَلُ ۖ فَسَوْفَ يَعْلَمُونَ﴾

﴾dharhum ya'kulū wa-yatamatta'ū wa-yulhihimu l-'amalu fa-sawfa ya'lamūn﴿

﴾Much will the faithless wish that they had been Muslims. Leave them to eat and enjoy and to be diverted by longings. Soon they will know﴿[125]

God ﷻ has alerted us that indulging in worldly pleasures and delighting in their bounties may lead to adopting the traits of disbelievers, not the traits of His righteous servants. In this regard, the following are some narrations that serve as warnings against prolonged hope:

One such narration is the Qudsi ḥadīth [divine saying]:

> O Mūsā, do not have prolonged hope in this worldly life, for it hardens your heart, and the one with a hard heart is far from Me.[126]

In his advice to Abū Dharr, Prophet Muḥammad ﷺ said,

> O Abū Dharr, beware of procrastinating with your [high] hopes, for verily you have today [at your disposal] and have not yet reached tomorrow.

---

[125] Sūrat al-Ḥijr, Verses 2–3.

[126] al-Ḥurr al-ʿĀmilī, Shaykh Muḥammad, *al-Jawāhir al-Saniyyah fī al-Aḥādīth al-Qudsiyyah*, p. 31.

When tomorrow comes to you, then be in it as you are in the present; [that way] even if you do not have tomorrow, you will not have regret for all that you neglected today. O Abū Dharr! How many people have met a day he did not complete? How many a waiter there is of tomorrow who does not find it! O Abū Dharr! If you knew the exact period you would live and realize your fate, you would hate hopes and their deception. O Abū Dharr! Be in the world like a stranger or pass by on a journey and count yourself among the graves' people. O Abū Dharr! When you wake up in the morning, do not talk to yourself about tonight; when night has come, do not worry about the morning.[127]

In another sermon by Imām ʿAlī 🕮, he said,

I am apprehensive for you on account of two things: submission to desire and cherishing of inordinate hope. As for desire, it prevents one from [realizing] the Truth [righteousness, God]; and as for inordinate hope, it makes man oblivious of the Hereafter.[128]

In another sermon, he 🕮 warned,

---

[127] Ṭabrisī, Shaykh Faḍl b. Ḥasan, *Makārim al-Akhlāq*, p. 459.

[128] Kulaynī, Shaykh Muḥammad b. Yaʿqūb, *al-Kāfī*, Vol. 2, p. 335.

> Know that prolonged hope distracts the mind and makes one forgetful of remembrance. So, reject prolonged hope, as it is delusional, and its companion is deluded.[129]

It was narrated that Usāmah b. Zayd bought a slave girl and set a time limit of one month for her to be set free. When the Prophet ﷺ was informed of this, he said,

> Are you not amazed at Usāmah setting a time limit of one month? Usāmah is indeed long in his hope (of life).[130]

In another narration, it is mentioned that two servants of God were conversing, and one asked the other,

> How short is your hope?

The other replied,

> My hope is such that when I wake up in the morning, I do not expect to live until evening, and when I go to sleep at night, I do not expect to wake up in the morning.

---

129 Sharīf Raḍī, Muḥammad b. al-Ḥusayn, *Nahj al-Balāghah*, Sermon 86.

130 Majlisī, 'Allāmah Muḥammad Bāqir, *Biḥār al-Anwār*, Vol. 70, p. 166.

The first person commented,

> You are long in your home, whereas I do not hope that I would live to take another breath after my current one, nor that I would exhale a breath if I take one.[131]

Some have pointed out the correlation between having long hopes in worldly desires and forgetting about the Hereafter, saying the following:

Expecting beloved worldly matters necessitates one to pay constant attention to them, and paying constant attention to them leads the self to turn away from considering the conditions of the Hereafter. In turn, the thought of the Hereafter fades from one's mind, and that is the meaning of forgetting it. Through this, eternal destruction and perpetual misery come about, and we seek refuge in God from that.[132]

Some have said that the reason for having prolonged hope [in life and worldly matters] is the love of this world. When a person becomes attached to worldly pleasures and delights, parting with them becomes burdensome, and they develop a strong attachment to the continuity of these pleasures. As a result, they do not contemplate death, which is the inevitable separation from this world. When

---

[131] Adab al-Nafs, Vol. 2, p. 27.

[132] Al-Ḥusaynī, Sayyid 'Alī Khān, *Riyāḍ al-Sālikīn*, Vol. 2, p. 147.

someone loves something, they dislike thinking about anything that may remove or negate it. Thus, they keep deluding themselves into thinking that they will continue to live in this world and have all their needs fulfilled regarding family, wealth, tools, and means. Their thoughts become engrossed in these matters, and death does not come to their mind. If the thought of death, repentance, and engaging in deeds for the Hereafter does cross their mind, they postpone it from one day to another, from one month to another, and from one year to another until they become old and their youth is long gone. They would say, "Once I finish this business, I will repent," or, "After I complete this construction project and marry my son to so-and-so or return from this trip, then I will repent." In this way, they keep procrastinating repentance; whenever they complete one worldly matter, another—or many others—grabs their attention until they are caught unaware by death, unprepared, and immersed in worldly matters. As a result, their regret grows longer, and their remorse increases in the Hereafter, which is a clear loss. We seek refuge in God from that.

Assuming that a person may know from someone who informs about God that they will live until a certain period, how can the meaning mentioned earlier be valid in this case?

The answer is that such information can only be about a predetermined lifespan that does not exceed the limits set by God. This is indicated by His saying:

﴿وَلَن يُؤَخِّرَ ٱللَّهُ نَفْسًا إِذَا جَآءَ أَجَلُهَا﴾

﴾*wa-lan yu'akhkhira llāhu nafsan 'idhā jā'a 'ajaluhā*﴿

﴾*But God will never respite anyone when his time has come*﴿[133]

As for an undetermined lifespan, it may be shortened, and this is what a believer fears, being taken by surprise if they come to know their predetermined time of death. And God is the one who grants success.

Repentance is an Obligation Upon All

Undoubtedly, anyone without immunity is not free from flaws or mistakes and may have committed some sins, small or large. The inclinations and tendencies towards disobedience, even if God has protected them from indulging in it, are all factors that distance one from the realm of God's mercy and lead to His displeasure. Therefore, every individual who has not been granted immunity must repent and seek forgiveness. Even the thought that one is not guilty of sin is a major sin, as they are not exempt from failing to fulfill their obligatory worship. Hence, it is prudent that everyone seek forgiveness. Rather, what we have discussed thus far implies that one must always seek repentance and forgiveness, hoping that he gets included in God's mercy so

[133] Sūrat al-Munāfiqūn, Verse 11.

He forgives and pardons him just as He promised His devoted servants.

Furthermore, by its nature, every potential existent is subject to imperfection. It inherently lacks what God, in His greatness, has decreed as necessary for it to progress from imperfection to perfection. No matter how elevated one's conduct may be in perfection and greatness, one will always remain imperfect based on one's potential, condition, and essence. To emerge from this imperfection, the servant must persist in holding onto the tail of God's mercy and the means of His power. The more they remain in this imperfection, the more they sense the distance and deprivation from the heights they have not yet attained. As they become aware of the vast and infinite distance between their current state and the exaltedness of their Lord, their sense of need for forgiveness and mercy intensifies.

Therefore, we should pay attention to the frequent seeking of forgiveness, the profound sorrow, and the strong drive of the pious servants of God to seek mercy and forgiveness for their shortcomings. Each time they overcome imperfection, they realize they need even more forgiveness and pardon.

There is textual evidence that indicates the general obligation of repentance and its inclusiveness for everyone. Let us take the following verses, for instance:

﴿وَتُوبُوٓاْ إِلَى ٱللَّهِ جَمِيعًا أَيُّهَ ٱلْمُؤْمِنُونَ لَعَلَّكُمْ تُفْلِحُونَ﴾

﴿*wa-tūbū 'ilā llāhi jamī'an 'ayyuha l-mu'minūna la'allakum tufliḥūna*﴾

﴿*Rally to God in repentance, O faithful, so that you may be felicitous*﴾[134]

﴿وَأَنِ ٱسْتَغْفِرُواْ رَبَّكُمْ ثُمَّ تُوبُوٓاْ إِلَيْهِ يُمَتِّعْكُم مَّتَٰعًا حَسَنًا﴾

﴿*wa-'ani staghfirū rabbakum thumma tūbū 'ilayhi yumatti'kum matā'an ḥasanan*﴾

﴿*Plead with your Lord for forgiveness, then turn to Him penitently. He will provide you with a good provision*﴾[135]

﴿وَيَٰقَوْمِ ٱسْتَغْفِرُواْ رَبَّكُمْ ثُمَّ تُوبُوٓاْ إِلَيْهِ يُرْسِلِ ٱلسَّمَآءَ عَلَيْكُم مِّدْرَارًا وَيَزِدْكُمْ قُوَّةً إِلَىٰ قُوَّتِكُمْ وَلَا تَتَوَلَّوْاْ مُجْرِمِينَ﴾

﴿*wa-yā-qawmi staghfirū rabbakum thumma tūbū 'ilayhi yursili s-samā'a 'alaykum midrāran wa-yazidkum quwwatan 'ilā quwwatikum wa-lā tatawallaw mujrimīna*﴾

﴿*'O my people! Plead with your Lord for forgiveness, then turn to Him penitently: He will send copious rains for you*

134 Sūrat an-Nūr, Verse 31.

135 Sūrat Hūd, Verse 3.

from the sky, and add power to your [present] power. So do not turn your backs [on Him] as guilty ones'﴾[136]

﴿وَٱسۡتَغۡفِرُواْ رَبَّكُمۡ ثُمَّ تُوبُوٓاْ إِلَيۡهِۚ إِنَّ رَبِّي رَحِيمٞ وَدُودٞ﴾

﴾*wa-staghfirū rabbakum thumma tūbū 'ilāyhi 'inna rabbī raḥīmun wadūdun*﴿

﴾*Plead with your Lord for forgiveness, then turn to Him penitently. My Lord is indeed Merciful, Affectionate*﴿[137]

Even though their context may refer to previous nations, these last four verses serve as a comprehensive general standard for the obligation of repentance for all accountable individuals. We all need God to provide us with good sustenance, send abundant rain upon us from the sky, and create us from the Earth and settle us therein. We all greatly depend on our Lord's mercy, affection, and kindness.

Other verses in this regard are the following:

﴿أَفَلَا يَتُوبُونَ إِلَى ٱللَّهِ وَيَسۡتَغۡفِرُونَهُۥۚ وَٱللَّهُ غَفُورٞ رَّحِيمٞ﴾

﴾*a-fa-lā yatūbūna 'ilā llāhi wa-yastaghfirūnahū wa-llāhu ghafūrun raḥīmun*﴿

136 Sūrat Hūd, Verse 52.

137 Sūrat Hūd, Verse 90.

﴿*Will they not repent to God and plead to Him for forgiveness? Yet God is Forgiving, Merciful*﴾[138]

This verse conveys a reminder and a warning against abandoning repentance and seeking forgiveness and encourages one to persist in this matter and constantly ask for pardon and mercy.

﴿أَوَلَا يَرَوْنَ أَنَّهُمْ يُفْتَنُونَ فِي كُلِّ عَامٍ مَّرَّةً أَوْ مَرَّتَيْنِ ثُمَّ لَا يَتُوبُونَ وَلَا هُمْ يَذَّكَّرُونَ﴾

﴿*a-wa-lā yarawna 'annahum yuftanūna fī kulli 'āmin marratan 'aw marratayni thumma lā yatūbūna wa-lā hum yadhdhakkarūn*[a]﴾

﴿*Do they not see that they are tried once or twice every year? Yet they neither repent, nor do they take admonition*﴾[139]

Perhaps mentioning the enticement once or twice every year is the least that God ﷻ tests His servants and alerts them to remember Him and repent to Him. It is well known that this verse, like its predecessors, is general.

﴿فَإِن يَتُوبُوا يَكُ خَيْرًا لَّهُمْ﴾

---

[138] Sūrat al-Mā'idah, Verse 74.

[139] Sūrat at-Tawbah, Verse 126.

﴿*fa-'in yatūbū yaku khayran lahum*﴾

﴿*Yet if they repent, it will be better for them*﴾[140]

﴿يَٰٓأَيُّهَا ٱلَّذِينَ ءَامَنُوا۟ تُوبُوٓا۟ إِلَى ٱللَّهِ تَوْبَةً نَّصُوحًا﴾

﴿*yā-'ayyuhā lladhīna 'āmanū tūbū 'ilā llāhi tawbatan naṣūḥan*﴾

﴿*O you who have faith! Repent to God with sincere repentance!*﴾[141]

Moreover, some verses praise those who repent and encourage seeking forgiveness. It is well understood that this implies urging and exhorting people to engage in these actions and warning against abandoning them. For instance, consider the following verses among many others that indicate the obligation of repentance, highlight its virtue, or extol the merits and benefits that result from repentance:

﴿إِلَّا ٱلَّذِينَ تَابُوا۟ وَأَصْلَحُوا۟ وَبَيَّنُوا۟ فَأُو۟لَٰٓئِكَ أَتُوبُ عَلَيْهِمْ وَأَنَا ٱلتَّوَّابُ ٱلرَّحِيمُ﴾

﴿*illā lladhīna tābū wa-'aṣlaḥū wa-bayyanū fa-'ulā'ika 'atūbu ʿalayhim wa-'ana t-tawwābu r-raḥīm*ᵘ﴾

140 Sūrat at-Tawbah, Verse 74.

141 Sūrat at-Taḥrīm, Verse 8.

﴾*except such as repent, make amends, and clarify—those I shall pardon, and I am the Clement, the Merciful*﴿[142]

﴿ٱلتَّـٰٓئِبُونَ ٱلۡعَـٰبِدُونَ ٱلۡحَـٰمِدُونَ ٱلسَّـٰٓئِحُونَ ٱلرَّٰكِعُونَ ٱلسَّـٰجِدُونَ﴾

﴾*ᵃt-tā'ibūna l-'ābidūna l-ḥāmidūna s-sā'iḥūna r-rāki'ūna s-sājidūna*﴿

﴾*[The faithful are] penitent, devout, celebrators of God's praise, wayfarers, who bow [and] prostrate [in prayer]*﴿[143]

﴿إِلَّا ٱلَّذِينَ تَابُواْ مِنۢ بَعۡدِ ذَٰلِكَ وَأَصۡلَحُواْ فَإِنَّ ٱللَّهَ غَفُورٞ رَّحِيمٌ﴾

﴾*illā lladhīna tābū min ba'di dhālika wa-'aṣlaḥū fa-'inna llāha ghafūrun raḥīmᵘⁿ*﴿

﴾*except such as repent after that and make amends, for God is Forgiving, Merciful*﴿[144]

إِلَّا ٱلَّذِينَ تَابُواْ وَأَصۡلَحُواْ وَٱعۡتَصَمُواْ بِٱللَّهِ وَأَخۡلَصُواْ دِينَهُمۡ لِلَّهِ فَأُوْلَـٰٓئِكَ مَعَ ٱلۡمُؤۡمِنِينَ﴾

﴾*illā lladhīna tābū wa-'aṣlaḥū wa-'taṣamū bi-llāhi wa-'akhlaṣū dīnahum li-llāhi fa-'ulā'ika ma'a l-mu'minīna*﴿

---

[142] Sūrat al-Baqarah, Verse 160.

[143] Sūrat at-Tawbah, Verse 112.

[144] Sūrat Āl 'Imrān, Verse 89.

﴾*except for those who repent and reform, and hold fast to God and dedicate their religion [exclusively] to God. Those are with the faithful*﴿[145]

﴿وَٱلَّذِينَ عَمِلُوا۟ ٱلسَّيِّـَٔاتِ ثُمَّ تَابُوا۟ مِنۢ بَعْدِهَا وَءَامَنُوٓا۟ إِنَّ رَبَّكَ مِنۢ بَعْدِهَا لَغَفُورٌ رَّحِيمٌ﴾

﴾*wa-lladhīna ʿamilū s-sayyiʾāti thumma tābū min baʿdihā wa-ʾāmanū ʾinna rabbaka min baʿdihā la-ghafūrun raḥīmun*﴿

﴾*Yet [to] those who commit misdeeds but repent after that, and believe—indeed, after that, your Lord shall surely be Forgiving, Merciful*﴿[146]

﴿ثُمَّ إِنَّ رَبَّكَ لِلَّذِينَ عَمِلُوا۟ ٱلسُّوٓءَ بِجَهَـٰلَةٍ ثُمَّ تَابُوا۟ مِنۢ بَعْدِ ذَٰلِكَ وَأَصْلَحُوٓا۟ إِنَّ رَبَّكَ مِنۢ بَعْدِهَا لَغَفُورٌ رَّحِيمٌ﴾

﴾*thumma ʾinna rabbaka li-lladhīna ʿamilū s-sūʾa bi-jahālatin thumma tābū min baʿdi dhālika wa-ʾaṣlaḥū ʾinna rabbaka min baʿdihā la-ghafūrun raḥīmun*﴿

---

[145] Sūrat an-Nisāʾ, Verse 146.

[146] Sūrat al-Aʿrāf, Verse 153.

﴾*Moreover, your Lord will indeed be forgiving and merciful to those who repent after they having committed evil out of ignorance and reform themselves*﴿[147]

﴿إِنَّ ٱللَّهَ يُحِبُّ ٱلتَّوَّٰبِينَ وَيُحِبُّ ٱلْمُتَطَهِّرِينَ﴾

﴾*inna llāha yuḥibbu t-tawwābīna wa-yuḥibbu l-mutaṭahhirīna*﴿

﴾*Indeed God loves the penitent and He loves those who keep clean*﴿[148]

﴿أَلَمْ يَعْلَمُوٓا۟ أَنَّ ٱللَّهَ هُوَ يَقْبَلُ ٱلتَّوْبَةَ عَنْ عِبَادِهِۦ وَيَأْخُذُ ٱلصَّدَقَٰتِ وَأَنَّ ٱللَّهَ هُوَ ٱلتَّوَّابُ ٱلرَّحِيمُ﴾

﴾*a-lam yaʿlamū ʾanna llāha huwa yaqbalu t-tawbata ʿan ʿibādihī wa-yaʾkhudhu ṣ-ṣadaqāti wa-ʾanna llāha huwa t-tawwābu r-raḥīmu*﴿

﴾*Do they not know that it is God who accepts the repentance of His servants and receives the charities, and that it is God who is the Clement, the Merciful?*﴿[149]

---

[147] Sūrat an-Naḥl, Verse 119.

[148] Sūrat al-Baqarah, Verse 222.

[149] Sūrat at-Tawbah, Verse 104.

One of the narrations that indicates the general and comprehensive obligation of repentance is an authentic [ṣaḥīḥ] narration from Muʿāwīyah b. Wahb. He said:

> I heard Imām Jaʿfar aṣ-Ṣādiq ﷺ saying:
>
> > If one truly repents, God likes to cover up his sins in the world and the Hereafter.
>
> I asked him,
>
> > How does God cover up the sins?
>
> The Imām ﷺ said,
>
> > He makes both guardian angels forget whatever they have recorded in the letter of deeds regarding his sins, He reveals to his body parts to cover up whatever sins he has done with them, and He reveals to the places on Earth where the sins were committed to cover up the sins. Thus, when he goes to meet his Lord in the Hereafter, nothing of his sins is left to bear witness against him.[150]

This narration has been mentioned previously.

---

[150] Kulaynī, Shaykh Muḥammad b. Yaʿqūb, *al-Kāfī*, Vol. 2, p. 430.

Furthermore, it is reported that Shaykh Bahā'ī ؒ explained the following:

The interpreters have mentioned various aspects of the true meaning of repentance described as nuṣūḥ [sincere]:

One aspect is that it means sincere repentance and advising others to do the same, encouraging them to seek the beautiful effects of repentance in themselves or urging others to quit committing sins and never return to them.

Another aspect is that sincerity in repentance is for the sake of God alone. This is derived from the saying that honey is pure [nuṣūḥ] when it is wax-free. Hence, in this context, it means to repent out of regret for the ugliness of sins or because they go against the pleasure of God, not out of fear of punishment, for example. Based on this, the great scholar al-Ṭūsī ؒ ruled in *al-Tajrīd* that remorse for sins out of fear of the Hellfire is not considered true repentance.[151]

Another aspect is that nuṣūḥ [sincerity] comes from the word naṣīḥah [advice]. It is like the sewing of torn fabric, where repentance mends what sins have torn, or it brings together the penitent with God's friends and beloved ones, just as sewing brings together pieces of cloth.

---

151 We have previously highlighted this notion.

Another aspect is that nuṣūḥ [sincerity] describes the repentant person and attributes repentance to him metaphorically, meaning that the repentance they advise themselves with should be brought in its complete form so it can entirely remove the traces of sins from their hearts. This is done by melting the self through regret and erasing the darkness of sins with the light of good deeds.

Another aspect is articulated in the authentic narration from Abū al-Ṣabbāḥ al-Kinānī, who said:

> I asked Imām Jaʿfar aṣ-Ṣādiq ﵇ about the verse:
>
> ﴿يَٰٓأَيُّهَا ٱلَّذِينَ ءَامَنُوا۟ تُوبُوٓا۟ إِلَى ٱللَّهِ تَوْبَةً نَّصُوحًا﴾
>
> ﴾*yā-ʾayyuhā lladhīna ʾāmanū tūbū ʾilā llāhi tawbatan naṣūḥan*﴿
>
> ﴾*O you who have faith! Repent to God with sincere repentance!*﴿[152]

He ﵇ said,

> The servant repents from the sin and then does not return to it.[153]

[152] Sūrat at-Taḥrīm, Verse 8.

[153] Kulaynī, Shaykh Muḥammad b. Yaʿqūb, *al-Kāfī*, Vol. 2, p. 432.

Muḥammad b. al-Fuḍayl also narrated,

> I asked Abū al-Ḥasan ﷺ about the same verse. He said,
>
> > It is repentance from the sin and not returning to it. The most beloved of servants to God ﷻ are those who are tested [with sins] and then repent.[154]

Shaykh Kulaynī reported in another authentic narration from Abū Baṣīr, who said,

> I asked Imām Jaʿfar aṣ-Ṣādiq ﷺ about the [last] verse.[155] He replied,
>
> > It is the sin that one does not return to ever again.
>
> I asked,
>
> > Which of us has not returned [to sins]?
>
> He said,

---

[154] Ibid.

[155] Sūrat at-Taḥrīm, Verse 8.

> O Abū Muḥammad, God loves from His servants the tested one who repents.[156]

Another narration that indicates the general obligation of repentance is the authentic narration of Muḥammad b. Muslim who reported from one of the Imāms regarding the verse:

﴿فَمَن جَآءَهُۥ مَوْعِظَةٌ مِّن رَّبِّهِۦ فَٱنتَهَىٰ فَلَهُۥ مَا سَلَفَ﴾

﴿fa-man jā'ahū maw'iẓatun min rabbihī fa-ntahā fa-lahū mā salafa﴾

﴿Whoever relinquishes [usury] on receiving advice from his Lord shall keep [the gains of] what is past﴾[157]

He said,

> The admonition is repentance.[158]

It should be known that persisting in sin is among the acts of disobedience that must be avoided. None of the servant's acts of obedience are accepted as long as he does not fear God. God ﷻ says,

---

[156] Kulaynī, Shaykh Muḥammad b. Ya'qūb, *al-Kāfī*, Vol. 2, p. 432.

[157] Sūrat al-Baqarah, Verse 275.

[158] Kulaynī, Shaykh Muḥammad b. Ya'qūb, *al-Kāfī*, Vol. 2, pp. 431–432.

﴿إِنَّمَا يَتَقَبَّلُ ٱللَّهُ مِنَ ٱلْمُتَّقِينَ﴾

﴿innamā yataqabbalu llāhu mina l-muttaqīn[a]﴾

﴿God accepts only from the Godwary﴾[159]

Through his authentic chain of narrators, Shaykh Kulaynī reported from Abū Baṣīr, who said,

> I heard Imām Jaʿfar aṣ-Ṣādiq ﷺ say,
>
> > No, by God! God does not accept any servant's obedience to Him while he persists in disobedience against Him.[160]

From these narrations, it can be understood that not initiating repentance is considered persistence in sin. Shaykh Kulaynī also reported the following through his chain of narrators from Jabir from Abū Jaʿfar ﷺ. Regarding the verse:

﴿وَلَمْ يُصِرُّوا۟ عَلَىٰ مَا فَعَلُوا۟ وَهُمْ يَعْلَمُونَ﴾

﴿wa-lam yuṣirrū ʿalā mā faʿalū wa-hum yaʿlamūn[a]﴾

---

[159] Sūrat al-Māʾidah, Verse 27.

[160] Kulaynī, Shaykh Muḥammad b. Yaʿqūb, *al-Kāfī*, Vol. 2, p. 288.

﴾and who knowingly do not persist in what [sins] they have committed﴿[161]

the Imām said,

> Persistence is when a person commits a sin and does not seek God's forgiveness nor resolves to repent; that is persistence.[162]

A small sin becomes significant through persistence, and as we know, neglecting repentance is a form of persistence. Kulaynī, through his chain of narrators, reported from ʿAbdullāh b. Sinān that Imām Jaʿfar aṣ-Ṣādiq ﷤ said,

> With persistence, no sin is minor, and with seeking forgiveness, no sin is major.[163]

Indeed, belittling a sin, regardless of its size, can lead to considering a minor sin as a major. Neglecting repentance for a sin can cause a person to persist in committing it, eventually becoming a major sin. Imām Jaʿfar aṣ-Ṣādiq ﷤ alluded to this meaning in the following narration:

---

161 Sūrat Āl ʿImrān, Verse 135.

162 Ibid.

163 Ibid.

The Imām said,

> Beware of those minor sins that you belittle, for they will not be forgiven.

I [the narrator] asked,

> What are those sins?

He replied,

> They are the ones which if a man commits, he says: I am prosperous if I do not commit any other sins [i.e., he is not afraid of this sin, seeing it as nothing really bad, and persists in it despite knowing it is wrong, following the mindset: how fortunate I am that it is not worse than that].[164]

Imām Mūsā al-Kāẓim ﷺ also indicated a similar concept when he said,

> Do not consider a great deal of good a great deal and do not consider a little sin very little; little sins accumulate and become a great deal. Have fear of God in private so you can do justice to yourselves.[165]

---

[164] Ibid., p. 287.

[165] Ibid.

Similarly, the Messenger of God ﷺ also warned about the sins people tend to overlook,

> Avoid minor sins that are belittled, for there is a searcher for everything, and the Recorder of sins writes whatever people offer to leave behind them.

﴿وَكُلَّ شَيْءٍ أَحْصَيْنَـٰهُ كِتَـٰبًا﴾

﴾*wa-kulla shay'in 'aḥṣaynāhu kitāba*ⁿ﴿

﴾*and We have figured everything in a Book*﴿[166]

Shaykh Kulaynī, through his chain of narrators, reported that Imām Ja'far aṣ-Ṣādiq al-Ṣādiq said,

> The Prophet ﷺ said,
>
> > Among the signs of wretchedness are hardened eyes, hardened hearts, and extreme eagerness in seeking worldly gains and persistence in committing sins.[167]

Shaykh Ṣadūq narrated through his chain of narrators from Imām Ja'far b. Muḥammad that his father said:

---

[166] Ibid., p. 288.

[167] al-Ḥurr al-'Āmilī, Shaykh Muḥammad b. al-Ḥasan, *Wasā'il al-Shī'ah*, Vol. 15, Chapter 48, p. 337.

> The Messenger of God ﷺ said,
>
> > Whoever sins while laughing will enter the Hellfire while weeping.[168]

As mentioned earlier, rejoicing in sinning leads the sinner away from repentance based on remorse.

Shaykh Kulaynī ؒ narrated through his chain of narrators that Mu'āwīyah b. 'Ammār said,

> I heard Imām Ja'far aṣ-Ṣādiq ؑ saying,
>
> > By God, no man has ever abandoned a sin while persisting in it; man can only abandon a sin by acknowledging it.[169]

---

[168] Ibid., p. 338.

[169] Ibid., Chapter 15, p. 59.

Benefit in Analyzing Repentance, Seeking Forgiveness, or Admitting Sins by the Infallible

After establishing the decisive evidence, whether intellectual or transmitted, of the infallibility of the prophets, Imāms ﷺ, Sayyidah Fāṭimah ﷺ, and the like, it becomes prudent to divert away from the apparent meaning of statements narrated from these holy personalities, which imply them to be admitting to sin or other such actions that are inconsistent with their natural course. This aligns with the approach of righteous scholars and seekers of the truth in dealing with the expressions found in reliable texts that attribute anthropomorphism or what accompanies it to the essence of the ﷻ. Thus, the question arises about the drive, wisdom, or necessity of such words and statements, not only in specific instances but also generally in other texts, such as those related to the Throne, Chair, and the apparent attribution of speech composed of sounds.

On certain occasions, we have stated that the words commonly used and employed to help the reader understand and comprehend the intended meaning are the ones that we *can* learn. The speaker, whoever they may be, is bound to limit their attempts to express [complex] meanings using such words. These words reveal the linguistic implications of what we can comprehend and understand. Regardless of their source, such words were designed to facilitate understanding and comprehension among humans and sometimes beyond them, like conversations between humans and angels or between them and some animals. Examples include what occurred between Prophet Sulaymān عليه السلام and the ant and between him and the hoopoe, in addition to what has been narrated about conversations between some infallibles and certain animals.

Since the speaker is limited to the circulated languages whose meanings we can comprehend, his efforts inevitably focus on choosing words in those languages as they are in terms of form and structural elements. This presents a problem in how these holy beings can express those lofty meanings, which are beyond our souls' reach or our intellect's comprehension, using common words confined to the prevalent languages or have become extinct altogether. Therefore, the speaker must employ allegorical and metaphorical expressions to help the listener or reader comprehend those lofty meanings, using hints and placing signs within the words to alert the rational mind to their intended meanings. Simultaneously, stern warnings are given to those not qualified to comprehend such expressions, similar to what is mentioned in the following verses:

﴿هُوَ ٱلَّذِيٓ أَنزَلَ عَلَيۡكَ ٱلۡكِتَٰبَ مِنۡهُ ءَايَٰتٞ مُّحۡكَمَٰتٌ هُنَّ أُمُّ ٱلۡكِتَٰبِ
وَأُخَرُ مُتَشَٰبِهَٰتٞۖ فَأَمَّا ٱلَّذِينَ فِي قُلُوبِهِمۡ زَيۡغٞ فَيَتَّبِعُونَ مَا تَشَٰبَهَ مِنۡهُ ٱبۡتِغَآءَ
ٱلۡفِتۡنَةِ وَٱبۡتِغَآءَ تَأۡوِيلِهِۦۗ وَمَا يَعۡلَمُ تَأۡوِيلَهُۥٓ إِلَّا ٱللَّهُۗ وَٱلرَّٰسِخُونَ فِي ٱلۡعِلۡمِ يَقُولُونَ
ءَامَنَّا بِهِۦ كُلّٞ مِّنۡ عِندِ رَبِّنَاۗ وَمَا يَذَّكَّرُ إِلَّآ أُوْلُواْ ٱلۡأَلۡبَٰبِ﴾

﴿huwa lladhī ʾanzala ʿalayka l-kitāba minhu ʾāyātun muḥkamātun hunna ʾummu l-kitābi wa-ʾukharu mutashābihātun fa-ʾammā lladhīna fī qulūbihim zayghun fa-yattabiʿūna mā tashābaha minhu btighāʾa l-fitnati wa-btighāʾa taʾwīlihī wa-mā yaʿlamu taʾwīlahū ʾillā llāhu wa-r-rāsikhūna fī l-ʿilmi yaqūlūna ʾāmannā bihī kullun min ʿindi rabbinā wa-mā yadhdhakkaru ʾillā ʾulū l-ʾalbābi﴾

﴾It is He who has sent down to you the Book. Parts of it are definitive verses, which are the mother of the Book, while others are metaphorical. As for those in whose hearts is deviance, they pursue what is metaphorical in it, courting temptation, and seeking its interpretation. But no one knows its interpretation except God and those firmly grounded in knowledge; they say, 'We believe in it; all of it is from our Lord.' And none takes admonition except those who possess intellect﴿[170]

and

﴿فَسْـَٔلُوٓا۟ أَهْلَ ٱلذِّكْرِ إِن كُنتُمْ لَا تَعْلَمُونَ﴾

﴾fa-sʾalū ʾahla dh-dhikri ʾin kuntum lā taʿlamūna﴿

﴾Ask the People of the Reminder if you do not know﴿[171]

---

[170] Sūrat Āl ʿImrān, Verse 7.

[171] Sūrat an-Naḥl, Verse 43.

In this context, Salmān al-Fārisī asked the Messenger of God ﷺ about the verse:

﴿وَٱلشَّمۡسِ وَضُحَىٰهَا﴾

﴿*wa-sh-shamsi wa-ḍuḥāhā*﴾

﴿وَٱلۡقَمَرِ إِذَا تَلَىٰهَا﴾

﴿*wa-l-qamari 'idhā talāhā*﴾

﴿*By the sun and her forenoon splendour,*
by the moon when he follows her﴾[172]

This highlights that it is necessary to place the narrated expressions about infallibility and purity in the context of those expressions, which definitive evidence and sound narrations prevent us from adopting their linguistic implications. This approach is not inferior to the transmitted texts and noble verses.

From this standpoint, ideas arose to research the true meanings and implications of what is narrated from these holy beings, which contradicts infallibility in their apparent meaning or naive understanding. Thus, various opinions and ideas emerged, some of which we summarize here in

---

[172] Sūrat ash-Shams, Verses 1–2.

appreciation of the efforts of our noble scholars. May God reward their beautiful endeavors.

The following, dear reader, is some of what can be presented hastily [each interpretation is specified as such in bold to separate between them]:

One interpretation is that the purpose of such expressions is to discipline people, teach them how to acknowledge and confess their shortcomings and sins and seek forgiveness and repentance from them.

Undoubtedly, it is evident that this aligns with the supplications that have been reported from the infallibles عليهم السلام in the context of teaching, such as the supplication of Amīr al-Mu'minīn عليه السلام, which he taught to Kumayl b. Ziyād قدس سره and the supplication that Imām ʿAlī b. al-Ḥusayn عليه السلام taught to his student Abū Ḥamza Thumālī. Also, some of the non-infallible individuals were taught certain Ziyārat, such as what was mentioned in the Ziyārah for the martyrs of the event of Taff, the companions of Imām Husayn عليهم السلام,

> My father and mother be sacrificed for you. Verily, you were pure; therefore, the land wherein you are buried has been purified...

The act of seeking intercession through the infallible's parents does not apply to anyone other than an infallible; it cannot be used for fallible people. Therefore, it can be understood that this practice is aimed at teaching and disciplining the one reading or listening to the Ziyārah.

Furthermore, this action concerns the apparent expressions and explicit texts some may not bear. For example, it is narrated about the great Prophet ﷺ that he used to seek forgiveness from God seventy times,[173] In another narration about him, he said,

> I repent to God a hundred times a day.[174]

This can only be reconciled by relying on the prelude we have pointed out and interpreting it in a way that does not contradict the decisive evidence of infallibility while leaving the uncovering of the truth to the one who possesses the authority of guidance and unveiling the hidden aspects of matters.

Another interpretation is that such expressions convey humility and acknowledge servitude, recognizing that humans are prone to shortcomings.[175] This means that everything mentioned in the supplications of the infallibles is an expression of humility for oneself and an acknowledgment that they are servants who do not possess immunity and guidance by their merit but that it is a gift

---

[173] Kulaynī, Shaykh Muḥammad b. Ya'qūb, *al-Kāfī*, Vol. 2, p. 438.

[174] Majlisī, 'Allāmah Muḥammad Bāqir, *Biḥār al-Anwār*, Vol. 90, p. 282.

[175] Al-Ḥusaynī, Sayyid 'Alī Khān, *Riyāḍ al-Sālikīn*, Vol. 2, p. 472.

from God ﷻ. Considering them as human beings, they are susceptible to shortcomings, thus always placing themselves among those who fall short.

In this context, the concept of humility is only realized when a person relinquishes their position or rights about the position of others, like when one of two companions walks slower than the other or sits with the other despite their lower position or status [sitting in a gathering regardless of position or status], or when one forsakes some titles in favor of titles given to their equal or inferior. Imām Ḥasan al-ʿAskarī ؑ said,

> Part of humility is greeting everyone man passes by and sitting in gatherings that are below his position or status.[176]

Imām Jaʿfar aṣ-Ṣādiq ؑ said,

> Humility is for a man to sit in gatherings that are below his position or status.[177]

Thus, humility is a relative concept or an additional meaning realized between two individuals, each according to their deserving position. If people humbly themselves

[176] al-Ḥarrānī, Ibn Shuʿba, *Tuḥaf al-ʿUqūl,* ninth sentence from the quotes of Imām Ḥasan al-ʿAskarī ؑ. Majlisī, ʿAllāmah Muḥammad Bāqir, *Biḥār al-Anwār*, Vol. 72, p. 466.

[177] Kulaynī, Shaykh Muḥammad b. Yaʿqūb, *al-Kāfī*, Vol. 2, p. 123.

and lower themselves beyond what they deserve, they have shown humility.

Based on this, it becomes difficult to depict humility between the servant and the worshiped or between the servant and the true Master because there is no position, reality, or truth of the servant relating to the Master that would warrant relinquishing some of those positions as an act of humility. Instead, everything he has is a favor and a gift bestowed upon him by the Master, whether it is an emanation or an additional emanation of divine light. Therefore, within those limits, only the light envelops the essence of the servant, and he does not act or comprehend, nor does he do or refrain [from something], except within that emanation and by that addition. Thus, the concept of humility is not realized in that context.

So, humility is a relative concept or an additional meaning realized between two individuals, each according to their deserving position. If one humbles themselves and lowers themselves beyond what they deserve, they have shown humility.

Based on this premise, it becomes difficult to depict humility between the servant and the worshiped or between the servant and the true Master because there is no position, reality, or truth of the servant towards the Master that would warrant relinquishing some of those positions as an act of humility. Everything the servant possesses is a favor and a gift from the Master, even an emanation or an additional emanation of divine light. Therefore, nothing is within those boundaries except the light that encompasses the essence of the servant. They neither move, perceive, act, nor refrain except within that emanation and by that addition, and thus, the true essence of humility is not realized there.

In the literature, we also see authentic narrations that emphasize the necessity of humility towards God, such as the following authentic narration from Muʿāwīyah b. ʿAmmār,

> I heard Imām Jaʿfar aṣ-Ṣādiq ﷺ say that there are two angels in the Heavens assigned to the servants, and whoever humbles themselves to God, they elevate him, and whoever becomes arrogant, they lower him.[178]

Another narration is the one from ʿAbd al-Rahman b. al-Ḥajjāj from Imām Jaʿfar aṣ-Ṣādiq ﷺ said,

> On a Thursday evening, the Messenger of God had completed his day's fasting, and dinner was served in the Mosque of Qubāʾ.
>
> He asked,
>
> Is there any drink?

[178] Ibid., p. 122.

> Aws b. Khawlī al-Anṣārī brought him a bowl of milk mixed with honey. When he touched it with his lips, he pushed it aside and said,
>
>> There are two drinks, each of which is enough as a drink for whoever has it, and I neither drink it nor prohibit it, but I humble myself to God. For whoever humbles themselves to God, God elevates them, and whoever shows arrogance, God lowers them, and whoever is moderate in their sustenance, God provides for them, and whoever gives generously, God makes things abundant for them, and whoever remembers death often, God loves them.[179]

These narrations and the like aim to highlight the detachment [Zuhd] of the Prophet ﷺ from the pleasures of this world, encouraging man to adhere to asceticism and find contentment with less than one's due rights towards others as a means of drawing closer to God. As narrated from Imām ʿAlī ؑ, the Prophet ﷺ was not served two different types of food in a single feast. The apparent meaning of this incident is that the Prophet ﷺ was entitled to drink the honeyed drink, as God had permitted it for him, just as Aws b. Khawlī was entitled to drink it. However, the Prophet ﷺ relinquished his right as an act of drawing closer to God. Therefore, humility, relinquishing

---

[179] Ibid.

one's rights towards others, is commendable when the ultimate goal is God, which means humility towards God.

Thus, the following narration from Imām Muḥammad al-Bāqir ‎ﷺ in the biography of Imām ʿAlī ‎ﷺ is also interpreted in this way:

> No two matters would be referred to him [Imām ʿAlī] at all for the sake of God and His pleasure except that he would opt for the more difficult one upon his body.[180]

Based on this understanding, the confessions and admissions of the infallibles ‎ﷺ regarding shortcomings, sins, seeking forgiveness, and repentance can be understood as a way for them to express and exercise humility.

This lends weight and reliability to what some people have articulated about the infallibles ‎ﷺ having their specific obligations different from ours. Their seeking forgiveness or admitting their sins and shortcomings, considering their specific obligations, does not diminish their elevated status. It is a matter of humility. For example, the obligation of a traveler is different from that of a resident, the obligation of a husband is different from that of a wife, the obligation of a religious authority is different from that of a follower, or

---

180 Majlisī, ʿAllāmah Muḥammad Bāqir, *Biḥār al-Anwār*, Vol. 40, p. 329 from *Manāqib Āl Abī Ṭālib* and Ṭūsī, Shaykh Muḥammad b. Ḥasan, *al-Amālī*, Vol. 40, p. 339.

the obligation of a prophet or an Imām is different from that on ordinary people. Yet, each person is held accountable if they intentionally neglect their obligations.

The claim that the good deeds of the righteous are the sins of those close to God only indicates differences in obligations. For example, an act that may not be considered a sin when done by someone with a weak personality, limited knowledge, and recently embraced faith might be considered a sin if done by someone else, according to religious standards. However, this does not mean that if it is considered sinful according to religious standards, it becomes contrary to infallibility.

Moreover, the assertion that the infallible place themselves in the position of one who falls short while being elevated with their honor above this lowly rank achieves the meaning of humility because, by doing so, they relinquish what is theirs and take what does not belong to them in the sight of God.

First, some supplications mention the admission of sin and the occurrence of shortcomings; for instance, in the twelfth supplication of *al-Ṣaḥīfah al-Sajjādīyyah*, we read,

> O God, three traits have prevented me from asking You and one trait has urged me on. I am prevented by a command You have commanded in which I have been slow [in fulfilling], a prohibition You have prohibited me from yet toward which I have

> hurried, and a favor through which You have favored for which I have not given sufficient thanks.

Until the Imām ﷺ says,

> Will my confession to You, my Lord, of the evil of what I have earned, benefit me? And will my acknowledgment of the ugliness of what I have committed save me from You?

As you can see, this does not seem to be mere humility on the surface.

Second, achieving the meaning of humility is only possible if it is established when a servant excels in their actions and avoids everything that incurs the displeasure of the Lord; it is genuinely attributed to God ﷻ, and it becomes a position with Him. However, the apparent meaning of the words of the Imāms ﷺ transmitted from them ﷺ is that everything the servant does is an outcome of servitude, and any good that comes from him is a result of God's favor. Indeed, it is impossible for anything other than honor and favors to be bestowed upon the sincere believers, as promised by God to the righteous; it is inconceivable for anything contrary to that promise to occur due to its ugliness and its inconsistency with the exalted position of His absolute sovereignty.

As for what follows this aspect (mankind being prone to falling short), it has become clear that it can only be attributed to them [the infallibles] in the sense that they might not have known the reality of what emanated from them, the outcome of their actions, and what they acquired. This interpretation is consistent with those who lost their infallibility and did not know the true nature of their actions, as indicated by some of what is mentioned in the supplication taught by Imām Zayn al-ʿĀbidīn to his student Abū Ḥamza Thumālī. He instructed him on how to confess to God regarding his state:

> O my Master, perhaps You have pushed me away from Your door and dismissed me from Your service! Or, perhaps You have noticed that I belittled the duties that You have made incumbent upon me, and You thus set me aside! Or, perhaps, You have seen me turning away from You, and thus You have turned away from me! Or, perhaps, You have found me in the manner of the liars, and thus You have rejected me! Or, perhaps, You have observed me showing no gratitude for Your graces, and thus You have deprived me of them! Or, perhaps, You have not found me in the meetings of the scholars, and thus, You have let me down! Or, perhaps, You have seen me among the inattentive ones, and thus You have made me despair of Your mercy! Or, perhaps You have found me fond of the wrongdoers' sessions and thus referred me to them! Or, perhaps, You have not willed to hear my

prayers and thus kept me away from You! Or,
perhaps You have punished me for my offenses and
sins! Or, perhaps, You have penalized me for my
shamelessness! If You forgive me, O Lord, then You
have occasionally forgiven the sinners like me
because Your compassion, O my Lord, is too great
to be compared to the punishment of the
negligent.

As for someone like Abū Ḥamza Thumālī, who is distant
from the status of infallibility, the honor of absolute
guardianship, and the realm of divine greatness, he might
find himself inclined towards falling short. He hovers
between fear and hope, fearing that he might be among the
negligent sinners while hoping for God's forgiveness and
mercy so that he is not held accountable for what befits his
situation. Instead, he hopes to be on the receiving end of
God's kindness and generosity, befitting His sublime status
and exaltedness. In this context, the meaning of what is
mentioned at the end of the supplication taught by Amīr
al-Mu'minīn 🕮 to his student, the devoted and ascetic
Kumayl b. Ziyād 🕮 becomes clear. The supplication says:

O He whose Name is a remedy, whose
remembrance is a cure, and whose obedience is
wealth! Have mercy upon him whose capital is
hope and whose weapon is tears! O Ample in
blessings! O Repeller of adversities! O Light of
those who are lonely in the darkness! O Knower,

> who was never taught! Bless Muḥammad and Muḥammad's household! And do with me what is worthy of You!...

Another interpretation [of the aforementioned admission of sin and pursuit of forgiveness and repentance by the infallible] or a way to look at it is that acknowledging sins and seeking forgiveness for them is only based on the assumption of their occurrence. The intended meaning is that if anything from these matters arises from me, then forgive me, considering that it is unnecessary for the truthfulness of the condition to validate each part separately.[181]

In this regard, it first contradicts the sincerity of the conditional cases that have been qualified descriptively, followed by the path of those who delve into deep understanding. It also contradicts explicitly what was mentioned in the second supplication from *al-Ṣaḥīfah al-Sajjādīyyah*.

Second, even though infallibility does not deprive the infallible of the capability of sinning—otherwise, there would be no merit to it—the occurrence of such sin from them is impossible due to their immunity, which precludes any possibility of ignorance as this status is given to them by God ﷻ.

---

[181] Al-Ḥusaynī, Sayyid ʿAlī Khān, *Riyāḍ al-Sālikīn*, Vol. 2, p. 472.

Third, the assumption of conditions in the context of acknowledgment and confession and the consideration of the intended meaning, expression, implications, and inferences between them is baseless.

Fourth, suppose the condition, whose truthfulness is not required in the context of assumption, means the loss of inherent immunity in the infallible. In that case, it only proves the intrinsic possibility, which does not negate the established practical impossibility based on infallibility. Suppose it is related to the influence of desires. In that case, God has absolved the infallibles from such desires, not in the sense of being exempt from human nature but due to the immunity resulting from their infallibility.

Nevertheless, this aspect of interpretation is acceptable when we struggle to understand the accurate expressions of their acknowledgment of shortcomings and acquiring what does not befit a servant. It implies that they seek continuous protection from God, as infallibility is divine grace, and the impossibility of committing sins is in the sense of eliminating the practical possibility. God knows best.

Another interpretation in this regard is that they [the infallibles] speak on behalf of their nation and followers. Their acknowledgment of sins is an acknowledgment of the sins of their nation and followers, and their seeking forgiveness is for their sake, as every leader is responsible for his followers. They merely associate the sins with their holy selves as a means of connection and influence. There is no stronger link than between the Prophet or the Imām ﷺ and their nation and followers. Do you not see that when a leader's people make a mistake or fall short, the leader apologizes on their behalf and attributes it to himself? And if they were to be reprimanded [for their actions], only the leader is addressed and reprimanded [on their behalf], even if he did not witness the wrongdoing or take any part in it. This usage [this interpretation] is well-known.[182]

This interpretation is supported by what was narrated in the understanding of the verse:

﴿لِّيَغْفِرَ لَكَ ٱللَّهُ مَا تَقَدَّمَ مِن ذَنۢبِكَ وَمَا تَأَخَّرَ﴾

﴿li-yaghfira laka llāhu mā taqaddama min dhanbika wa-mā ta'akhkhara﴾

﴿that God may forgive you what is past of your sin and what is to come﴾[183]

It is reported that the Messenger of God ﷺ said:

---

[182] Ibid., pp. 472–473.

[183] Sūrat al-Fatḥ, Verse 2.

> O 'Alī, God ﷻ had me carry the sins of your Shī'ah [followers] and then forgave them for me.[184]

This is about God's statement in the last verse.

Regarding the same verse, 'Alī b. Ibrāhīm also reported with his chain of narrators from Imām Ja'far aṣ-Ṣādiq ؑ that he said,

> He ['Alī] had no sin, nor did he seek to commit any. But God had him carry the sins of his Shī'ah and then forgave them for him.[185]

Likewise, a chain of narrators from Muḥammad b. Sa'īd al-Marwazī narrated the following:

> I asked a man [Imām al-Hadi ؑ],
>
>> Did the Messenger of God ﷺ ever sin?
>
> He replied,
>
>> No.
>
> I said,

[184] al-Baḥrānī, Hāshim al-Tūbilī, *Tafsīr al-Burhān*, as found in Ṣadūq, Shaykh Muḥammad b. 'Alī, *'Ilal al-Sharāi'*, Vol. 1, p. 172.

[185] al-Baḥrānī, Hāshim al-Tūbilī, *Tafsīr al-Burhān*, Vol. 1, p. 112, from al-Qummī, 'Alī b. Ibrāhīm, *Tafsīr al-Qummī*, Vol. 2, p. 214.

> Then what about the verse "*that God may forgive you what is past of your sin and what is to come*"?[186]

He said,

> God ﷻ had Muḥammad ﷺ carry the sins of the Shīʿah of ʿAlī ؑ, then He forgave him for what preceded [the sins of the Shīʿah that transpired in the past] and what will follow [the sins of the Shīʿah that will happen in the future].[187]

Similarly, Sharaf ad-Dīn al-Najafī said,

> This is supported by what is narrated—elevated [marfūʿ], directly related to the Prophet—from Imām ʿAlī al-Hādī ؑ. He was asked about the verse: "*that God may forgive you what is past of your sin and what is to come*".[188]
>
> He ؑ said,
>
> > What sin could there be for the Messenger of God ﷺ, whether preceding or following?

[186] Sūrat al-Fatḥ, Verse 2.

[187] al-Baḥrānī, Hāshim al-Tūbilī, *Tafsīr al-Burhān*, Vol. 9, p. 113 as found in *Ta'wīl al-Ayāt*, Vol. 2, p. 591.

[188] Sūrat al-Fatḥ, Verse 2.

Rather, God had him carry the sins of the Shī'ah of 'Alī ☀, those that occurred in the past and those that will come; then He forgave them for him.[189]

Moreover, al-Ṭabrisī ☀ said that al-Mufaḍḍal b. 'Umar narrated on the authority of Imām Ja'far aṣ-Ṣādiq ☀ the following:

A man asked the Imām about this [aforementioned] verse, so he said,

By God, he [Imām 'Alī] had no sin, but God ☀ guaranteed him to forgive the sins of the Shī'ah of 'Alī ☀, both those that have passed and those that will come to pass in the future.[190]

It is not far-fetched that the greatest Messenger ☀ and the infallible Imāms ☀ shouldered the responsibility of seeking forgiveness for their Shī'ah [followers]. This is an act of compassion and mercy from them towards their Shī'ah, considering what the Shī'ah endure and continue to endure in their devotion and love for their Imāms ☀. This

---

189 Al-Baḥrānī, Hāshim al-Tūbilī, *Tafsīr al-Burhān*, Vol. 9, p. 113; *Ta'wīl al-Āyāt*, Vol. 2, p. 395.

190 Ibid., pp. 113–114. Ṭabrisī, Shaykh Faḍl b. Ḥasan, *Majma' al-Bayān fī Tafsīr al-Qur'ān*, Vol. 9, p. 168

notion is also reinforced in an authentic narration reported by Ibn Wahb, who said,

> I heard Imām Jaʿfar aṣ-Ṣādiq ﷺ supplicating while in prostration:
>
>> O You Who has honored us with nobility, promised us intercession, entrusted us with the [divine] will of the messengers, granted us knowledge of the past and the future, and made the hearts of people incline towards us. Forgive me and my brothers [in faith] and the shrine visitors of my grandfather al-Ḥusayn, those who have spent their wealth and risked their lives seeking our pleasure and what is with You in our connection. [O Lord, forgive them] for the joy they bring to Your Prophet, the way they heed our commands and the anger they trigger in our enemies [with their visit] seeking Your pleasure. Grant them complete contentment on our behalf and provide them with protection day and night. Reward their families and children left behind with the best rewards and companionship. Keep them safe from the evil of every tyrant, obstinate oppressor, and every weak and powerful individual among Your creations. Protect them from the mischief of the devils among humans

> and jinn. Bestow upon them what they longed for while being away from their homelands and what they preferred for us over their children, families, and relatives. O God, our enemies reproached them for coming to us, but that did not stop them from coming to us lovingly and persistently, opposing those who opposed us. O God, have mercy on those faces that the sun has changed, and have mercy on those cheeks turned from side to side over the grave of Abī ʿAbdillāh al-Ḥusayn. Have mercy on those eyes that shed tears out of compassion for us, and have mercy on those hearts that felt sorrow and burned in love for us. Have mercy on that cry that was made for our sake. O God, I entrust to You those souls and bodies until You gather them at the Pond [in Paradise] on the Day of the Great Thirst.

When Ibn Wahb found this abundance of supplications to be too much for the visitors of al-Ḥusayn ﵇ and expressed this accordingly, Imām Jaʿfar aṣ-Ṣādiq ﵇ said to him,

> Indeed, those who supplicate for the visitors of al-Ḥusayn ﵇ in the Heavens are more numerous than those who supplicate for them on earth.[191]

Regarding the verse

﴿إِنَّا فَتَحْنَا لَكَ فَتْحًا مُّبِينًا﴾

﴾*innā fataḥnā laka fatḥan mubīnan*﴿

﴾*Indeed We have inaugurated for you a clear victory*﴿[192]

the narrations reported in the interpretation of this verse are weak in their chain of transmission. Moreover, their content suggests that the Prophet ﷺ is entrusted with seeking forgiveness specifically for the sins of his followers (Shīʿah), implying that he should seek forgiveness for them. The content of the supplications confirms the acknowledgment of committing actions that necessitate seeking forgiveness, and it shows the great concern for seeking forgiveness from God. The two meanings harmoniously complement each other.

Furthermore, the discussion regarding the admission to sin by all the infallibles from our father Ādam ﵇ to the end of

---

[191] al-Qummī, Ibn Qūlawayh, *Kāmil al-Zīyārāt*, Chapter 40, ḥadīth 2. Ṣadūq, Shaykh Muḥammad b. ʿAlī, *Thawāb al-Aʿmāl*, pp. 94–96. Kulaynī, Shaykh Muḥammad b. Yaʿqūb, *al-Kāfī,* Vol. 4, pp. 582–583.

[192] Sūrat al-Fatḥ, Verse 1.

the chain of Imāmate does not align with the established narrations, and many expressions in the supplications reject or exclude this interpretation.

Regarding the authentic statement of Ibn Wahb, it is like the clear narration that reports that the Imām ﷺ seeks forgiveness for his followers and supporters, indicating the infallibles' association with the sins of their followers and their accountability for them.

As for the analogy of a community leader who, if there is a mistake or shortcoming among his people, stands up to apologize for them and attributes it to himself and so on, it mixes two different positions. One is the intercession of the community leader for those he leads, an honorable position adopted and endorsed by every sincere leader for his people. This elevated and noble position belongs to the Master of Messengers ﷺ on the Day of Judgment, which is referred to in God's statement:

﴿عَسَىٰٓ أَن يَبۡعَثَكَ رَبُّكَ مَقَامًا مَّحۡمُودًا﴾

﴾ʿasā ʾan yabʿathaka rabbuka maqāman maḥmūdaⁿ﴿

﴾It may be that your Lord will raise you to a praiseworthy station﴿[193]

[193] Sūrat al-Isrā', Verse 79.

It is the most hopeful verse in the Qur'ān. However, the focus here is on acknowledging mistakes [admission to sin] and the obligation of repentance, and the distinction between these two positions should not be obscured. The second [position] is for the leader to acknowledge his shortcomings and apologize for his negative actions towards his people. Some leaders may do this, but such an action would not come from the infallible, let alone the Prophet ﷺ. Rather, the opposite is true, and the Prophet ﷺ says something in this regard as mentioned in the Noble Qur'ān:

﴿وَقَالَ ٱلرَّسُولُ يَٰرَبِّ إِنَّ قَوْمِي ٱتَّخَذُواْ هَٰذَا ٱلْقُرْءَانَ مَهْجُورًا﴾

﴿wa-qāla r-rasūlu yā-rabbi 'inna qawmī ttakhadhū hādhā l-qur'āna mahjūran﴾

﴿And the Apostle will say, 'O my Lord! Indeed my people consigned this Qur'ān to oblivion'﴾[194]

None of the texts that acknowledge the need for repentance support this meaning. If we found evidence for it, there would be no obstacle in accepting this interpretation.

[194] Sūrat al-Furqān, Verse 30.

Another interpretation within this topic is what Shaykh ʿAlī b. ʿIsā al-Irbilī ﵀ mentioned.[195] He said that the prophets and Imāms ﵈ spend their time in remembrance of God, their hearts absorbed, and their thoughts attached to the higher realm. They are constantly in a state of mindfulness, as Imām ʿAlī ﵇ said,

> Worship God as if you see Him, and if you do not see Him, surely He sees you.[196]

They are always turned towards Him, fully devoted. Whenever they deviate from this exalted position and high station to be occupied with mundane matters such as eating, drinking, engaging in lawful marital relations, and other permissible activities, they consider it a deficiency and thus seek forgiveness from God. To illustrate this with an example, consider this: if some servants of people in this world were seen eating, drinking, and engaging in lawful marital relations while knowing that their master is observing and listening, they would be blamed by the people and considered negligent in their duty of serving their master and owner. Now, put this into perspective and this context [the infallibles towards God]: God is the Master of the universe and the Owner of all dominions.

---

[195] al-Irbilī, ʿAlī b. ʿIsā Hakkārī, *Kashf al-Ghummah fī Maʿrifat al-Aʾimma.*

[196] Ṭabrisī, Shaykh Faḍl b. Ḥasan, *Makārim al-Akhlāq*, p. 459.

What do you think now? This is what the Prophet ﷺ indicated when he said,

> Verily, it is close to my heart, and I seek God's forgiveness seventy times a day.[197]

The same is implied when he ﷺ said,

> The good deeds of the righteous are sins for those who are close [to God].[198]

His discourse concludes with a concise summary in *Riyāḍ al-Sālikīn*[199], which he greatly approved of, saying that it is the best way to dispel doubts.

The same meaning is also attributed[200] when explaining the statement of the Prophet ﷺ,

> Verily, it is close to my heart, and I seek God's forgiveness one hundred times a day.

I say [in my view]: I have not come across any compelling reason for endorsing this viewpoint that is attributed to the

---

[197] Majlisī, ʿAllāmah Muḥammad Bāqir, *Biḥār al-Anwār*, Vol. 25, pp. 204–205.

[198] Ibid., p. 205.

[199] Al-Ḥusaynī, Sayyid ʿAlī Khān, *Riyāḍ al-Sālikīn*.

[200] Al-Bayḍāwī, Qāḍī Nāṣir al-Dīn, *Sharḥ al-Maṣābīḥ*.

eminent scholar Sayyid ʿAlī Khān al-Ḥusaynī ﷺ, as it contains the following issues:

First, the infallible ones, may God's blessings and peace be upon them, do not engage in permissible activities except when necessitated by worldly life and its possibilities. In such cases, their engagement becomes obligatory in fulfilling their responsibilities. However, it has been reported that the lifestyle of the righteous, who followed the path of those infallible ones in refining themselves, did not reach the level of the Imāms ﷺ. Some pious jurists even mentioned that they did not engage in any permissible act for forty years. Perhaps their engagement in such activities was solely to clarify their rulings, as they must convey and clarify the divine law.

Furthermore, even if their engagement in those permissible activities was with divine permission, as indicated in His statement,

﴿قُلْ مَنْ حَرَّمَ زِينَةَ ٱللَّهِ ٱلَّتِيٓ أَخْرَجَ لِعِبَادِهِۦ وَٱلطَّيِّبَٰتِ مِنَ ٱلرِّزْقِۚ قُلْ هِيَ لِلَّذِينَ ءَامَنُواْ فِي ٱلْحَيَوٰةِ ٱلدُّنْيَا خَالِصَةً يَوْمَ ٱلْقِيَٰمَةِۗ كَذَٰلِكَ نُفَصِّلُ ٱلْأٓيَٰتِ لِقَوْمٍ يَعْلَمُونَ﴾

﴿qul man ḥarrama zīnata llāhi llatī ʾakhraja li-ʿibādihī wa-ṭ-ṭayyibāti mina r-rizqi qul hiya li-lladhīna ʾāmanū fī l-ḥayāti d-dunyā khāliṣatan yawma l-qiyāmati ka-dhālika nufaṣṣilu l-ʾāyāti li-qawmin yaʿlamūn[a]﴾

﴾*Say, 'Who has forbidden the adornment of God which He has brought forth for His servants, and the good things of [His] provision?' Say, 'These are for the faithful in the life of this world, and exclusively for them on the Day of Resurrection.' Thus do We elaborate the signs for a people who have knowledge*﴿[201]

It does not make sense to consider it a sin, attributing it to Shayṭān's influence or the like. Rather, benefiting from the blessings bestowed by the Bestower and expressing enjoyment before Him is a form of obligatory gratitude, both rationally and religiously.

Moreover, it is strange to give the example of some worldly servants sitting and eating... to the point where he says they would be blamed. This example implies that if the servant sits with permission and authorization from the Master, the wise still criticizes his sitting. If he sits without permission and at a time when it is not permitted for him, without the Master specifying the time for his rest, he would be deserving of blame from the wise and punishment from the Master. Where does this example fit in the context of the Imāms ﷺ status in relation to the Lord of the Worlds?

Furthermore, the narration ("the good deeds of the righteous are sins for those who are close [to God]") linking righteous deeds to sinful acts is very peculiar. If this

[201] Sūrat al-Aʿrāf, Verse 32.

attribution is true for the infallible, it would imply that the obligations differ based on different ranks. Those who attain higher ranks in divine proximity might commit sins according to their ranks, and what might be considered a sin for one might not be so for someone in a lower rank and status.

It is also inappropriate to conclude the differentiation of actions based on ranks about divine wisdom. For instance, some parts of an obligatory action might be superior to others, such as prostration during prayer. Prostration is the best part of prayer, and this differentiation exists in obligatory and recommended acts and divine obligations. However, this does not mean that abandoning what is superior at a time or circumstance that favors the recommended act constitutes degradation for the performer. For example, neither performing prayer nor occupying oneself with another recommended act of worship (the time and condition of which has come) implies a downgrade from a higher to a lower status. Real degradation occurs when one chooses the inferior or lesser act over the superior or greater act. However, he can adhere to what is superior; he chooses to yield to his whims and desires and succumb to psychological comfort.

In light of this, we know that the infallibles عليهم السلام do not act, speak, or desire anything except what is willed by God in all stages of their lives, as indicated in the Qur'ān:

﴿وَمَا يَنطِقُ عَنِ ٱلْهَوَىٰٓ﴾

❨wa-mā yanṭiqu ʿani l-hawā❩

﴿إِنْ هُوَ إِلَّا وَحْيٌ يُوحَىٰ﴾

❨in huwa ʾillā waḥyun yūḥā❩

❨*Nor does he speak out of [his own] desire: it is just a
revelation that is revealed [to him]*❩[202]

and

﴿وَمَا تَشَآءُونَ إِلَّآ أَن يَشَآءَ ٱللَّهُ رَبُّ ٱلْعَٰلَمِينَ﴾

❨wa-mā tashāʾūna ʾillā ʾan yashāʾa llāhu rabbu l-ʿālamīnᵃ❩

❨*but you will not wish unless it is wished by God,
the Lord of all the worlds*❩[203]

Additionally, we have the narration that describes how
Imām ʿAlī ☙, whenever he was presented with two options
that would please God, chose the harder of the two for

---

[202] Sūrat al-Najm, Verses 3–4.

[203] Sūrat at-Takwīr, Verse 29.

himself [paraphrased].[204] Thus, how can one reconcile the notion presented in such narrations and verses with the idea articulated in the statement of the eminent scholar that the infallibles could be occupied with permissible activities to the extent that it might be seen as neglecting other devotional acts or behaving like regular humans—like us? It is also well-known that they are superior to angels, about whom God says:

﴿لَا يَسْبِقُونَهُۥ بِٱلْقَوْلِ وَهُم بِأَمْرِهِۦ يَعْمَلُونَ﴾

﴾*lā yasbiqūnahū bi-l-qawli wa-hum bi-ʾamrihī yaʿmalūna*﴿

﴾*They do not venture to speak ahead of Him, and they act by His command*﴿[205]

The statement suggests that they are preoccupied with permissible activities instead of acts of worship. However, what the infallibles do in permissible activities is worship with a secondary designation.

Another interpretation is as follows: It is said that the perfect servant of God encompasses all levels of worship. Worship can be categorized into sincere hopeful believers' devotion and fearful sinners' devotion. The infallible Imām

---

[204] Majlisī, ʿAllāmah Muḥammad Bāqir, *Biḥār al-Anwār*, Vol. 40, p. 329.

[205] Sūrat al-Anbiyāʾ, Verse 27.

seeks to worship God with complete servitude and traverse all stages of worship. Sometimes, he lowers himself to the level of a sinful sinner and mentions in his supplications what a transgressor might say while committing various sins. This is only because he acknowledges the heights of worship in all its aspects and reaches the pinnacle of servitude through all its paths. This is evident in the words of Imām Zayn al-ʿĀbidīn ☙ in his supplication on abasing himself before God, which is supplication number 53 in *al-Ṣaḥīfah al-Sajjādiyyah*,

> I have brought myself to a halt in the halting place of the abased sinners, the halting place of the wretched and insolent, those who think lightly of Your promise...

In this supplication, the Imām expresses his deep humility before God and demonstrates his understanding and empathy for those who might be in a state of sin or weakness while at the same time remaining firmly committed to the path of perfection in worship and servitude to God.

Ultimately, within this interpretation, this is the intended meaning behind all mentioned in the supplications of the infallibles ☙, where they acknowledge their sins and transgressions. This concludes the discussion.

I say [in my view]: First, those who have attained the highest ranks in their spiritual journey have no desire for worldly ranks. God ﷻ says:

﴿قَالَ أَتَسْتَبْدِلُونَ ٱلَّذِي هُوَ أَدْنَىٰ بِٱلَّذِي هُوَ خَيْرٌ﴾

﴿*qāla 'a-tastabdilūna lladhī huwa 'adnā bi-lladhī huwa khayrun*﴾

﴿*He said, 'Do you seek to replace what is superior with that which is inferior?'*﴾[206]

Moreover, this is considered contemptible by the wise.

Second, attributing sins they have not committed to themselves and branding themselves with shameful actions contrary to reality is reprehensible from two perspectives: it involves falsehood and placing oneself among the condemned and the misguided before their Lord.

Third, feeling pleasure in worship, humility, and servitude is a station of honor and a position attained by those who have reached a level where the obligations are transformed into desired and wanted actions. It is a noble station coveted by people like us. However, for those who have surpassed this stage and have reached the level of obligatory

[206] Sūrat al-Baqarah, Verse 61.

existence,[207] where the veils have been lifted, including the veil of greatness and the erasure of boundaries, such a station, though esteemed by comparison, becomes undesirable. This is because it depends on feeling the pleasure necessary for a limited existence, and they [the worshipers] realize that they are in a station where they enjoy seeing, worshiping, and obeying. Our pure masters are far above this level. They do not find pleasure in worship because they only seek God. Some of their supplications indicate that if they were to be expelled—God forbid, assuming the impossible—they would not abandon and leave the gate of His presence. Therefore, in their exalted position and their ultimate pleasure, they do not seek anything but Him. Hence, it is not reasonable to suggest that they ﷵ seek refuge and pleasure in worship such that they even find pleasure in worshiping those at lower levels.

As for what is recited in the supplication of Imām Zayn al-ʿĀbidīn ؑ, the expression does not mean what the proponent of this view understood. It is evident in the acknowledgment of the sins and transgressions that we are discussing here.

[207] Translator's note: The "obligatory existence" is the highest level of spiritual realization and closeness to God, where the individual's actions and thoughts are entirely guided by divine purpose. They find complete contentment and fulfillment in fulfilling their duty to God without attachment to personal desires or pleasures.

What the Observation Implies

It should be noted that the sources of doubt are not limited to the mentioned supplication alone. There are multiple and diverse sources of doubt, all of which invite contemplation and investigation to find the proper alignment between them and infallibility. Here are some of them:

1. The confession of the infallible about the influence of the cursed Shayṭān over him, accompanied by seeking refuge in God, seeking deliverance from the evil of that cursed one, and being affected by or showing empathy towards the actions of the accursed Iblīs.

2. The acknowledgment of committing sins by all bodily organs, as mentioned in the supplication attributed to Imām Mūsā al-Kāẓim 🕮 and the supplication of the Imām al-Ḥusayn 🕮 on the Day of 'Arafah, and others.

3. Humbling oneself before God, seeking repentance, and earnestly seeking forgiveness necessitates genuine acknowledgment of committing sins and God's acceptance of repentance and granting forgiveness.

4. His evident and manifest fear, accompanied by genuine dread of Hellfire, can only arise from firm belief and realization of deserving it.

5. The content of several other supplications, such as the supplication of Monday found in the appendices of *al-Ṣaḥīfah al-Sajjādīyyah*, as narrated by the esteemed narrator Shaykh ʿAbbās al-Qummī ﵀. In this supplication, the infallible acknowledges having transgressed against others and implores God to mediate between him and those he has wronged and fulfill the servants' rights upon him.

These are the sources of doubt that confront the observer, and one may imagine them to contradict infallibility, particularly in the sense we believe regarding the Prophet ﷺ and the infallible Imāms from his lineage ﵈ that they have not committed even the slightest of these actions.

A single answer is insufficient to address all of these doubts. Each matter we have mentioned has its specific aspect and analysis relevant to dispel what we perceive as contradictory to infallibility. Therefore, let us delve into these matters, seeking help from God:

The First Aspect

It should be known that Iblīs and his allies, among the jinn and mankind, constantly seek, by their wickedness and animosity towards goodness and its people, to harbor resentment and envy for the blessings God has bestowed upon the righteous servants in terms of the honor of nearness and the dignity of worship with sincerity. They strive to divert the infallible and righteous individuals, as well as others, from their path. This endeavor includes creating obstacles, which is part of the dominion of the evil forces over worldly means and material facilities. God allows this dominion to take place so that it exposes the wicked nature and malicious intentions of these forces, thus serving as evidence against them and a clarification for others regarding the severity of their punishment on the Day of Judgment. Moreover, this dominion provides an opportunity for the righteous to attain honor, as the greater the effort, the greater the reward, and the more the obstacles, the more intense the effort. The greater the trial, the greater the merit of the deeds; as mentioned,

The best deeds are the most difficult ones.[208]

From this perspective, Iblīs and his allies strive by all means and employ every possible method to harm the righteous servants of God. They seize control over the wealth and children of God's righteous followers, either through illness, murder, and displacement or through misguidance if the person is not divinely protected against sin [via infallibility]. They do this to cause harm and hindrance, according to their wicked illusion, to prevent God's righteous followers from continuing on the path of obedience to God and ascending the ranks of servitude to elevate their status and position before Him. This is just as

---

[208] Majlisī, 'Allāmah Muḥammad Bāqir, *Biḥār al-Anwār*, Vol. 67, p. 190. al-Bahā'ī, Shaykh Muḥammad, *Miftāḥ al-Falāḥ*, p. 45.

Iblīs managed to overpower Qābīl, deceive him, and use him to kill Hābīl.

Moreover, the cursed Iblīs may seek assistance from certain allies to him among humans, so he employs an enemy from the foes of God to afflict the righteous person's wealth, causing its destruction, or to afflict their child with illness or to lead them astray. This causes pain and suffering to the righteous, yet through this ordeal, they attain a degree [in faith and honor before God for their steadfastness despite hardship], thus disappointing Iblīs and his allies among the jinn and humans.

Similarly, the enemies of God, both the jinn and humans, seek to afflict the body of God's righteous servants with physical illnesses to hinder them from continuing in their acts of obedience to God. The righteous servants may suffer from a disease that debilitates them and causes pain in their bodies, creating obstacles that make the path difficult. The souls of the righteous servants then feel anguish because these ailments prevent them from engaging in what they desire, hope for, and aspire to achieve through their actions. However, God ﷻ rewards them for their intention to persist on the path they were on before facing these physical afflictions.

Even the infallible ones may experience physical weakness, as mentioned in *Ḥadīth al-Kisā'* [Ḥadīth of the Cloak], where the Prophet Muḥammad ﷺ said,

I see weakness in my body.

Similarly, the infallible ones may experience physical weakness when confronted with challenges and battle, as happened to Imām al-Ḥusayn ﷺ. When his wounds became one too many, he became weak and unable to continue fighting. Moreover, there is no doubt that the infallible ones go through stages of childhood, adolescence, adulthood, and old age.

However, some individuals who claim to be associated with Shīʿah Islām have misunderstood this concept [i.e., that Iblīs or his wicked allies would attack the body of the infallible] and imagined that Imām al-Ḥusayn ﷺ could not be killed. They deluded themselves into believing that he was not killed but was raised to the heavens and that his enemies killed someone resembling him, similar to what is claimed about Prophet ʿĪsā ﷺ. This misconception spread among some naive Shīʿah Muslims. Therefore, the great guardian of God, Imām Muḥammad al-Mahdī ﷺ, issued a decree of condemnation upon those who believe that Imām al-Ḥusayn ﷺ was not martyred.

The difference between the sincere, aware Shīʿah believer who acknowledges that the oppressor can control the body of an infallible without affecting their intellect and those insincere ones who believe that weakness can overpower [the infallible's] intellect and mind. This leads to the emergence of blasphemous statements made against the

Greatest Messenger ﷺ, and this, in turn, obligates their [the people who make such statements and hold such beliefs] to excommunication and ostracization by the Muslim community.

Likewise, the accursed devil, along with his allies from among the jinn and humans, tries to gain control over their self, thoughts, and intellect. Here, the infallibles distinguish themselves from others. They have been granted immunity, spiritual strength, and insight into their soul and intellect. The accursed devil and his followers cannot influence the infallibles, as they cannot take away anything from their levels of devotion and sincerity. God ﷻ has equipped the infallible with what they need to fulfill their duties.

Indeed, the infallible suffer from infallible suffer from pain caused by the attempts of the accursed Iblīs and his allies to influence their mind and soul. They create obstacles before the infallible infallible, causing them pain while they [the infallibles] strive to overcome them. To remain sufficient and overcome these struggles, they continuously seek the help of God ﷻ.

This is supported by what is mentioned in the Qur'ān and narrations regarding Prophet Ayyūb ؑ.

﴿وَٱذْكُرْ عَبْدَنَآ أَيُّوبَ إِذْ نَادَىٰ رَبَّهُۥٓ أَنِّي مَسَّنِيَ ٱلشَّيْطَٰنُ بِنُصْبٍ وَعَذَابٍ﴾

﴾*wa-dhkur ʿabdanā ʾayyūba ʾidh nādā rabbahū ʾannī massaniya sh-shayṭānu bi-nuṣbin wa-ʿadhābi*[n-i]﴿

﴾*And remember Our servant Ayyūb [in the Qurʾān]. When he called out to his Lord, 'The devil has visited on me hardship and torment'*﴿[209]

Iblīs had depleted his wealth, destroyed his children, and afflicted him with severe diseases and excruciating pain.

The esteemed Sayyid Hāshim al-Baḥrānī ﵀ has narrated[210] the traditions that support what we mentioned about Iblīs going after the blessings God ﷻ has granted to man in this world. The Imāms ﵈ has also mentioned in narrations, which the Sayyid reported in his interpretation of the verse above, that God tested His Prophet Ayyūb ﵇ without any wrongdoing on his part. He reported these narrations from the *ʿIlal al-Sharāiʿ*, *Tafsīr al-Qummī*, *al-Kāfī*, and others.

This notion is also highlighted in what is written in the margins of the book *Mafātīḥ al-Jinān—al-Baqiyat as-Salihat* with the following supplication:

> O God, indeed Iblīs, one of Your servants, sees me from where I cannot see him, and You see him from where he cannot see You. You are Powerful

---

[209] Sūrat Ṣād, Verse 41.

[210] al-Baḥrānī, Hāshim al-Tūbilī, *Tafsīr al-Burhān*.

> over him, but he has no power over anything from Your affairs. I seek Your help against him, O Lord, as I have no strength or ability except with You. O God, if he intends harm for me, fend him off, and if he plots against me, undo his plotting. Protect me from his evil and make his deceit backfire on him by Your mercy, O the Most Merciful. May God's blessings be upon Muḥammad and his pure family.

What is even clearer is God's command to the Prophet ﷺ to seek refuge in God from the accursed devil, which is evident in many verses.[211]

As for the non-infallible, his foot may slip, and then Iblīs can tempt him. He may deviate from faith or righteousness or exhibit negligence and inadequacy when turning to God ﷻ and expressing gratitude for His blessings. He may forget, neglect, or intentionally abandon, seeking refuge in God and seeking His help against the accursed. His condition may deteriorate to yielding to the desires and succumbing to the deceptions of Iblīs as his wickedness and desire cloud his judgment. May God protect us from his plots, aid us in overcoming them, and grant us the strength to endure hardships. Indeed, He is the Powerful, the Praiseworthy.

In light of this, we should pay attention to two points:

---

[211] Such as in Sūrat al-Aʿrāf, Verse 200, Sūrat an-Naḥl, Verse 98, Sūrat Fuṣṣilat, Verse 36, and others.

First, the devil is the enemy of man, as God ﷻ said,

﴿يَٰٓـَٔادَمُ إِنَّ هَٰذَا عَدُوٌّ لَّكَ وَلِزَوْجِكَ﴾

﴿*yā-'ādamu 'inna hādhā 'aduwwun laka wa-li-zawjika*﴾

﴿*O Ādam! This is indeed an enemy of yours and your mate's*﴾[212]

And He also narrated the story of the words of Prophet Mūsā ﷺ:

﴿قَالَ هَٰذَا مِنْ عَمَلِ ٱلشَّيْطَٰنِ ۖ إِنَّهُۥ عَدُوٌّ مُّضِلٌّ مُّبِينٌ﴾

﴿*qāla hādhā min 'amali sh-shayṭāni 'innahū 'aduwwun muḍillun mubīn*[un]﴾

﴿*He said, 'This is of Shayṭān's doing. Indeed he is clearly a misguiding enemy*﴾[213]

And God said,

﴿إِنَّ ٱلشَّيْطَٰنَ لَكُمْ عَدُوٌّ فَٱتَّخِذُوهُ عَدُوًّا﴾

---

[212] Sūrat Ṭā Hā, Verse 117.

[213] Sūrat al-Qaṣaṣ, Verse 15.

﴿*inna sh-shayṭāna lakum 'aduwwun fa-ttakhidhūhu 'aduwwan*﴾

﴿*Shayṭān is indeed your enemy, so treat him as an enemy*﴾[214]

and

﴿وَلَا يَصُدَّنَّكُمُ ٱلشَّيْطَٰنُ ۖ إِنَّهُۥ لَكُمْ عَدُوٌّ مُّبِينٌ﴾

﴿*wa-lā yaṣuddannakumu sh-shayṭānu 'innahū lakum 'aduwwun mubīn*[un]﴾

﴿*Do not let Shayṭān bar you [from the way of God]. Indeed he is your manifest enemy*﴾[215]

As a result of the nature of the enemy, he hates what benefits his adversary and is inclined toward what harms him. This is the principle of envy and the origin of this malady. When the devil is referred to as the "misleader" or when he threatens to mislead the servants, it does not mean that misguidance occurs inevitably. Rather, it signifies that he and his followers strive to fool people, succeeding with some individuals while failing with others. Nevertheless, they manage to cause harm to all. For instance, consider this verse:

---

[214] Sūrat Fāṭir, Verse 6.

[215] Sūrat az-Zukhruf, Verse 62.

﴿وَلَقَدْ أَضَلَّ مِنكُمْ جِبِلًّا كَثِيرًا ۖ أَفَلَمْ تَكُونُوا تَعْقِلُونَ﴾

﴿*wa-la-qad ʾaḍalla minkum jibillan kathīran ʾa-fa-lam takūnū taʿqilūna*﴾

﴿*Certainly, he has led astray many of your generations. Have you not exercised your reason?*﴾[216]

That is in line with what the accursed devil says, which the Qurʾān articulated as follows:

﴿وَلَأُضِلَّنَّهُمْ وَلَأُمَنِّيَنَّهُمْ وَلَآمُرَنَّهُمْ فَلَيُبَتِّكُنَّ آذَانَ الْأَنْعَامِ وَلَآمُرَنَّهُمْ فَلَيُغَيِّرُنَّ خَلْقَ اللَّهِ ۚ وَمَن يَتَّخِذِ الشَّيْطَانَ وَلِيًّا مِّن دُونِ اللَّهِ فَقَدْ خَسِرَ خُسْرَانًا مُّبِينًا﴾

﴿*wa-la-ʾuḍillannahum wa-la-ʾumanniyannahum wa-la-ʾāmurannahum fa-la-yubattikunna ʾādhāna l-ʾanʿāmi wa-la-ʾāmurannahum fa-la-yughayyirunna khalqa llāhi wa-man yattakhidhi sh-shayṭāna waliyyan min dūni llāhi fa-qad khasira khusrānan mubīnan*﴾

﴿*'and I will lead them astray and give them [false] hopes, and prompt them to slit the ears of cattle, and I will prompt them to alter God's creation.' Whoever takes Shayṭān as a*

[216] Sūrat Yā Sīn, Verse 62.

guardian instead of God has certainly incurred a manifest loss﴾[217]

As for the exception in the verse

﴿وَلَأُغْوِيَنَّهُمْ أَجْمَعِينَ﴾

﴿*wa-la-'ughwiyannahum 'ajma'īna*﴾

﴿إِلَّا عِبَادَكَ مِنْهُمُ ٱلْمُخْلَصِينَ﴾

﴿*illā 'ibādaka minhumu l-mukhlaṣīna*﴾

﴿*and I will surely pervert them, all except Your dedicated servants among them*﴾[218]

it does not mean an exception from what the devil does, but it refers to an exception from those who will fall under the devil's influence. The devil's pursuit of misleading everyone to the extent he can is described in God's statement:

﴿وَمَآ أَرْسَلْنَا مِن قَبْلِكَ مِن رَّسُولٍ وَلَا نَبِيٍّ إِلَّآ إِذَا تَمَنَّىٰٓ أَلْقَى ٱلشَّيْطَٰنُ فِيٓ أُمْنِيَّتِهِۦ فَيَنسَخُ ٱللَّهُ مَا يُلْقِي ٱلشَّيْطَٰنُ ثُمَّ يُحْكِمُ ٱللَّهُ ءَايَٰتِهِۦۗ وَٱللَّهُ عَلِيمٌ حَكِيمٌ﴾

---

217 Sūrat an-Nisā', Verse 119.

218 Sūrat al-Ḥijr, Verse 40.

﴾*wa-mā ʾarsalnā min qablika min rasūlin wa-lā nabiyyin ʾillā ʾidhā tamannā ʾalqā sh-shayṭānu fī ʾumniyyatihī fa-yansakhu llāhu mā yulqī sh-shayṭānu thumma yuḥkimu llāhu ʾāyātihī wa-llāhu ʿalīmun ḥakīm*^{un}﴿

﴾*We did not send any apostle or prophet before you but that when he recited [the scripture] Shayṭān interjected [something] in his recitation. Thereat God nullifies whatever Shayṭān has interjected, and then God confirms His signs, and God is Knowing, Wise*﴿[219]

In this context, God ﷻ says in the following verses:

﴿وَإِمَّا يَنزَغَنَّكَ مِنَ ٱلشَّيۡطَٰنِ نَزۡغٞ فَٱسۡتَعِذۡ بِٱللَّهِۚ﴾

﴾*wa-ʾimmā yanzaghannaka mina sh-shayṭāni nazghun fa-staʿidh bi-llāhi*﴿

﴾*Should a temptation from Shayṭān disturb you, invoke the protection of God*﴿[220]

﴿فَإِذَا قَرَأۡتَ ٱلۡقُرۡءَانَ فَٱسۡتَعِذۡ بِٱللَّهِ مِنَ ٱلشَّيۡطَٰنِ ٱلرَّجِيمِ﴾

﴾*fa-ʾidhā qaraʾta l-qurʿāna fa-staʿidh bi-llāhi mina sh-shayṭāni r-rajīm*^{i}﴿

---

[219] Sūrat al-Ḥajj, Verse 52.

[220] Sūrat al-Aʿrāf, Verse 200.

﴾*When you recite the Qur'ān, seek the protection of God against the outcast Shayṭān*﴿[221]

﴾وَقُل رَّبِّ أَعُوذُ بِكَ مِنْ هَمَزَٰتِ ٱلشَّيَٰطِينِ﴿

﴾*wa-qul rabbi 'a'ūdhu bika min hamazāti sh-shayāṭīn*ⁱ﴿

﴾*Say, 'My Lord! I seek Your protection from the promptings of devils'*﴿[222]

﴾قُلْ أَعُوذُ بِرَبِّ ٱلْفَلَقِ﴿

﴾*qul 'a'ūdhu bi-rabbi l-falaq*ⁱ﴿

﴾*Say, 'I seek the protection of the Lord of the daybreak'*﴿[223]

﴾قُلْ أَعُوذُ بِرَبِّ ٱلنَّاسِ﴿

﴾*qul 'a'ūdhu bi-rabbi n-nās*ⁱ﴿

﴾*Say, 'I seek the protection of the Lord of humans'*﴿[224]

---

221 Sūrat an-Naḥl, Verse 98.

222 Sūrat al-Mu'minūn, Verse 87.

223 Sūrat al-Falaq, Verse 1.

224 Sūrat al-Nas, Verse 1.

In the same sense, the Qur'ān narrates what Prophet Yūsuf ﷺ said:

﴿وَقَدۡ أَحۡسَنَ بِيٓ إِذۡ أَخۡرَجَنِي مِنَ ٱلسِّجۡنِ وَجَآءَ بِكُم مِّنَ ٱلۡبَدۡوِ مِنۢ بَعۡدِ أَن نَّزَغَ ٱلشَّيۡطَٰنُ بَيۡنِي وَبَيۡنَ إِخۡوَتِيٓۚ﴾

﴿wa-qad 'aḥsana bī 'idh 'akhrajanī mina s-sijni wa-jā'a bikum mina l-badwi min ba'di 'an nazagha sh-shayṭānu baynī wa-bayna 'ikhwatī﴾

﴿He was certainly gracious to me when He brought me out of the prison and brought you over from the desert after that Shayṭān had incited ill feeling between me and my brothers﴾[225]

God ﷻ also said:

﴿وَقُل لِّعِبَادِي يَقُولُواْ ٱلَّتِي هِيَ أَحۡسَنُۚ إِنَّ ٱلشَّيۡطَٰنَ يَنزَغُ بَيۡنَهُمۡۚ إِنَّ ٱلشَّيۡطَٰنَ كَانَ لِلۡإِنسَٰنِ عَدُوّٗا مُّبِينٗا﴾

﴿wa-qul li-'ibādī yaqūlū llatī hiya 'aḥsanu 'inna sh-shayṭāna yanzaghu baynahum 'inna sh-shayṭāna kāna li-l-'insāni 'aduwwan mubīnaⁿ﴾

[225] Sūrat Yūsuf, Verse 100.

❰*Tell My servants to speak in a manner which is the best.
Indeed Shayṭān incites ill feeling between them, and
Shayṭān is indeed man's manifest enemy*❱226

In this context, all that is mentioned in the supplications of
the infallible infallible 🕌 is also applicable, just as it is
stated in the Sunday supplication of Imām Zayn al-ʿĀbidīn
🕌:

> I seek refuge in You, O Lord, from the whispers of
> Shayṭān and I seek protection with Your authority
> from the tyranny of tyrants.

The second point is that it is narrated in the traditions that
the devil harms the infallibles 🕌 by attempting to hinder
their efforts in guiding people and striving to obstruct their
worship of God 🕌. Although he may not succeed in
achieving his ultimate goal, through his attempts, he can
harm the infallibles 🕌 either by his actions or with the
help of his allies from among the jinn and mankind, as well
as the worldly necessities. In *Munājāt al-Zāhidīn* by Imām
Zayn al-ʿĀbidīn 🕌, he says,

> My God, You have settled us in an abode which has
> dug for us pits of deception, and You have fastened
> us by the hands of death in the snares of that
> abode's treachery! In You, we seek asylum from the
> tricks of its guile, and to You, we hold fast lest the

---

226 Sūrat al-Isrāʾ, Verse 53.

> glitter of its ornaments deludes the glitter of its ornaments delude us! It destroys its pursuers and ruins its settlers; it is stuffed with blights and calamities.

Despite feeling the pain of being bound to the material world, he ﷺ seeks help from God ﷻ to overcome the requirements of this realm, thus acknowledging his self-sufficiency that is coupled with the necessity of existence.

This is added to what is mentioned in the narrations for Muʿtabarah Hishām b. Salīm reported that Imām Jaʿfar aṣ-Ṣādiq ﷺ said,

> The most severely afflicted people are the prophets, then those who follow them, and then the best among others.[227]

Many other narrations convey the same meaning.

Abū Ḥamzah Thumālī narrated that Imām Jaʿfar aṣ-Ṣādiq ﷺ said,

> The Messenger of God ﷺ said,
>
> > Indeed, God has made a covenant with the believer [to exercise patience] in the face of four afflictions. The first and the easiest of

[227] Kulaynī, Shaykh Muḥammad b. Yaʿqūb, *al-Kāfī*, Vol. 2, p. 252.

> these is a fellow believer who envies him; the second is a hypocrite who follows his tracks and uncovers his faults; the third is a devil who tries to tempt and mislead him; an unbeliever against whom jihād (working hard in the way of God) is necessary may cause him suffering. What remains of a believer after (all) this?[228]

Similarly, ʿAbdullāh b. Sinān narrated that Imām Jaʿfar aṣ-Ṣādiq ﷺ said,

> To every believer God has assigned four things: a devil who seeks to mislead him, an unbeliever who fights him, a believer who envies him—it is the most difficult one—and a hypocrite who tracks down his faults (for evil purposes).[229]

It is reported that Imām Jaʿfar aṣ-Ṣādiq ﷺ said,

> Indeed, God ﷻ tests the believer with every affliction and can cause him to die with every manner of death, but He does not test him by taking away his intellect and mind. Do you not see how Ayyūb was afflicted by the devil over his wealth, his children, his family, and everything he

---

[228] Ibid., p. 246.

[229] Majlisī, ʿAllāmah Muḥammad Bāqir, *Biḥār al-Anwār*, Vol. 65, p. 222.

> had, but he was not given power over his mind, which was left to him so that he may worship God with it and maintain his belief in Him.[230]

Among these narrations is also the one from Muʿtabar b. Miskān narrated that Imām Jaʿfar aṣ-Ṣādiq ﵇ said:

> A believer cannot escape from one of three problems, and all three can happen to him at once. Either a person with whom he lives in the same house will close the door and not let him in to hurt him, or there is a neighbor who will bother him, or someone will trouble him on his way to work. Even if a believer lives on top of a mountain, God will send a devil to him to harm him,[231] but He will make his belief a source of comfort and companionship, and with it, he does not feel frightened of anyone or lonely.[232]

It has been narrated that when the Messenger of God ﷺ fell ill, the angel Jibrāʾīl ﵇ sought refuge for him in God with

---

[230] Kulaynī, Shaykh Muḥammad b. Yaʿqūb, *al-Kāfī*, Vol. 2, p. 256.

[231] It means that He opens the way for the devil to reach the believer, intending to harm him.

[232] Kulaynī, Shaykh Muḥammad b. Yaʿqūb, *al-Kāfī*, Vol. 2, pp. 249–250.

the last two sūrahs of the Qur'ān (Sūrat al-Falaq and Sūrat an-Nās).[233]

It is also narrated that at the time of the Prophet's ﷺ birth, his mother sought refuge for him at the command of the hidden caller (the caller to the unseen realms), saying,

> I seek refuge for him with the One from the evil of every envier and every malevolent creature that takes its place in the paths of destiny, whether standing or sitting.[234]

The Prophet ﷺ sought refuge for Imām al-Ḥasan al-Mujtabā and Imām al-Ḥusayn ﵉ by saying,

> I seek refuge for you both in the perfect words of God, from every devil and harmful creature, and every evil eye.[235]

Thus, it is evident that the enemies of the righteous, Iblīs and his followers, strive to deceive everyone, and some may slip into their traps. While Iblīs cannot overpower those given strength and protection, they are still vulnerable to some harm from which they seek refuge in God. The devils

---

233 Shahrūdī, Shaykh 'Alī Namāzī, *Mustadrak Safīnat al-Biḥār*, Vol. 7, p. 476.

234 Majlisī, 'Allāmah Muḥammad Bāqir, *Biḥār al-Anwār*, Vol. 15, p. 271.

235 Ibid., Vol. 43, p. 282, Vol. 62, p. 277, and Vol. 63, p. 18.

among jinn and mankind have gone after the righteous servants of God, causing them to be killed, scattered, or torn apart. So, the righteous complain to God about Iblīs and his allies due to the harm they inflict and their attempts to obstruct their path, but this does not contradict their infallibility.

Attention:

The scholars—may God be pleased with them all—have stated various forms of wisdom behind the affliction of the devil and the disbelievers upon the believer:

1. It serves as an expiation for the believer's sins.

2. It tests the believer's patience and includes them among the patient ones.

3. The afflictions help prevent the believer from becoming too attached to the worldly life so that they do not become complacent and find it difficult to detach themselves from it.

These aspects apply to both the infallible and non-infallible individuals.

4. Moreover, the afflictions lead the believer to seek proximity to the Truth, glorified be He, in times of

distress, and encourage them to resort to supplication to ward off afflictions, thus elevating their status.[236]

5. Additionally, the afflictions foster the believer's detachment from the creation and draw them closer to the Lord of the worlds. This is exemplified in how Ḍarār b. Ḍamrah al-Laythī described Imām ʿAlī ﷺ as someone who found comfort in the night and solitude, was deeply insightful and contemplative, and often addressed his soul [self-address] and whispered to his Lord.[237]

The last two aspects apply to both the infallible and non-infallible individuals.

Another aspect to consider is that human beings, in their innate disposition, are imperfect in strength, yet some possess nobility and luminous qualities. They are inclined towards sacred matters and greatly desire the Hereafter. On the other hand, some individuals have despicable qualities. Darkness dominates them, and they are inclined towards physical desires. They prioritize gratification of their passions and anger over nobility.

However, if there were no allurements and temptations, and if the soul and desires were not inclined towards

---

[236] Majlisī, ʿAllāmah Muḥammad Bāqir, *Mirʾāt al-ʿUqūl fī Sharḥ Akhbār Āl al-Rasūl*, Vol. 2, p. 222.

[237] Ibid.

certain tendencies, it would contradict divine wisdom, as the human souls would remain on a single level of purity and simplicity, with no opportunity for growth and improvement. As per divine wisdom, the construction of this world relies on souls of diverse inclinations and varied tendencies that seek to fulfill urgent lowly needs and not on rigid souls.[238] In this regard, let us consider what is narrated in the divine narration [Ḥadīth Qudsi],

> Verily, I made the disobedience of Ādam a means of construction for the world.[239]

Also, it is narrated in a tradition,

> If it were not for the fact that you commit sins, God would have destroyed you and brought forth a people who commit sins.[240]

This last aspect was chosen by the distinguished scholar Mullā Ṣadrā[241], and Sayyid ʿAlī Khān al-Ḥusaynī

---

[238] In the Arabic text, the word جسا is used to describe the souls in this case, and it is derived from جَسَأَ which means to become dry and hard. It refers to something that dries up, solidifies, or becomes rigid. (Source: *Al-Miṣbāḥ al-Munīr*, Ḥadīth 140).

[239] Ṣadrā, Mullā, *Tafsīr Mullā Ṣadrā*, Vol. 6, p. 94.

[240] Ibid.

[241] Mullā Ṣadrā, *Tafsīr Mullā Ṣadrā*, Vol 6, pp. 92–95.

summarized it[242]. However, although it contains valuable insights, this aspect pertains to non-infallible individuals.

And the closest understanding—and God knows best—is that the infallibles, due to their innate and acquired gifts and their steadfastness despite the intense enmity of the enemies of God upon them, become a source of exaltation for others, guiding the seekers of truth and serving as proof against the misguided.

To elaborate, the presence of the infallibles, their attributes, their qualities, and all that emanates from them are all bestowed upon them by God or acquired through their journey toward divine proximity. All of this confers honor upon them and makes them a source of guidance, direction, and enlightenment for all creatures, leading them from the darkness of this temporal world to the eternal Hereafter.

It is also known that the intense animosity of the accursed devil towards mankind intensifies his hatred for the righteous among men and drives him to expend all his efforts, means, and allies in harming and obstructing the righteous leaders of the believers since they serve as the beacons guiding the world from this lowly darkness to the Hereafter. The devil knows that without these pious individuals who are close to God, humanity would have gone astray, becoming doomed to Hellfire. Hence, the devil

242 Al-Ḥusaynī, Sayyid ʿAlī Khān, *Riyāḍ al-Sālikīn*, Vol. 3, p. 185.

exerts all his power to harm these righteous individuals and hinder their efforts. If people were to witness the steadfastness of the allies of God on the path of righteousness, their refusal to follow their whims and desires, their immunity to the deception and delusion of the devil, their detachment from worldly temptations, and their immunity to the allure of this transient world, all of this would call upon all servants of God among mankind to adhere and hold fast to the path of God. The allies of God, through their mere existence, become signs that guide the misguided and serve as beacons of guidance. They support people in their pursuit of closeness to God and advancement through the innumerable stages of servitude to Him. People follow their light both during their physical presence in this life and the people's memories after they depart from this world.

People are invited to stand at their graves and recite the narrated Ziyārāt, seeking enlightenment from them. For instance, we read in some Ziyārāt:

> I bear witness that you were a light in illustrious loins and purified wombs. Ignorance could not defile you with its impurities, nor did you wear the tattered clothes of its people. I bear witness to the fact that you were among the pillars of religion and the supporters of the believers.[243]

---

243 From the Ziyārat of Imām al-Ḥusayn ﷵ (Ziyārat Wārith).

Similarly, in the Ziyārah of Amīr al-Mu'minīn ☸, passages recall his steadfastness in adhering to the truth, such as:

> You worship God sincerely, striving patiently for His sake. You were always mindful of yourself, accountable for your deeds, and acted by His Book and the tradition of His Prophet. You performed prayer, paid alms, enjoined good, and forbade evil to the best of your ability, seeking what God has promised. You were not afraid of difficulties nor hesitant in fighting...

The same is articulated in other paragraphs in this Ziyārah.

In summary, the devil's effort to harm God's infallible allies is intense, and their trials and tribulations are the strongest and most severe. However, their patience on the path of God is greater. This becomes a source of goodness for them, a guiding torch for those who seek guidance, and evidence against those who fail to benefit from the light of their guidance.

The Second Aspect

The next aspect to consider is the Imām ☸, acknowledging committing sins with all his organs and limbs.

Contemplating the meaning of sin and its implications reveals that it can be divided into two fundamental elements:

1. The first is departing from obedience to the Lord, either by an absolute departure or in the sense that the one committing it does not achieve what he aspires to or desires in the realm of divine closeness.

2. The second is that sin obstructs the servant's journey in the stages of divine proximity and the ascension towards the highest principles. Whoever faces such obstacles experiences more hardship and difficulty than the physical punishment that a person may deserve for disobeying God. The spiritual torment is more severe and harder to bear than the physical one. This is why the greatest Prophet ﷺ compared what he encountered from his enemies to what previous prophets faced and said,

   No prophet was afflicted as I have been afflicted.[244]

Even though it is known that other prophets were harmed, imprisoned, and killed, the burden that the greatest Prophet ﷺ carried weighed heavily on his sacred soul. The afflictions from previous prophets were mainly physical, whereas the burden experienced by the Prophet ﷺ was more spiritual. This meaning is also implied in the supplication taught by Imām ʿAlī ﷷ to his disciple Kumayl b. Ziyād, where he says,

---

[244] Majlisī, ʿAllāmah Muḥammad Bāqir, *Biḥār al-Anwār,* Vol. 39, p. 55. Al-Irbilī, ʿAlī b. ʿIsā Hakkārī, *Kashf al-Ghummah fī Maʿrifat al-A'imma*, Vol. 2, p. 537.

> Suppose that I can endure the heat of Your fire; how can I endure separation from You?

Therefore, the servant's suffering due to the hindrance of his journey caused by this aspect is more severe.

The souls of the infallibles ﷺ and their pure selves are distinguished from the souls of all other servants in terms of their elevated creation and sublime status. They were created from the light of greatness. Their descent into this world and connection to their material bodies were by divine wisdom, to become sources of guidance and shining lights for nations in the darkness of materialism.

In this regard, it is narrated that Imām Jaʿfar aṣ-Ṣādiq ؑ said,

> By God if it were not for the fact that God has ordained our Wilāyah, love, and kinship, we would not have let you enter our houses or stand at our doors.

All of this was the reason for their distance from their original abode above the higher realm and their descent from the abode of holiness. Their souls were attached to the divine throne, fortunate in that abode, living in its spiritual vicinity, and continuously engaged in worship, glorification, and sanctification of the Supreme Principle. Their descent was connected to the promise of their return to the same sublime station, with an increase in their blessedness due to what they would endure in guiding humanity.

Thus, their souls became connected to their material bodies. This connection and the inevitable necessities of living in this world, such as the need for food, drink, and sleep, the pain, hunger, thirst, and weariness, along with being restrained by their physical senses and limbs, all became barriers and obstacles preventing the return of their souls to their original abode. Amīr al-Mu'minīn ﷺ alluded to this when describing the pious in his sermon:

> And were it not for the predetermined term, their souls would not remain in their bodies for the twinkling of an eye due to their yearning for meeting [with their Lord].

Despite being within the framework of the comprehensive divine law, all that pertains to the requirements of this body, including its limbs and organs, their movements and functions, are considered barriers and obstacles. Everything that emanates from these bodily parts, being necessities of the impediments, is, in fact, the barriers themselves. Even though they lead to higher ranks and elevated stations, they bring about spiritual distress as they delay the return of this holy soul to its original abode. This is because all these aforementioned physical body elements physical body elements are derived from attachment to the lower worldly realm. All of these are expressed by the term "sins," although they are shaped within the molds of divine law for more significant purposes within the entity called sin, and hence they are called "sins."

In this context, the actions that, despite being within the bounds of compliance with divine law, were called "sins." "sin" originally meant "to take responsibility for something's sin." It is said, "I have sinned it; I have incurred its sin." The term is used for every action that carries a consequence, considering the sin of that thing. Thus, the term "sin" refers to the result or outcome of an action. As such, all that emanates from the infallibles as what is attributed to them from "sins" is only because of what we have mentioned, as it implies a sense of distance and that these matters delay them from their goal, which is to return to their original abode. For this reason, Imām al-Ḥusayn ﷺ says in his supplication on 'Arafah,

> O my God, You have ordered us to refer to the traces; therefore, (please do) make me refer to You with the garb of lights and the guidance of insight so that I will return to You in the same way as I have entered to You from them as being too protected to look at them and too determining to depend upon them, for You have power over all things. O my God, this is my humiliation; it manifests itself before You. This is my manner; it cannot be concealed against You. From You do I beseech soaring to You, and through You do I take the way to You. So, (please do) guide me to You

> through Your Light and make me stand up before Your Hands with true servitude to You.

In another part of the supplication, he says,

> O my God, fate awakens my hope and whim has enchained me with the firm chains of lust; so, (please do) be my Supporter so that You shall back me and show me the right path.

Thus, the term "sin" is applied to everything that hinders the progress of the infallible towards their original abode. "Sin" refers to actions that slow down reward attainment. As the poet said:

> Falsehoods murder Beauty
>
> When lies spread desolation.[245]

From this perspective, "disobedience" is also used, and although it refers to going against obedience, as we mentioned earlier, "sin" contains two elements: One is what prevents reaching the ultimate goal or hinders swift progress, as we discussed earlier. The other can be understood in two ways:

---

[245] al-Iṣfahānī, al-Rāghib, *al-Mufradāt fī Gharīb al-Qur'ān*.

First, it refers to going against obedience and rebelling against the Lord, consistently or temporarily, which contradicts infallibility.

Second, it implies not achieving what one aspires to in the realm of divine proximity, which they express through words such as "leaving the preferred" (refraining from attaining the higher spiritual stations). This has been attributed to some of the previous prophets ﻉ, as mentioned in the context of what happened with Prophet Dāwūd ﻉ when two angels blocked his access to a certain place. Or it can be understood in what is related to Prophet Ādam ﻉ. Some supplications of the prophets towards their people can also be interpreted similarly. The patience displayed by Prophet Muḥammad ﷺ and the infallible Imāms ﻉ is a great example of how they persevered and endured trials.[246]

The Third Aspect

In this regard, there are several points:

The first point is the repentance of the infallibles ﻉ.

---

[246] As for our esteemed teacher and scholar ﺭﻩ, he clarified in the discussions related to the verses that are used as evidence for the lack of infallibility that nothing has been reported from Ādam and other prophets, indicating the concept of "leaving the better option," and what suggests to this is the attainment of higher ranks after the occurrence of what is referred to as "leaving the better option."

We understand that repentance is returning, as mentioned earlier. The trial of the infallibles ﷺ in this worldly life and its people, on the one hand, and the attachment of their pure souls and spirits to the material bodies, on the other hand, make them feel a distance from their original abode, the sanctuary of the divine presence within the highest assembly. They beseech God ﷻ to help them swiftly detach from these attachments and their implications, which cause them intense psychological pain due to their longing for what God has promised them of returning to their places with increased favor and elevated ranks.

The second point is earnestly seeking forgiveness.

We should know that forgiveness is covering up, and it is achieved by overlooking shortcomings and faults and removing them. Sin is considered a deficiency as it leads to degradation for its perpetrator. Therefore, anything that a person perceives or considers a deficiency is considered a sin. Seeking forgiveness is thus considered a rational and obligatory request based on the wisdom of every refined soul.

As for the infallibles ﷺ, they consider their attachment to this world with all its aspects and necessities as burdens, the physical body and its ensuing needs posing as a source of feeling incomplete. This contrasts those blinded by this world's "wonderful" yet deceptive pleasures, thus mostly occupied with satisfying their needs.

Hence, these holy people of God suffer from their stay in this world and the resulting feeling of incompleteness and seek solace in seclusion with God ﷻ and private supplications to Him. It has been reported that the Prophet ﷺ would sometimes say to his caller to prayer, Bilāl,

> Grant us some respite, O Bilāl [i.e., the respite of the time of prayer].

When ʿAmmār ؓ was martyred, Imām ʿAlī ؑ said:

> O Death, you are not leaving anyone.
>
> Spare me, for you have taken all my beloved friends.
>
> I see you vigilant over those whom I love,
>
> As if you are heading towards them with a clear sign.

Similarly, Imām ʿAlī ؑ expressed his intense pain from worldly life and its attractions when he said,

> Get away from me, O' world. Your rein is on your shoulders as I have released myself from your ditches, removed myself from your snares, and avoided walking into your slippery places. Where are those whom you have deceived by your jokes? Where are those communities whom you have enticed with your embellishments? They are all

> confined to graves and hidden in burial places. By God, if you had been a visible personality and a body capable of feeling, I would have awarded you the penalties fixed by God because of the people whom you deceived through desires, the communities whom you threw into destruction, and the rulers whom you consigned to ruin and drove to places of distress after which there is neither going nor returning...

Until he ﷺ says,

> Get away from me, for, by God, I do not bow before you so that you may humiliate me, nor do I let loose the reins for you so that you may drive me away. I swear by God an oath wherein I, except for the will of God, shall so train myself that it will feel joyful if it gets one loaf for eating...[247]

and so on until the end of his ﷺ letter.

The pain of the infallibles from this world and their repentance express their strong and certain longing to return to their original abode and quickly rid themselves of the obstacles. Perhaps this is what Imām Ja'far aṣ-Ṣādiq ﷺ indicated in the narration attributed to him:

---

[247] Sharīf Raḍī, Muḥammad b. al-Ḥusayn, *Nahj al-Balāghah*, an excerpt from his ﷺ letter to his governor in Baṣrah, 'Uthmān b. Ḥunayf, letter no. 45.

> Repentance is the rope of God and the extension
> of His care. The servant must continue repenting
> in all circumstances. Every group of worshipers has
> their repentance. So, the repentance of the
> prophets is from the agitation of the secret, the
> repentance of the close friends of God [Awliyā'; i.e.,
> pious, God-conscious people devoted to God and
> close to Him] is from the diversions, and the
> repentance of the righteous is from seeking
> comfort.[248]

The agitation of the secret refers to the turmoil of the soul;
it is agitated to return to the sacred sanctuary due to the
pressure and heaviness of its attachment to the world and
corruption. This attachment forces them to engage in
permissible acts, as previously mentioned.

And what is meant by seeking comfort is that the
righteous, due to the attachment of their souls to their
bodies, feel the need for the body's comfort, which is one
of its necessities.

What the diversions mean is the matters in which the
bodies of those devoted to God are deficient. They
experience the dangers of what the body lacks regarding
food, drink, protection from heat and cold, pain, and
seeking comfort that follows the body's comfort.

---

[248] Imām Jaʿfar aṣ-Ṣādiq ☀, *Miṣbāḥ al-Sharīʿah*, Chapter 44: *Fī al-Tawbah* [on repentance].

In contrast, others feel pain for the worldly life, as their hearts become attached to it, leading them to fall into pitfalls and disasters. Even if they are encompassed by mercy and guided by providence, they still struggle to turn to obedience, seeking God's help to free themselves from the clutches of their deeds that they have burdened themselves with due to their attachment to worldly life and their dip into its pleasures. Perhaps the following saying attributed to Imām Jaʿfar aṣ-Ṣādiq 🕮 refers to this:

> And the repentance of the general public is from sins.[249]

Know that among the prophets, those who are devoted to God, and righteous individuals, on one hand, and the common people, on the other hand, there is a group referred to as the Khawāṣṣ [the elite], and their repentance is related to their preoccupation with things other than God. This means they become absorbed in some permissible matters to enjoy the allowable pleasures.

The third point

God's response to the repentance of the penitent varies according to their state and status. For the penitent sinner, God's forgiveness means covering their flaws until reckoning and punishment arrive or erasing their sins. As for the repentance and forgiveness of the infallibles, it is

---

[249] Ibid.

accompanied by God's bounties, elevating their ranks and opening paths to excellence, thereby alleviating their عليهم السلام sense of pain from being tested with the worldly life and its people and dwelling among those who enjoy it and desire to indulge in it even more.

The Fourth Aspect

It should be known that the attachment of the infallible souls, regardless of their ranks, to their physical bodies and their requirements distances them forcibly from the world of abstraction while they are, at the same time, obliged to protect their bodies from anything that may harm them. They are bound to provide for their bodily needs accordingly. However, in their conviction, this attachment to things does not befit their station because it impedes them from worshiping in the realm of abstraction, which is considered the highest and noblest level of devotion. This situation instills fear in them of Hellfire, as they are unable to attain the state they once achieved, basking under the shelter of the Throne of Mercy *and* unable to worship as they did before due to their attachment to worldly affairs, as mentioned before. This feeling of inadequacy creates fear of punishment and hellfire, so we find them عليهم السلام confessing their shortcomings in worship and seeking repentance in their supplications.

Overall, the involuntary withdrawal from the realm of abstraction, where they were soaring in the lofty ranks of worship, and their being bound by the worldly realm and

its requirements—including being commanded to seek
well-being for their bodies and providing sustenance in the
various forms that the body lacks—forces them to abide by
a lower level of worship in the worldly realm and
experience divine love in a smaller proportion compared to
what they were used to and aspire to return to after their
souls separate from their bodies. All of this creates a sense
of deficiency and, even more, a sense of falling short in
fulfilling the rights of worship and the obligations of love
and devotion to the Beloved. This sense of falling short
leads to fear of punishment. That is why it is narrated that
Imām Zayn al-ʿĀbidīn 🕊 considered not fulfilling his duty
of worship as a terrifying sin.

Testifying that they 🕊 are not satisfied with their worship
being constrained by their bodies, as it is beneath what they
desire and wish for, Imām Zayn al-ʿĀbidīn 🕊 said,

> My God, were it not incumbent to accept Your
> command, I would declare You far too exalted for
> me to remember You. However, I remember You in
> my measure, not in Your measure, and my scope
> can hardly reach the point where I may be a locus
> for calling You holy!...[250]

And so on until the end of his supplication.

---

[250] Part of *Munājāt al-Dhākirīn*; see books of supplication such as
Mafātīḥ al-Jinān.

If you argue that the attachment of the infallible ones to their human bodies is involuntary and that their adherence to the necessities of dwelling in this world, the realm of the universe and corruption, is linked to the divine formation, and they do what is within their capacity in terms of worship, then from where does this feeling of inadequacy arise?

When the infallible looks at the vast difference and distance between the worship they engaged in during their state of detachment and the worship they performed. At the same time, bound to this world and its requirements, this contrast makes them lament over what they cannot do. Moreover, when they witness the divine purity of God, the fact that He has not bound them to this world to keep them away from higher ranks of worship but rather to pave the way for them to achieve superior levels beyond what they were capable of before the attachment, they realize that God has not deprived them of the ability to worship at the highest levels. From this, they sense their inability to reach those elevated worship ranks is on them, not God ﷻ. Therefore, the same apology a servant gives the Master for not attaining the highest level of obedience is seen as an acknowledgment of their shortcomings.

The Fifth Aspect

This is an acknowledgment of sins committed while surpassing the boundaries and transgressing against others who are also servants of God. It is similar to what is mentioned in the Monday supplication:

> O God, I pray forgiveness from You for every vow I have vowed, every promise I have made, and every pledge I have pledged and then I failed to keep for You. I ask You concerning the complaints of Your servants against me: If there is a servant from among Your servants or a bondmaid from among Your bondmaids who has against me a complaint because I have wronged him in respect to himself, his reputation, his property, his wife or his child, or because evil words I have spoken about him in his absence, an imposition upon him through inclination, caprice, scorn, zeal, false show, bigotry, whether he be absent or present, alive or dead, such that my hand has fallen short and my capacity has been too narrow to make restitution to him or to annul my obligation to him, I ask You, O He who owns all objects of need, which are granted by His will and hasten to His desire that You bless Muḥammad and the Household of Muḥammad, and make [the one I have wronged] satisfied with me in the manner that You will, ... [until the end of the supplication].

It is evident that the term ʿabd (servant) is not exclusive to humans, jinn, and angels; rather, it encompasses all living beings, including animals, as mentioned in the verse:

﴿وَمَا مِن دَآبَّةٍ فِي ٱلۡأَرۡضِ وَلَا طَـٰٓئِرٍ يَطِيرُ بِجَنَاحَيۡهِ إِلَّآ أُمَمٌ أَمۡثَالُكُم﴾

﴾wa-mā min dābbatin fī l-'arḍi wa-lā ṭā'irin yaṭīru bi-janāḥayhi 'illā 'umamun 'amthālukum mā farraṭnā fī l-kitābi min shay'in thumma 'ilā rabbihim yuḥsharūna﴿

﴾There is no animal on land, nor a bird that flies with its wings, but they are communities like yourselves. We have not omitted anything from the Book﴿[251]

Even all entities, including plants and inanimate objects, fall under the title of ʿabd (servants), as stated in the verse:

﴿تُسَبِّحُ لَهُ ٱلسَّمَـٰوَٰتُ ٱلسَّبۡعُ وَٱلۡأَرۡضُ وَمَن فِيهِنَّۚ وَإِن مِّن شَيۡءٍ إِلَّا يُسَبِّحُ بِحَمۡدِهِۦ وَلَـٰكِن لَّا تَفۡقَهُونَ تَسۡبِيحَهُمۡۚ إِنَّهُۥ كَانَ حَلِيمًا غَفُورًا﴾

﴾tusabbiḥu lahu s-samāwātu s-sabʿu wa-l-'arḍu wa-man fīhinna wa-'in min shay'in 'illā yusabbiḥu bi-ḥamdihī wa-lākin lā tafqahūna tasbīḥahum 'innahū kāna ḥalīman ghafūran﴿

﴾The seven heavens glorify Him, and the earth [too], and whoever is in them. There is not a thing but celebrates His praise, but you do not understand their glorification. Indeed, He is Forbearing, Forgiving﴿[252]

---

[251] Sūrat al-Anʿām, Verse 38.

[252] Sūrat al-Isrā', Verse 44.

The act of praising and exalting God applies to everything in the Heavens and the earth, as well as to the very Heavens and earth themselves. For instance, God says:

﴿ثُمَّ ٱسْتَوَىٰٓ إِلَى ٱلسَّمَآءِ وَهِيَ دُخَانٌ فَقَالَ لَهَا وَلِلْأَرْضِ ٱئْتِيَا طَوْعًا أَوْ كَرْهًا قَالَتَآ أَتَيْنَا طَآئِعِينَ﴾

﴿thumma stawā ʾilā s-samāʾi wa-hiya dukhānun fa-qāla lahā wa-li-l-ʾarḍi ʾtiyā ṭawʿan ʾaw karhan qālatā ʾataynā ṭāʾiʿīna﴾

﴿Then He turned to the heaven, and it was smoke, and He said to it and to the earth, 'Come, willingly or unwillingly!' They said, 'We come obediently'﴾[253]

Moreover, in the verse:

﴿وَإِذَا ٱلْوُحُوشُ حُشِرَتْ﴾

﴿wa-ʾidhā l-wuḥūshu ḥushirat﴾

﴿when the wild beasts are mustered﴾[254]

all creatures are included in the concept of being held accountable. The narration from Muʿāwīyahh b. ʿAmmār

[253] Sūrat Fuṣṣilat, Verse 11.

[254] Sūrat at-Takwīr, Verse 5.

supports this understanding who reported that Imām Jaʿfar aṣ-Ṣādiq was once approached with a remark that a bird of prey was on the Kaʿbah and that it hit every pigeon that passed. The Imām said,

> Catch and kill it because it has committed deviation.[255]

Likewise, ʿAbdullāh b. Maymūn narrated from Imām Jaʿfar aṣ-Ṣādiq from Imām Muḥammad al-Bāqir that Prophet Yaʿqūb said to his son Prophet Yūsuf,

> O my son, do not commit wrongdoing, for if a bird were to commit wrongdoing, its feathers would scatter.[256]

Similarly, the submission of birds and other creatures to the obedience of Prophet Sulaymān is another evidence of this concept. God says:

﴿وَحُشِرَ لِسُلَيْمَـٰنَ جُنُودُهُۥ مِنَ ٱلْجِنِّ وَٱلْإِنسِ وَٱلطَّيْرِ﴾

﴿wa-ḥushira li-sulaymāna junūduhū mina l-jinni wa-l-ʾinsi wa-ṭ-ṭayri﴾

---

[255] Kulaynī, Shaykh Muḥammad b. Yaʿqūb, *al-Kāfī*, Vol. 4, p. 227.

[256] Ṣadūq, Shaykh Muḥammad b. ʿAlī, *Man Lā Yaḥḍuruh al-Faqīh*, Vol. 4, p. 13. Kulaynī, Shaykh Muḥammad b. Yaʿqūb, al-Kāfī, Vol. 5, p. 542, and al-Barqī, Aḥmad b. Muḥammad b. Khālid, *al-Maḥāsin*.

﴾[Once] Sulaymān's hosts were marched out for him, comprising jinn, humans and birds﴿[257]

and

﴿وَٱلطَّيْرَ مَحْشُورَةً كُلٌّ لَّهُۥٓ أَوَّابٌ﴿

﴾wa-ṭ-ṭayra maḥshūratan kullun lahū 'awwāb^un^﴿

﴾and the birds [as well], mustered [in flocks]; all echoing him [in a chorus]﴿[258]

Furthermore, a narration reports that Imām Zayn al-ʿĀbidīn ﷺ might have raised his whip intending to discipline his camel for not walking properly, but then he refrained and said,

> Ah! If it were not for retribution (i.e., accountability).

This indicates that one must be prepared for accountability for any action that transgresses the permissible boundaries set by the divine law. Any misconduct or wrongdoing towards any creature is considered a transgression and injustice. An example of this principle can also be seen in the prohibition of urinating in stagnant water, with the

---

257 Sūrat al-Naml, Verse 17.

258 Sūrat Ṣād, Verse 19.

explanation that it has living beings that might be harmed. Ultimately, the expression attributed to the Imām ☙ in the earlier paragraph encompasses all we have referred to:

> Our Lord, suffice us with Your mercy and make our lives as guided by Your wisdom.

And among what is in line with this meaning in the supplications is the saying of Imām Zayn al-ʿĀbidīn ☙ in the supplication known as *Makārim al-Akhlāq* [Supplication for Noble Moral Traits]:

> O God, make what Shayṭān throws into my heart, of desires, suspicion, and envy, be (a cause of) remembrance of Your might pondering over Your power, and planning against Your enemy. Make what he (Shayṭān) makes me utter, of indecent and obscene words, reviling a good reputation, false evidence speaking ill of an absent believer, or abusing one who is present, and other similar things, (let all this) be a speech in Your praise.

Therefore, we say: Indeed, the recognized matters in which the person under judgment is not restricted by mental existence, whether realized or predetermined nor by external existence, are true in an absolute sense. This occurs when the analysis converges with the conditionality, meaning there is no observation or consideration of the subject's realization. Instead, the judgment is based on the fact that whatever is characterized by the nominal description is estimated to exist externally or mentally, and accordingly, these matters are governed. These issues are found in the reported words of the supplications of the infallibles ﷺ. For instance, when the Imāms ﷺ say "any servant...," it means that if the subject were to be realized through this nominal description, then what is mentioned in the sections of the supplication would be required from God ﷻ. It is well-known that true matters do not necessitate the realization of the subject or its characterization with the nominal description in any circumstance, whether external or mental. This explains what is mentioned in the sections of the supplication of Amīr al-Mu'minīn ﷺ, which his disciple Kumayl b. Ziyād ﷺ learned from him, such as his saying,

> O God, forgive me those sins which tear apart safeguards! O God, forgive me those sins which draw down adversities! O God, forgive me those sins which alter blessings! O God, forgive me those sins which hold back supplication! O God, forgive me those sins which cut down the hopes!

Although, this supplication is beyond the scope of discussion, as it came in the context of teaching, similar to the supplication of Abū Ḥamza Thumālī, which he learned from Imām Zayn al-'Ābidīn ﷺ.

Barriers and Obstacles to Repentance

Know, my brother, that numerous barriers and obstacles prevent the servant from initiating repentance and push him towards stumbling in his life. Consequently, the servant is driven towards disobedience and persists in ignorance, delving deeper into the darkness of this worldly life. This continues until death surprises him, and regrets then overcome him. Thus, he becomes a living example of the divine saying:

﴿رَبِّ لَوْلَآ أَخَّرْتَنِيٓ إِلَىٰٓ أَجَلٍ قَرِيبٍ فَأَصَّدَّقَ وَأَكُن مِّنَ ٱلصَّٰلِحِينَ﴾

﴿*rabbi law-lā ʾakhkhartanī ʾilā ʾajalin qarībin fa-ʾaṣṣaddaqa wa-ʾakun mina ṣ-ṣāliḥīna*﴾

﴿وَلَن يُؤَخِّرَ ٱللَّهُ نَفْسًا إِذَا جَآءَ أَجَلُهَاۚ وَٱللَّهُ خَبِيرُۢ بِمَا تَعْمَلُونَ﴾

﴿*wa-lan yuʾakhkhira llāhu nafsan ʾidhā jāʾa ʾajaluhā wa-llāhu khabīrun bi-mā taʿmalūna*﴾

﴿*'My Lord, why did You not respite me for a short time so that I could give charity and become one of the righteous!' But God will never respite anyone when his time has come, and God is well aware of what you do*﴾[259]

The transgressor might also persist in his defiance and aggression against himself, his Creator, and his Master,

---

[259] Sūrat Munāfiqūn, Verses 10–11.

continuing to rebel against his Lord. He may suddenly meet his end, thus becoming among the losers.

Some are in worse conditions than these two. They remember repentance and its obligation and become aware of their transgressions and deviations. They become aware of what they must do to achieve their salvation, yet they delay repentance. Indeed, the one who remembers and then procrastinates is worse than those who persist in their ignorance without self-awareness. This procrastination is often preceded by reminders from various sources so that no one can present an excuse before God. Rather, He has the ultimate argument over everything.

In the following, we will address some of these barriers and obstacles. We will all turn to ourselves, strive to overcome these obstacles, and endeavor to free ourselves from the shadows of these hindrances. It is well-known that no one has achieved this, nor will anyone do so, except by the encompassing mercy of God. May we remember and fear accordingly.

Among those reasons and obstacles are the following:

Weakness of Faith in God, His Messenger ﷺ, and the Hereafter

This weakness can arise from persisting in consuming what is prohibited [ḥarām] and excessive love for the worldly life. The situation may reach a point where an individual—and we seek refuge in God from such a state—empties their heart of complete faith. Even though they may consider themselves Muslims or believers, there is no trace of true faith within them. They may mock religious rituals, belittle religious figures, and cast doubt on miracles and extraordinary events, even if they are well-documented. They often view many spiritual practices as superstitions, believe they are outdated, or think that such practices lead to divisions among Muslims.

In some cases, this skepticism extends to doubting the infallibility of the Imāms عليهم السلام. While they may acknowledge the infallibility of the Prophets and Imāms عليهم السلام, they still regard them as mere humans in their conversations about them. For instance, they promote the idea of minimizing the condolences and gatherings dedicated to commemorating Imām Ḥusayn, suggesting that expressions of grief such as crying and self-flagellation should be abandoned as much time has passed since then. They fail to realize that these practices are essential for the continuity of the religion and the preservation of Islām. They also belittle Ziyārāt and similar practices, arguing that visiting the Imāms' shrines is useless since the Imām is in Paradise and does not benefit from it. Such individuals are not inclined towards seeking forgiveness because, in reality, they lack faith in the Day of Resurrection. They may, however, engage in these practices out of habit or to avoid social consequences, and this category of individuals are hypocrites who, in reality, do not truly believe in the power of supplication. They might utter prayers without considering seeking forgiveness and repentance. God alludes to people of this nature in the verse:

﴿وَإِذَا قِيلَ لَهُمْ تَعَالَوْا۟ يَسْتَغْفِرْ لَكُمْ رَسُولُ ٱللَّهِ لَوَّوْا۟ رُءُوسَهُمْ وَرَأَيْتَهُمْ يَصُدُّونَ وَهُم مُّسْتَكْبِرُونَ﴾

﴾*wa-'idhā qīla lahum ta'ālaw yastaghfir lakum rasūlu llāhi lawwaw ru'ūsahum wa-ra'aytahum yaṣuddūna wa-hum mustakbirūn*[a]﴿

﴿سَوَآءٌ عَلَيْهِمْ أَسْتَغْفَرْتَ لَهُمْ أَمْ لَمْ تَسْتَغْفِرْ لَهُمْ لَن يَغْفِرَ ٱللَّهُ لَهُمْ﴾

﴾*sawā'un 'alayhim 'a-staghfarta lahum 'am lam tastaghfir lahum lan yaghfira llāhu lahum*﴿

﴾*When they are told, 'Come, that God's Apostle may plead for forgiveness for you,' they twist their heads, and you see them turn away disdainfully. It is the same for them whether you plead for forgiveness for them, or do not plead for forgiveness for them: God will never forgive them*﴿[260]

Their state is also described by God ﷻ in this verse:

﴿ذَٰلِكَ بِأَنَّهُمْ ءَامَنُوا۟ ثُمَّ كَفَرُوا۟ فَطُبِعَ عَلَىٰ قُلُوبِهِمْ فَهُمْ لَا يَفْقَهُونَ﴾

[260] Sūrat al-Munāfiqūn, Verses 5–6.

﴿*dhālika bi-'annahum 'āmanū thumma kafarū fa-ṭubi'a 'alā qulūbihim fa-hum lā yafqahūna*﴾

﴿*That is because they believed and then disbelieved, so their hearts were sealed. Hence, they do not understand*﴾[261]

And know, my dear brother, that individuals like these can be found in all Islāmic societies, even within the righteous group and perhaps even among religious figures.

The Accumulation of Rust Upon the Heart

When the accountable individual delves into sins, consumes the forbidden and the doubtful, and his flesh grows upon these actions, his spiritual faculties become obscured by the weight of his wrongful deeds. Despite the divine warnings, admonitions, and constant reminders throughout his life, he persists in his transgressions, thus darkening his heart and weakening the essence of faith. This is alluded to in the saying of God:

﴿كَلَّاۖ بَلۡۜ رَانَ عَلَىٰ قُلُوبِهِم مَّا كَانُواْ يَكۡسِبُونَ﴾

﴿*kallā bal rāna 'alā qulūbihim mā kānū yaksibūna*﴾

261 Sūrat al-Munāfiqūn, Verse 3.

﴿*No, that is not the case! Rather, their hearts have been sullied by what they have been earning*﴾[262]

And

﴿وَإِن يَرَوْاْ سَبِيلَ ٱلْغَيِّ يَتَّخِذُوهُ سَبِيلًا﴾

﴿*wa-'in yaraw sabīla l-ghayyi yattakhidhūhu sabīlan*﴾

﴿*And if they see the way of error they will take it as [their] way*﴾[263]

These individuals do not stand alone; they have counterparts who share their ways, collaborating in sin, aggression, and persisting in transgression, as highlighted in this verse:

﴿وَإِخْوَٰنُهُمْ يَمُدُّونَهُمْ فِي ٱلْغَيِّ ثُمَّ لَا يُقْصِرُونَ﴾

﴿*wa-'ikhwānuhum yamuddūnahum fī l-ghayyi thumma lā yuqṣirūn*[a]﴾

﴿*But their brethren, they draw them into error, and then they do not spare [any harm]*﴾[264]

---

262 Sūrat al-Muṭaffifīn, Verse 14.

263 Sūrat al-A'rāf, Verse 146.

264 Sūrat al-A'rāf, Verse 202.

They are impervious to sincere advice and the warnings of admonishers, as emphasized by the words of God:

﴿وَلَا يَنفَعُكُمْ نُصْحِيٓ إِنْ أَرَدتُّ أَنْ أَنصَحَ لَكُمْ﴾

﴿*wa-lā yanfaʿukum nuṣḥī ʾin ʾaradtu ʾan ʾanṣaḥa lakum*﴾

﴿*My exhorting will not benefit you,*
much as I may seek to exhort you﴾[265]

Such individuals may outwardly pretend to seek forgiveness or repent, mimicking the genuine repenters, but their repentance does not spring from the depths of their will. Imām ʿAlī ﷺ referred to such people in his discussion of the stages of repentance, where he said,

> The fifth [stage] is to aim at the flesh grown as a result of unlawful earning so that you may melt it by grief (of repentance) till the skin touches the bone and a new flesh grows between them...[266]

The entirety of his statement has been previously elaborated upon.[267]

---

[265] Sūrat Hūd, Verse 34.

[266] Sharīf Raḍī, Muḥammad b. al-Ḥusayn, *Nahj al-Balāghah,* Saying 417.

[267] It was discussed in the sixth condition of repentance.

This case of this group is considered less severe than the first, and one remains hopeful that they eventually heed their situation, even though the possibility of them being affected by admonitions and warnings is weak. It is narrated in some reports that when Imām al-Ḥusayn ﷺ, the Master of Martyrs, intended to advise the wayward, some of them raised their voices and shouted to prevent themselves from hearing his words.

He said,

> I call you to the path of guidance. Whoever obeys me will be among the guided, and whoever disobeys me will be among the doomed. All of you are disobedient to my command, not listening to my words. Your stomachs have been filled with the forbidden, and it has been sealed onto your hearts. Woe to you! Don't you listen? Don't you hear?[268]

The consequence of their behavior is well-known to us all. Therefore, a strong warning is issued against consuming what is doubtful and forbidden. It is also known that associating with sinners and those who mock God's religion and His laws can lead to such a state. Hence, we are prohibited from mingling with sinners and are instructed to distance ourselves from idle gatherings and the company of those who disregard religion. Interacting with such individuals can lead to a similar condition.

---

[268] Majlisī, ʿAllāmah Muḥammad Bāqir, *Biḥār al-Anwār,* Vol. 45, p. 8.

Hardness of the Heart

When a person continues to be indifferent and unconcerned about the divine law despite performing obligatory duties and persists in committing minor sins without refraining from major ones when the opportunity arises, their heart becomes hardened. It does not soften to listen to admonitions nor yield to the influence of advice. Even if it produces listening, the heart's hardness prevents them from resorting to repentance, and not a single tear is shed in fear of God. They weep for what they miss out on in the world and cry out in anguish over the loss of family, friends, and children, yet no tears appear in the corners of their eyes out of fear of the ﷻ.

Some verses refer to this group, such as the following:

﴿ثُمَّ قَسَتْ قُلُوبُكُم مِّنْ بَعْدِ ذَٰلِكَ فَهِيَ كَٱلْحِجَارَةِ أَوْ أَشَدُّ قَسْوَةً﴾

﴾thumma qasat qulūbukum min baʿdi dhālika fa-hiya ka-l-ḥijārati ʾaw ʾashaddu qaswatan﴿

﴾Then your hearts hardened after that; so they are like stones, or even harder﴿[269]

﴿فَوَلَٰكِن قَسَتْ قُلُوبُهُمْ وَزَيَّنَ لَهُمُ ٱلشَّيْطَٰنُ مَا كَانُوا۟ يَعْمَلُونَ﴾

---

269 Sūrat al-Baqarah, Verse 74.

﴿*wa-lākin qasat qulūbuhum wa-zayyana lahumu sh-shayṭānu mā kānū ya'malūn*[a]﴾

﴿*But their hearts had hardened, and Shayṭān had made what they had been doing seem decorous to them*﴾[270]

﴿فَطَالَ عَلَيۡهِمُ ٱلۡأَمَدُ فَقَسَتۡ قُلُوبُهُمۡۖ وَكَثِيرٞ مِّنۡهُمۡ فَٰسِقُونَ﴾

﴿*fa-ṭāla 'alayhimu l-'amadu fa-qasat qulūbuhum wa-kathīrun minhum fāsiqūn*[a]﴾

﴿*Time took its toll on them and so their hearts were hardened, and many of them are transgressors*﴾[271]

﴿فَبِمَا نَقۡضِهِم مِّيثَٰقَهُمۡ لَعَنَّٰهُمۡ وَجَعَلۡنَا قُلُوبَهُمۡ قَٰسِيَةٗۖ﴾

﴿*fa-bi-mā naqḍihim mīthāqahum la'annāhum wa-ja'alnā qulūbahum qāsiyatan*﴾

﴿*Then, because of their breaking their covenant We cursed them and made their hearts hard*﴾[272]

God ﷻ warned against the hardness of the heart, saying:

---

[270] Sūrat al-An'ām, Verse 43.

[271] Sūrat al-Ḥadīd, Verse 13.

[272] Sūrat al-Mā'idah, Verse 13.

﴿فَوَيْلٌ لِّلْقَـٰسِيَةِ قُلُوبُهُم مِّن ذِكْرِ ٱللَّهِ﴾

﴾*fa-waylun li-l-qāsiyati qulūbuhum min dhikri llāhi*﴿

﴾*So woe to those whose hearts have been hardened to the remembrance of God*﴿[273]

The case of this group is less severe than the previous ones, especially when the person is among those who believe in God and His Messenger. When divine wisdom is necessitated, mercy encompasses them, and they become aware of their situation. They seek guidance and admonishment and take the initiative to rectify themselves. A transformation occurs from one state to another, similar to what happened to Ḥurr b. Yazīd al-Riyāḥī ؓ. Thus, the repentant who once used to steal shrouds during the time of the Prophet ﷺ and many other similar examples and instances serve as evidence of this.

Being Deluded by Respite

Sometimes, a person may think that God ﷻ has favored him in this world, so he indulges in sins and transgressions. The devil leads him to believe that God will overlook his actions and forgive him without the need for repentance and atonement for his wrongdoing. He does not realize that these worldly blessings and respite are a means of leading him astray. This verse refers to such people as

---

273 Sūrat az-Zumar, Verse 22.

﴿فَلَمَّا نَسُوا۟ مَا ذُكِّرُوا۟ بِهِۦ فَتَحْنَا عَلَيْهِمْ أَبْوَٰبَ كُلِّ شَىْءٍ حَتَّىٰٓ إِذَا فَرِحُوا۟ بِمَآ أُوتُوٓا۟ أَخَذْنَٰهُم بَغْتَةً فَإِذَا هُم مُّبْلِسُونَ﴾

﴿fa-lammā nasū mā dhukkirū bihī fataḥnā ʿalayhim ʾabwāba kulli shayʾin ḥattā ʾidhā fariḥū bi-mā ʾūtū ʾakhadhnāhum baghtatan fa-ʾidhā hum mublisūna﴾

﴿So when they forgot what they had been admonished of, We opened for them the gates of all [good] things. When they ﴿became proud of what they were given, We seized them suddenly, whereat, behold, they were despondent﴾[274]

These individuals overlook that the forgiveness of sins and the encompassing of His mercy, as mentioned in many verses, are conditioned upon repentance. Consider the following verses:

﴿فَخَلَفَ مِنۢ بَعْدِهِمْ خَلْفٌ أَضَاعُوا۟ ٱلصَّلَوٰةَ وَٱتَّبَعُوا۟ ٱلشَّهَوَٰتِ ۖ فَسَوْفَ يَلْقَوْنَ غَيًّا﴾

﴿fa-khalafa min baʿdihim khalfun ʾaḍāʿū ṣ-ṣalāta wa-ttabaʿū sh-shahawāti fa-sawfa yalqawna ghayyan﴾

﴿إِلَّا مَن تَابَ وَءَامَنَ وَعَمِلَ صَٰلِحًا فَأُو۟لَٰٓئِكَ يَدْخُلُونَ ٱلْجَنَّةَ وَلَا يُظْلَمُونَ شَيْـًٔا﴾

[274] Sūrat al-Anʿām, Verse 44.

﴾*illā man tāba wa-ʾāmana wa-ʿamila ṣāliḥan fa-ʾulāʾika yadkhulūna l-jannata wa-lā yuẓlamūna shayʾa*[n]﴿

﴾*But they were succeeded by an evil posterity who neglected the prayer, and followed [their base] appetites. So they will soon encounter [the reward of] perversity, barring those who repent, believe, and act righteously. Such will enter paradise, and they will not be wronged in the least*﴿[275]

﴿فَأَمَّا مَن تَابَ وَءَامَنَ وَعَمِلَ صَٰلِحٗا فَعَسَىٰٓ أَن يَكُونَ مِنَ ٱلۡمُفۡلِحِينَ﴾

﴾*fa-ʾammā man tāba wa-ʾāmana wa-ʿamila ṣāliḥan fa-ʿasā ʾan yakūna mina l-mufliḥīn*[a]﴿

﴾*As for him who repents, has faith and acts righteously, maybe he will be among the felicitous*﴿[276]

﴿وَمَن يَبۡتَغِ غَيۡرَ ٱلۡإِسۡلَٰمِ دِينٗا فَلَن يُقۡبَلَ مِنۡهُ وَهُوَ فِي ٱلۡأٓخِرَةِ مِنَ ٱلۡخَٰسِرِينَ﴾

﴾*wa-man yabtaghi ghayra l-ʾislāmi dīnan fa-lan yuqbala minhu wa-huwa fī l-ʾākhirati mina l-khāsirīn*[a]﴿

﴿كَيۡفَ يَهۡدِي ٱللَّهُ قَوۡمٗا كَفَرُواْ بَعۡدَ إِيمَٰنِهِمۡ وَشَهِدُوٓاْ أَنَّ ٱلرَّسُولَ حَقّٞ
وَجَآءَهُمُ ٱلۡبَيِّنَٰتُۚ وَٱللَّهُ لَا يَهۡدِي ٱلۡقَوۡمَ ٱلظَّٰلِمِينَ﴾

---

275 Sūrat Maryam, Verses 59–60.

276 Sūrat al-Qaṣaṣ, Verse 67.

﴾kayfa yahdī llāhu qawman kafarū baʿda ʾīmānihim wa-shahidū ʾanna r-rasūla ḥaqqun wa-jāʾahumu l-bayyinātu wa-llāhu lā yahdī l-qawma ẓ-ẓālimīna﴿

﴾أُوْلَٰٓئِكَ جَزَآؤُهُمْ أَنَّ عَلَيْهِمْ لَعْنَةَ ٱللَّهِ وَٱلْمَلَٰٓئِكَةِ وَٱلنَّاسِ أَجْمَعِينَ﴿

﴾ulāʾika jazāʾuhum ʾanna ʿalayhim laʿnata llāhi wa-l-malāʾikati wa-n-nāsi ʾajmaʿīna﴿

﴾خَٰلِدِينَ فِيهَا لَا يُخَفَّفُ عَنْهُمُ ٱلْعَذَابُ وَلَا هُمْ يُنظَرُونَ﴿

﴾khālidīna fīhā lā yukhaffafu ʿanhumu l-ʿadhābu wa-lā hum yunẓarūna﴿

﴾إِلَّا ٱلَّذِينَ تَابُواْ مِنۢ بَعْدِ ذَٰلِكَ وَأَصْلَحُواْ فَإِنَّ ٱللَّهَ غَفُورٌ رَّحِيمٌ﴿

﴾illā lladhīna tābū min baʿdi dhālika wa-ʾaṣlaḥū fa-ʾinna llāha ghafūrun raḥīmun﴿

﴾Should anyone follow a religion other than Islām, it shall never be accepted from him, and he will be among the losers in the Hereafter. How shall God guide a people who have disbelieved after their faith and [after] bearing witness that the Apostle is true, and [after] manifest proofs had come to them? God does not guide the wrongdoing lot. Their requital is that there shall be upon them the curse of God, the angels, and all mankind. They will remain in it [forever], and their punishment will not be lightened, nor will they be

granted any respite, except such as repent after that and make amends, for God is Forgiving, Merciful﴿[277]

It seems that what is meant by "disbelief" here is to depart from obedience, and it is not intended to be disbelief in faith. For disbelief in faith cannot coexist with bearing witness to the truth of prophethood—the prophethood of the Messenger of God ﷺ. God ﷻ said:

﴿ثُمَّ إِنَّ رَبَّكَ لِلَّذِينَ عَمِلُوا۟ ٱلسُّوٓءَ بِجَهَٰلَةٍ ثُمَّ تَابُوا۟ مِنۢ بَعْدِ ذَٰلِكَ وَأَصْلَحُوٓا۟ إِنَّ رَبَّكَ مِنۢ بَعْدِهَا لَغَفُورٌ رَّحِيمٌ﴾

﴾*thumma 'inna rabbaka li-lladhīna ʿamilū s-sū'a bi-jahālatin thumma tābū min baʿdi dhālika wa-'aṣlaḥū 'inna rabbaka min baʿdihā la-ghafūrun raḥīm*[un]﴿

﴾*Moreover, your Lord will indeed be forgiving and merciful to those who repent after they having committed evil out of ignorance and reform themselves*﴿[278]

Narrations have conveyed what means the following: Do not be among those who hope for God's mercy without deeds [that is, without striving].

---

[277] Sūrat Āl ʿImrān, Verses 85–89.

[278] Sūrat an-Naḥl, Verse 119.

Delusion by Promised Rewards for Recommended Actions

The narrations mention recommended acts for which abundant rewards and the promise of Paradise are assured. Such acts include visiting the Master of Martyrs ﴿عليه السلام﴾, performing the night prayer, and other recommended deeds. The conceited person imagines that performing these recommended acts, all or most, would exempt him from the need for repentance. He might stop committing sins and satisfy himself with these recommended acts, thinking they suffice as a substitute for repentance for his past deeds. Alternatively, his arrogance may overpower him, leading him to persist in his sins while disregarding the fact that God ﷻ grants the promised rewards for recommended actions and others only if accepted. God only accepts them from the pious God-conscious people. God ﷻ said:

﴿إِنَّمَا يَتَقَبَّلُ ٱللَّهُ مِنَ ٱلْمُتَّقِينَ﴾

﴾*innamā yataqabbalu llāhu mina l-muttaqīn*[a]﴿

﴾*God accepts only from the Godwary*﴿[279]

This God-consciousness and piety cannot coexist with neglecting obligatory divine duties, such as repentance.

---

[279] Sūrat al-Mā'idah, Verse 27.

Belittling Sins, Trivializing Them, and Relying on Them

Perhaps the servant falls as easy prey into the clutches of the accursed devil, where his evil-prone self drives him towards destruction that will consume him in the Hereafter and perhaps even in this world. This destruction is when he perceives his sin as insignificant compared to the sins of others, or he considers it inconsequential in the face of God's mercy. Another side to this is that he might believe that he has committed only this sin while ignoring his other, more grave transgressions, or he belittles his sin and disregards the enormity of having disobeyed, rebelled, and done wrong against the Exalted Lord. Zayd al-Shaḥḥām said,

> Imām Jaʿfar aṣ-Ṣādiq ﷺ said,
>
> > Beware of those minor sins that you belittle, for they will not be forgiven.
>
> I [the narrator] asked,
>
> > What are those sins?
>
> He replied,
>
> They are the ones which if a man commits, he says: I am prosperous if I do not commit any other sins [i.e., he is not afraid of this sin, seeing it as nothing

> really bad, and persists in it despite knowing it is wrong, following the mindset: how fortunate I am that it is not worse than that].[280]

In a similar vein, Samāʿah b. Mahārān said,

> I heard Abū al-Hasan ﷷ say,
>
> > Do not consider a great deal of good a great deal, and do not consider a little sin very little; little sins accumulate and become a great deal. Have a fear of God in private so you can do justice to yourselves.[281]

It was also narrated that Imām Jaʿfar aṣ-Ṣādiq ﷷ said,

> The Messenger of God ﷺ stopped, during a journey on barren land, for rest and asked his companions to collect firewood. The companions said,
>
> > O Messenger of God, we are in a barren land with no firewood around here.
>
> He said,
>
> > Let everyone bring whatever he can.

---

[280] Kulaynī, Shaykh Muḥammad b. Yaʿqūb, *al-Kāfī*, Vol. 2, p. 287.

[281] Ibid., pp. 287–288.

They collected firewood and placed one piece over the other in a heap before him. The Messenger of God ﷺ then said,

> This is how sins accumulate.

Then he said,

> Avoid minor sins that are belittled, for there is a searcher for everything, and the Recorder of sins writes whatever people offer to leave behind them.

﴿وَكُلَّ شَيْءٍ أَحْصَيْنَاهُ كِتَابًا﴾

﴾*wa-kulla shay'in 'aḥṣaynāhu kitāban*﴿

﴾*and We have figured everything in a Book*﴿[282] [283]

Wrongly Assuming One's Disobedience is Forgiven

Perhaps a person is deluded due to his foolishness and lack of understanding, and he imagines or believes that the sins he commits are among minor transgressions and are

---

[282] Sūrat an-Naba', Verse 29.

[283] Kulaynī, Shaykh Muḥammad b. Ya'qūb, *al-Kāfī*, Vol. 2, p. 288.

forgiven without the need for repentance. He thinks this way because God ﷻ says:

﴿إِن تَجْتَنِبُوا۟ كَبَآئِرَ مَا تُنْهَوْنَ عَنْهُ نُكَفِّرْ عَنكُمْ سَيِّـَٔاتِكُمْ وَنُدْخِلْكُم مُّدْخَلًا كَرِيمًا﴾

﴿in tajtanibū kabā'ira mā tunhawna 'anhu nukaffir 'ankum sayyi'ātikum wa-nudkhilkum mudkhalan karīman﴾

﴿If you avoid the major sins that you are forbidden, We will absolve you of your misdeeds and admit you to a noble abode﴾[284]

Such a person overlooks or neglects two matters:

1. Insistence on committing a minor sin makes it significant. 'Abdullāh b. Sinān narrated that Imām Ja'far aṣ-Ṣādiq ﵇ said,

   With persistence, no sin is minor, and with seeking forgiveness, no sin is major.[285]

   And Abū Baṣīr narrated:

   I heard Imām Ja'far aṣ-Ṣādiq ﵇ saying,

---

[284] Sūrat an-Nisā', Verse 31.

[285] Kulaynī, Shaykh Muḥammad b. Ya'qūb, *al-Kāfī*, Vol. 2, p. 288.

> No, by God! God does not accept any servant's obedience to Him while he persists in disobedience against Him.[286]

2. God ﷻ promised to overlook one's minor sins if he avoids major sins, except when they [the minor sins] are done with persistence. Jābir narrated from Abū Jaʿfar ؑ regarding the saying of God ﷻ:

﴿وَلَمْ يُصِرُّواْ عَلَىٰ مَا فَعَلُواْ وَهُمْ يَعْلَمُونَ﴾

﴾*wa-lam yuṣirrū ʿalā mā faʿalū wa-hum yaʿlamūna*﴿

﴾*and who knowingly do not persist in what [sins] they have committed*﴿[287]

The Imām said,

> Persistence is when a person commits a sin and does not seek God's forgiveness nor resolves to repent; that is persistence.[288]

---

[286] Ibid.

[287] Sūrat Āl ʿImrān, Verse 135.

[288] Kulaynī, Shaykh Muḥammad b. Yaʿqūb, *al-Kāfī*, Vol. 2, p. 288.

Despairing of the Mercy of God and Losing Hope in His Forgiveness

God ﷻ says:

﴿لَا تَقْنَطُوا۟ مِن رَّحْمَةِ ٱللَّهِ﴾

﴿lā taqnaṭū min raḥmati llāhi﴾

﴿do not despair of the mercy of God﴾[289]

Of course, this is with repentance, and all that is necessary to earn forgiveness. In this regard, consider what God has said in the following verses:

﴿قَالَ وَمَن يَقْنَطُ مِن رَّحْمَةِ رَبِّهِۦٓ إِلَّا ٱلضَّآلُّونَ﴾

﴿qāla wa-man yaqnaṭu min raḥmati rabbihī
ʾillā ḍ-ḍāllūna[a]*﴾*

﴿He said, 'Who despairs of his Lord's mercy
except the astray?!'﴾[290]

﴿وَإِن تُصِبْهُمْ سَيِّئَةٌۢ بِمَا قَدَّمَتْ أَيْدِيهِمْ فَإِنَّ ٱلْإِنسَـٰنَ كَفُورٌ﴾

---

[289] Sūrat az-Zumar, Verse 53.

[290] Sūrat al-Ḥijr, Verse 56.

﴿*wa-'in tuṣibhum sayyi'atun bi-mā qaddamat 'aydīhim fa-'inna l-'insāna kafūr*[un]﴾

﴿*but should an ill visit him because of what his hands have sent ahead, then man is very ungrateful*﴾[291]

﴿وَإِن مَّسَّهُ ٱلشَّرُّ فَيَـُٔوسٌ قَنُوطٌ﴾

﴿*wa-'in massahu sh-sharru fa-ya'ūsun qanūṭ*[un]﴾

﴿*and should any ill befall him, he becomes hopeless and despondent*﴾[292]

﴿وَإِذَا مَسَّهُ ٱلشَّرُّ كَانَ يَـُٔوسًا﴾

﴿*wa-'idhā massahu sh-sharru kāna ya'ūsa*[n]﴾

﴿*but when an ill befalls him, he is despondent*﴾[293]

In this regard, it has been narrated that 'Abdullāh al-Bazzāz al-Nīsābūrī said,

> There was a trade between me and Ḥamīd b. Qaḥṭabah, and after I returned from a trip, he summoned me. I went to see him wearing travel

291 Sūrat ar-Rūm, Verse 48.

292 Sūrat Fuṣṣilat, Verse 49.

293 Sūrat al-Isrā', Verse 83.

clothes. I entered upon him, and it was midday in the blessed month of Ramaḍān. He had a dish and a jug brought for him. He washed his hands, and I was ordered to do the same. I washed my hands and forgot that it was the month of Ramaḍān. After the food was brought, I remembered that it was the month of Ramaḍān, so I sat apart.

Ḥamīd asked,

> Why aren't you eating?

I said,

> O Amīr, it is the blessed month [of Ramaḍān], and I am neither sick nor have any other excuse to break the fast. The Amīr can have an excuse.

He wept and said,

> I also have no excuse, and I am not sick.

Then tears streamed down his cheeks. After he finished eating, I asked him about the reason for his weeping.

He answered,

> When Hārūn ar-Rashīd (may the curse of God be upon him) was in Ṭūs, he sent for

me one night. When I entered him, I saw a lit candle and a green-colored sword without its sheath beside him. When he saw me, he asked:

> How is your obedience to Amīr al-Mu'minīn?

I said:

> With my soul and wealth.

He allowed me to leave. It did not take long until he sent it to me again and repeated the same question.

I said:

> With my soul, wealth, family, children, and religion.

He laughed and said:

> Take this sword. As soon as the servant guides you to someone, kill him.

So I took the sword, and when the servant guided me, I followed him. He took me to a house, the door of which was locked. After it was opened, we entered, and I saw a pit in the middle. The house had four rooms, each locked. He opened the door of one of them, and I saw twenty people, both old and young, in chains. All of them were from the children of ʿAlī and Fāṭimah ﷺ.

The servant said:

> You must kill them all.

He brought them one by one, and I severed their heads and threw them into the pit until they were all killed. Then he opened the second room door, which was the same as the first. I killed them all and threw their heads into the pit. The third room was the same as the first two. I killed them all. Only one old man remained. He said to me:

> What excuse will you have on the Day of Resurrection when they stand before you in the presence of my grandfather, the Messenger of God ﷺ, and ask you about killing sixty members of his family without any sin?

I trembled with fear, and my limbs shivered. I killed that old man, too, and I threw his head into the pit. What benefit is

> there in prayer and fasting for someone who killed sixty members of the family of the Messenger of God ﷺ? I am certain that I will be eternally damned in Hellfire. For this reason, I do not fast in the month of Ramaḍān.[294]

In light of this narration, it is reported that after the arrival of Imām 'Alī ar-Riḍā ﷷ to Khurāsān, 'Abdullāh al-Nīsābūrī recounted the story of that accursed person and his despair of his Lord to the Imām ﷷ. The Imām ﷷ said,

> Woe to him! Ḥamīd's despair in divine mercy is a greater sin than killing sixty descendants of the Ahl al-Bayt.[295]

Benefits of Repentance

It has been mentioned that repentance is required from everyone, and as previously stated, it varies from individual to individual. There is the repentance of the infallibles and that of others. Thus, the anticipated outcomes, benefits, and intended purposes of repentance for each category of repenters differ in terms of what is hoped for, what is

---

[294] Ṣadūq, Shaykh Muḥammad b. 'Alī, *'Uyūn Akhbār al-Riḍā* ﷷ, Vol. 1, p. 108. Majlisī, 'Allāmah Muḥammad Bāqir, *Biḥār al-Anwār*, Vol. 48, p. 176.

[295] Shīrāzī, Āyatullāh 'Abdul Ḥusayn Dastaghīb, *al-Dhunūb al-Kabīrah*, margin p. 73.

intended, and what results from the corresponding repentance.

As for the repentance of the infallibles ﷺ, it entails returning to God to free oneself from worldly attachments and their dwellings, which, due to the challenges they present, elevate their ranks; they are tested by the world, contending against its people and battling with its demands. However, these attachments prevent them from joining the higher assembly and returning to the sanctuary of holiness, which is their ultimate goal. For this reason, they dismiss the world, even if its utility comes at the cost of compromising their exalted positions in the Hereafter. Imām ʿAlī ﷺ divorced the globe three times, as previously mentioned in the account attributed to Ḍarār b. Ḍamrah.

The world was also presented to Prophet Muḥammad ﷺ, with the option of staying within it for as long as it endures, without anything being deducted from his share in the Hereafter. However, he chose the Hereafter based on the words of God ﷻ:

﴿وَلَلْآخِرَةُ خَيْرٌ لَّكَ مِنَ الْأُولَىٰ﴾

﴿*wa-la-l-ʾākhiratu khayrun laka mina l-ʾūlā*﴾

﴿وَلَسَوْفَ يُعْطِيكَ رَبُّكَ فَتَرْضَىٰ﴾

﴿*wa-la-sawfa yuʿṭīka rabbuka fa-tarḍā*﴾

﴾*and the Hereafter shall be better for you than the world. Soon your Lord will give you [that with which] you will be pleased*﴿[296]

This is also consistent with the station of the infallible repenters, as indicated by the verse:

﴿إِنَّ ٱللَّهَ ٱشْتَرَىٰ مِنَ ٱلْمُؤْمِنِينَ أَنفُسَهُمْ وَأَمْوَٰلَهُم بِأَنَّ لَهُمُ ٱلْجَنَّةَ ۚ يُقَٰتِلُونَ فِي سَبِيلِ ٱللَّهِ فَيَقْتُلُونَ وَيُقْتَلُونَ ۖ وَعْدًا عَلَيْهِ حَقًّا فِي ٱلتَّوْرَىٰةِ وَٱلْإِنجِيلِ وَٱلْقُرْءَانِ ۚ وَمَنْ أَوْفَىٰ بِعَهْدِهِۦ مِنَ ٱللَّهِ ۚ فَٱسْتَبْشِرُوا۟ بِبَيْعِكُمُ ٱلَّذِي بَايَعْتُم بِهِۦ ۚ وَذَٰلِكَ هُوَ ٱلْفَوْزُ ٱلْعَظِيمُ﴾

﴾*inna llāha shtarā mina l-mu'minīna 'anfusahum wa-'amwālahum bi-'anna lahumu l-jannata yuqātilūna fī sabīli llāhi fa-yaqtulūna wa-yuqtalūna wa'dan 'alayhi ḥaqqan fī t-tawrāti wa-l-'injīli wa-l-qur'āni wa-man 'awfā bi-'ahdihī mina llāhi fa-stabshirū bi-bay'ikumu lladhī bāya'tum bihī wa-dhālika huwa l-fawzu l-'aẓīm*[u]﴿

﴿ٱلتَّٰٓئِبُونَ ٱلْعَٰبِدُونَ ٱلْحَٰمِدُونَ ٱلسَّٰٓئِحُونَ ٱلرَّٰكِعُونَ ٱلسَّٰجِدُونَ ٱلْءَامِرُونَ بِٱلْمَعْرُوفِ وَٱلنَّاهُونَ عَنِ ٱلْمُنكَرِ وَٱلْحَٰفِظُونَ لِحُدُودِ ٱللَّهِ ۗ وَبَشِّرِ ٱلْمُؤْمِنِينَ﴾

﴾[a]*t-tā'ibūna l-'ābidūna l-ḥāmidūna s-sā'iḥūna r-rāki'ūna s-sājidūna l-'āmirūna bi-l-ma'rūfi wa-n-nāhūna 'ani l-*

[296] Sūrat aḍ-Ḍuḥā, Verses 4–5.

munkari wa-l-ḥāfiẓūna li-ḥudūdi llāhi wa-bashshiri l-mu'minīna﴾

﴿*Indeed God has bought from the faithful their souls and their possessions for paradise to be theirs: they fight in the way of God, kill, and are killed. A promise binding upon Him in the Torah and the Evangel and the Qur'ān. And who is truer to his promise than God? So rejoice in the bargain you have made with Him, and that is the great success. [The faithful are] penitent, devout, celebrators of God's praise, wayfarers, who bow [and] prostrate [in prayer], bid what is right and forbid what is wrong, and keep God's bounds—and give good news to the faithful*﴾[297]

Indeed, the offering of one's self is the highest form of generosity and the utmost submission to the obedience of God.

Those whom the verse referred to have indeed traded themselves and their wealth. This transaction descends from the higher realm to the lower. The two matters were mentioned together because worship is physical and financial, and there is no third option. It is narrated that God ﷻ is the merchant of the believers, and He raised the price for them [i.e., the value of the believers' actions and efforts is greatly magnified in the eyes of God], thus granting them Paradise. Ṭabrisī ؒ narrated that Imām Ja'far aṣ-Ṣādiq ؑ used to say,

[297] Sūrat at-Tawbah, Verses 111–112.

> O you with no aspirations, indeed the only price for your souls is Paradise. Do not sell them for anything other than that.

In this regard, al-Aṣmaʿī composed the following lines for Imām Jaʿfar aṣ-Ṣādiq:

> I value the precious soul through its Lord,
>
> For among creation, there is no price for it.
>
> With it, we buy the Heavens. If I were to sell it,
>
> For anything else, that would be unjust.
>
> When my soul departs with this world, I obtain it,
>
> For this world has gone, and so has the price.[298]

It is well known that the qualities mentioned in the two aforementioned verses are collectively found only in the infallibles, as established in *Majmaʿ al-Bayān* on the principles of Imāmiyyah. This is further emphasized by what is narrated that this pledge, which is alluded to, was from Amīr al-Mu'minīn, his brother Jaʿfar, and his uncle Ḥamzah, as mentioned in the Ziyārah of Amīr al-Mu'minīn on the Day of Ghadīr. Al-ʿAyyāshī and al-Qummī narrated that this verse was revealed regarding the

298 Ṭabrisī, Shaykh Faḍl b. Ḥasan, *Majmaʿ al-Bayān fī Tafsīr al-Qur'ān*, Vol. 5, p. 130.

Imāms ﷺ, as it describes a quality that does not apply to others.[299]

One of the consequences of the repentance of the infallibles ﷺ is the elevation of their ranks. The repentance of our father Ādam (peace be upon him and his family) was accompanied by outcomes that are indicated by the words of God ﷻ:

﴿إِنَّ ٱللَّهَ ٱصۡطَفَىٰٓ ءَادَمَ وَنُوحٗا وَءَالَ إِبۡرَٰهِيمَ وَءَالَ عِمۡرَٰنَ عَلَى ٱلۡعَٰلَمِينَ﴾

﴾*inna llāha ṣṭafā ʾādama wa-nūḥan wa-ʾāla ʾibrāhīma wa-ʾāla ʿimrāna ʿalā l-ʿālamīna*﴿

﴾*Indeed God chose Ādam and Nūḥ, and the progeny of Ibrāhīm and the progeny of ʿImrān above all the nations*﴿[300]

and

﴿ثُمَّ ٱجۡتَبَٰهُ رَبُّهُۥ فَتَابَ عَلَيۡهِ وَهَدَىٰ﴾

﴾*thumma jtabāhu rabbuhū fa-tāba ʿalayhi wa-hadā*﴿

---

[299] Al-Qummī, ʿAlī b. Ibrāhīm, *Tafsīr al-Qummī*, Vol. 1, p. 306. Fayḍ Kāshānī, Mullā Muḥammad b. Murtaḍā, *al-Tafsīr al-Ṣāfī*, Vol. 1, p. 734.

[300] Sūrat Āl ʿImrān, Verse 33.

﴿*Then his Lord chose him, and turned to him clemently, and guided him*﴾[301]

Likewise, in the case of the Prophet Yūnus ﷺ, the Qur'ān mentions:

﴿لَّوْلَآ أَن تَدَارَكَهُۥ نِعْمَةٌ مِّن رَّبِّهِۦ لَنُبِذَ بِٱلْعَرَآءِ وَهُوَ مَذْمُومٌ﴾

﴿*law-lā 'an tadārakahū ni'matun min rabbihī la-nubidha bi-l-'arā'i wa-huwa madhmūm*[un]﴾

﴿فَٱجْتَبَـٰهُ رَبُّهُۥ فَجَعَلَهُۥ مِنَ ٱلصَّـٰلِحِينَ﴾

﴿*fa-jtabāhu rabbuhū fa-ja'alahū mina ṣ-ṣāliḥīn*[a]﴾

﴿*Had it not been for a blessing that came to his rescue from his Lord, he would surely have been cast on the bare shore, being blameworthy. So his Lord chose him and made him one of the righteous*﴾[302]

---

[301] Sūrat Ṭā Hā, Verse 122.

[302] Sūrat al-Qalam, Verses 49–50.

In the case of the Prophet Dāwūd ﷺ, it is stated[303]:

﴿وَظَنَّ دَاوُۥدُ أَنَّمَا فَتَنَّٰهُ فَٱسۡتَغۡفَرَ رَبَّهُۥ وَخَرَّ رَاكِعٗا وَأَنَابَ ۩﴾

﴿*wa-ẓanna dāwūdu 'annamā fatannāhu fa-staghfara rabbahū wa-kharra rāki'an wa-'anāb[a]*﴾

﴿فَغَفَرۡنَا لَهُۥ ذَٰلِكَۖ وَإِنَّ لَهُۥ عِندَنَا لَزُلۡفَىٰ وَحُسۡنَ مَـَٔابٖ﴾

﴿*fa-ghafarnā lahū dhālika wa-'inna lahū 'indanā la-zulfā wa-ḥusna ma'āb[in]*﴾

﴿يَٰدَاوُۥدُ إِنَّا جَعَلۡنَٰكَ خَلِيفَةٗ فِي ٱلۡأَرۡضِ فَٱحۡكُم بَيۡنَ ٱلنَّاسِ بِٱلۡحَقِّ﴾

﴿*yā-dāwūdu 'innā ja'alnāka khalīfatan fī l-'arḍi fa-ḥkum bayna n-nāsi bi-l-ḥaqqi*﴾

﴿*Then Dāwūd knew that We had tested him, whereat he pleaded with his Lord for forgiveness, and fell down in prostration and repented. So We forgave him that, and indeed he has [a station of] nearness with Us and a good destination. 'O Dāwūd! Indeed, We have made you a vicegerent on the earth. So judge between people with justice, and do not follow your desires, or they will lead you astray*

---

303 ۩ This symbol in the Qur'ān indicates an āyah of sajdah (verse of prostration). When recited or heard, performing sujūd (prostration) is mandatory (*wājib*) for specific verses and recommended (*mustaḥabb*) for others.

from the way of God. Indeed there is a severe punishment for those who stray from the way of God, because of their forgetting the Day of Reckoning❳[304]

Similarly, for every prophet mentioned, their repentance is followed by God's declaration of granting them virtue, higher status, or blessings.

The ranks of the infallibles cannot be measured by worldly standards, as they do not bind them. They do not bind them. Their ranks are only known to God ﷻ or themselves ﷺ. The best outcome of their repentance is to free themselves from the disturbances of the inner self.

As for the repentance of the close friends of God [Awliyā'; i.e., pious, God-conscious people devoted to God and close to Him], the best outcome that follows it is the liberation from the disturbances arising from the connection of their souls with corporeal bodies and their dwelling among the people of the material world.

The repentance of the righteous liberates them from the discomfort that arises from the necessary expression of their connection with bodies, which require nourishment and rest. In turn, God ﷻ grants them strength to continue their efforts in drawing closer to Him, and they persist on His path, hastening towards the ranks of proximity to His

[304] Sūrat Ṣād, Verses 24–26.

sacred presence. Perhaps the statement of Imām Mūsā al-Kāẓim ﵇ during his imprisonment alludes to this:

> O God, You know that I asked You to free me for Your worship, and You have done so. Praise be to You.[305]

As for the repentance of the special individuals, God ﷻ takes care of their affairs, liberates their deeds for His sake, and purifies their hearts from all else.

The repentance of the common people who have committed sins results in their absolution from the wrongdoings they burdened themselves with. Various verses, including the following, indicate his various verses, including the following indicate this:

﴿إِنَّمَا ٱلتَّوْبَةُ عَلَى ٱللَّهِ لِلَّذِينَ يَعْمَلُونَ ٱلسُّوٓءَ بِجَهَـٰلَةٍ ثُمَّ يَتُوبُونَ مِن قَرِيبٍ فَأُو۟لَـٰٓئِكَ يَتُوبُ ٱللَّهُ عَلَيْهِمْ ۗ وَكَانَ ٱللَّهُ عَلِيمًا حَكِيمًا﴾

﴾*innamā t-tawbatu ʿalā llāhi li-lladhīna yaʿmalūna s-sūʾa bi-jahālatin thumma yatūbūna min qarībin fa-ʾulāʾika yatūbu llāhu ʿalayhim wa-kāna llāhu ʿalīman ḥakīma*[n]﴿

﴾*[Acceptance of] repentance by God is only for those who commit evil out of ignorance and then repent promptly. It is*

[305] Mufīd, Shaykh Muḥammad, *Kitāb al-Irshād*, Vol. 2, p. 240. Majlisī, ʿAllāmah Muḥammad Bāqir, *Biḥār al-Anwār*, Vol. 47, p. 107.

﴾such whose repentance God will accept, and God is Knowing, Wise﴿[306]

If a person is unaware or ignorant of a wrongdoing, the fault does not remain with him.

﴿فَمَن تَابَ مِنۢ بَعۡدِ ظُلۡمِهِۦ وَأَصۡلَحَ فَإِنَّ ٱللَّهَ يَتُوبُ عَلَيۡهِ﴿

﴾fa-man tāba min baʿdi ẓulmihī wa-ʾaṣlaḥa fa-ʾinna llāha yatūbu ʿalayhi﴿

﴾But whoever repents after his wrongdoing, and reforms, then God shall accept his repentance﴿[307]

﴿وَمَن تَابَ وَعَمِلَ صَٰلِحٗا فَإِنَّهُۥ يَتُوبُ إِلَى ٱللَّهِ مَتَابٗا﴿

*﴾wa-man tāba wa-ʿamila ṣāliḥan fa-ʾinnahū yatūbu ʾilā llāhi matāba*ⁿ*﴿*

﴾And whoever repents and acts righteously indeed turns to God with due penitence﴿[308]

﴿وَأَنِ ٱسۡتَغۡفِرُواْ رَبَّكُمۡ ثُمَّ تُوبُوٓاْ إِلَيۡهِ يُمَتِّعۡكُم مَّتَٰعًا حَسَنًا﴿

---

306 Sūrat an-Nisāʾ, Verse 17.

307 Sūrat al-Māʾidah, Verse 39.

308 Sūrat al-Furqān, Verse 71.

﴾wa-ʾani staghfirū rabbakum thumma tūbū ʾilayhi yumattiʿkum matāʿan ḥasanan﴿

﴾Plead with your Lord for forgiveness, then turn to Him penitently. He will provide you with a good provision﴿[309]

Among the consequences of repentance for the general people, in addition to the forgiveness of sins they have repented from, is an increase in sustenance, offspring, and blessings. This has been narrated from the infallibles عليهم السلام[310] and is indicated by what God said in this verse:

﴿فَقُلْتُ ٱسْتَغْفِرُوا۟ رَبَّكُمْ إِنَّهُۥ كَانَ غَفَّارًا﴾

﴾fa-qultu staghfirū rabbakum ʾinnahū kāna ghaffāra^{n}﴿

﴿يُرْسِلِ ٱلسَّمَآءَ عَلَيْكُم مِّدْرَارًا﴾

﴾yursili s-samāʾa ʿalaykum midrāra^{n}﴿

﴿وَيُمْدِدْكُم بِأَمْوَٰلٍ وَبَنِينَ وَيَجْعَل لَّكُمْ جَنَّٰتٍ وَيَجْعَل لَّكُمْ أَنْهَٰرًا﴾

﴾wa-yumdidkum bi-ʾamwālin wa-banīna wa-yajʿal lakum jannātin wa-yajʿal lakum ʾanhāra^{n}﴿

---

309 Sūrat Hūd, Verse 3.

310 Ṭabrisī, Shaykh Faḍl b. Ḥasan, *Makārim al-Akhlāq*, ḥadīth 3 and 4.

﴾*telling [them]: 'Plead to your Lord for forgiveness. Indeed, He is Forgiving. He will send for you abundant rains from the sky, and aid you with wealth and sons, and provide you with gardens and provide you with streams'*﴿[311]

Likewise, in the story of Hūd, He says:

﴿وَيَـٰقَوْمِ ٱسْتَغْفِرُوا۟ رَبَّكُمْ ثُمَّ تُوبُوٓا۟ إِلَيْهِ يُرْسِلِ ٱلسَّمَآءَ عَلَيْكُم مِّدْرَارًا وَيَزِدْكُمْ قُوَّةً إِلَىٰ قُوَّتِكُمْ وَلَا تَتَوَلَّوْا۟ مُجْرِمِينَ﴾

﴾*wa-yā-qawmi staghfirū rabbakum thumma tūbū 'ilayhi yursili s-samā'a 'alaykum midrāran wa-yazidkum quwwatan 'ilā quwwatikum wa-lā tatawallaw mujrimīn*[a]﴿

﴾*'O my people! Plead with your Lord for forgiveness, then turn to Him penitently: He will send copious rains for you from the sky, and add power to your [present] power. So do not turn your backs [on Him] as guilty ones.'*﴿[312]

Furthermore, it is narrated that a man said to Imām Ja'far aṣ-Ṣādiq ﷺ,

> I pray to God to keep my soul in service for your cause; I have not been granted any children.

---

[311] Sūrat Nūḥ, Verses 10–12.

[312] Sūrat Hūd, Verse 52.

The Imām ﷺ replied,

> When you return to your country and then decide to go to bed with your wife, read,

﴿وَذَا ٱلنُّونِ إِذ ذَّهَبَ مُغَـٰضِبًا فَظَنَّ أَن لَّن نَّقْدِرَ عَلَيْهِ فَنَادَىٰ فِي ٱلظُّلُمَـٰتِ أَن لَّآ إِلَـٰهَ إِلَّآ أَنتَ سُبْحَـٰنَكَ إِنِّي كُنتُ مِنَ ٱلظَّـٰلِمِينَ﴾

﴿*wa-dhā n-nūni 'idh dhahaba mughāḍiban fa-ẓanna 'an lan naqdira ʿalayhi fa-nādā fī ẓ-ẓulumāti 'an lā 'ilāha 'illā 'anta subḥānaka 'innī kuntu mina ẓ-ẓālimīn*[a]﴾

﴿*And [remember] the Man of the Fish, when he left in a rage, thinking that We would not put him to hardship. Then he cried out in the darkness, 'There is no god except You! You are immaculate! I have indeed been among the wrongdoers!'*﴾[313]

Read up to [these] three verses:

﴿فَٱسْتَجَبْنَا لَهُۥ وَنَجَّيْنَـٰهُ مِنَ ٱلْغَمِّ ۚ وَكَذَٰلِكَ نُـۨجِي ٱلْمُؤْمِنِينَ﴾

﴿*fa-stajabnā lahū wa-najjaynāhu mina l-ghammi wa-ka-dhālika nunjī l-mu'minīn*[a]﴾

﴿وَزَكَرِيَّآ إِذْ نَادَىٰ رَبَّهُۥ رَبِّ لَا تَذَرْنِي فَرْدًا وَأَنتَ خَيْرُ ٱلْوَٰرِثِينَ﴾

---

[313] Sūrat al-Anbiyā', Verse 87.

﴾*wa-zakariyyā 'idh nādā rabbahū rabbi lā tadharnī fardan wa-'anta khayru l-wārithīn*[a]﴿

﴿فَٱسْتَجَبْنَا لَهُۥ وَوَهَبْنَا لَهُۥ يَحْيَىٰ وَأَصْلَحْنَا لَهُۥ زَوْجَهُۥٓ ۚ إِنَّهُمْ كَانُوا۟ يُسَٰرِعُونَ فِى ٱلْخَيْرَٰتِ وَيَدْعُونَنَا رَغَبًا وَرَهَبًا ۖ وَكَانُوا۟ لَنَا خَٰشِعِينَ﴾

﴾*fa-stajabnā lahū wa-wahabnā lahū yaḥyā wa-'aṣlaḥnā lahū zawjahū 'innahum kānū yusāri'ūna fī l-khayrāti wa-yad'ūnanā raghaban wa-rahaban wa-kānū lanā khāshi'īn*[a]﴿

﴾*So We answered his prayer and delivered him from the agony; and thus do We deliver the faithful. And [remember] Zakariyyā, when he cried out to his Lord, 'My Lord! Do not leave me without an heir, and You are the best of inheritors.' So We answered his prayer, and gave him John, and cured for him his wife [of infertility]. Indeed, they were active in [performing] good works, and they would supplicate Us with eagerness and awe and were humble before Us*﴿[314]

> The will of God will grant you a child. The will of God will grant you a child.[315]

Among the consequences of repentance is that it brings about the love of God for His repentant servant. This is

---

[314] Sūrat al-Anbiyā', Verses 88–90.

[315] Kulaynī, Shaykh Muḥammad b. Ya'qūb, *al-Kāfī*, Vol. 6, p. 10.

because such a servant is a good-doer, refining his self, character, and deeds, for

﴿وَٱللَّهُ يُحِبُّ ٱلْمُحْسِنِينَ﴾

﴿*wa-llāhu yuḥibbu l-muḥsinīn*[a]﴾

﴿*and God loves the virtuous*﴾[316]

Moreover, the repentant surely becomes patient and steadfast, restraining himself and keeping it in the line of obedience to God and rectifying the slip-ups that arise from being lured by the world, for

﴿وَٱللَّهُ يُحِبُّ ٱلصَّٰبِرِينَ﴾

﴿*wa-llāhu yuḥibbu ṣ-ṣābirīn*[a]﴾

﴿*and God loves the steadfast*﴾[317]

Indeed, repentance places its bearer among the ranks of God-conscious people, and

﴿فَإِنَّ ٱللَّهَ يُحِبُّ ٱلْمُتَّقِينَ﴾

﴿*fa-ʾinna llāha yuḥibbu l-muttaqīn*[a]﴾

---

[316] Sūrat Āl ʿImrān, Verse 134.

[317] Sūrat Āl ʿImrān, Verse 146.

﴾*God indeed loves the Godwary*﴿[318]

We should also not overlook that repentance purifies a person from all forms of impurity and wipes away the afflictions of sins from their soul. The person thus becomes purified and is then classified into a distinguished category, as indicated by what God ﷻ says in this verse:

﴾فِيهِ رِجَالٌ يُحِبُّونَ أَن يَتَطَهَّرُوا۟ ۚ وَٱللَّهُ يُحِبُّ ٱلْمُطَّهِّرِينَ﴿

﴾*fīhi rijālun yuḥibbūna ʾan yataṭahharū wa-llāhu yuḥibbu l-muṭṭahhirīn*a﴿

﴾*Therein are men who love to keep pure, and God loves those who keep pure*﴿[319]

Furthermore, it must be understood that repentance elevates a person from the category of wrongdoers who oppress themselves to that of reformers who establish justice. He thus belongs to a group referred to by God ﷻ in the following verse:

﴾وَأَقْسِطُوٓا۟ ۖ إِنَّ ٱللَّهَ يُحِبُّ ٱلْمُقْسِطِينَ﴿

﴾*wa-ʾaqsiṭū ʾinna llāha yuḥibbu l-muqsiṭīn*a﴿

[318] Sūrat Āl ʿImrān, Verse 76.

[319] Sūrat at-Tawbah, Verse 108.

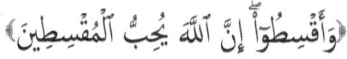

﴾*and do justice. Indeed God loves the just*﴿[320]

Repentance is a struggle against the self—it is one of its best forms. The repentant person struggles and strives in the way of God; thus, what God says in this verse applies to him:

﴿إِنَّ ٱللَّهَ يُحِبُّ ٱلَّذِينَ يُقَٰتِلُونَ فِي سَبِيلِهِۦ صَفًّا كَأَنَّهُم بُنۡيَٰنٞ مَّرۡصُوصٞ﴾

﴾*inna llāha yuḥibbu lladhīna yuqātilūna fī sabīlihī ṣaffan ka-ʾannahum bunyānun marṣūṣ*[un]﴿

﴾*Indeed God loves those who fight in His way in ranks, as if they were a compact structure*﴿[321]

Without a doubt, the repentant one follows the commands of God and His Prophet ﷺ; therefore, they are beloved to Him ﷻ as stated in His saying:

﴿قُلۡ إِن كُنتُمۡ تُحِبُّونَ ٱللَّهَ فَٱتَّبِعُونِي يُحۡبِبۡكُمُ ٱللَّهُ وَيَغۡفِرۡ لَكُمۡ ذُنُوبَكُمۡۚ وَٱللَّهُ غَفُورٞ رَّحِيمٞ﴾

﴾*qul ʾin kuntum tuḥibbūna llāha fa-ttabiʿūnī yuḥbibkumu llāhu wa-yaghfir lakum dhunūbakum wa-llāhu ghafūrun raḥīm*[un]﴿

---

[320] Sūrat al-Ḥujurāt, Verse 9.

[321] Sūrat al-Ṣaff, Verse 4.

﴾*Say, 'If you love God, then follow me; God will love you and forgive you your sins, and God is Forgiving, Merciful'*﴿[322]

It is also important, dear reader, that you know that the noblest degrees of repentance arise from a person's love for God. Such a person feels as though he has distanced himself from the domain of those who love Him ﷻ due to their slip-ups, and through his repentance and return to Him, he becomes attached to Him and His love and seeks to remove what has created barriers between him and his true Beloved. The more his love for God ﷻ increases, the closer he becomes to Him, and the higher the rank of his repentance rises. This confirms what God ﷻ says in this verse:

﴿وَٱلَّذِينَ ءَامَنُوٓاْ أَشَدُّ حُبًّا لِّلَّهِ﴾

﴾*wa-lladhīna 'āmanū 'ashaddu ḥubban li-llāhi*﴿

﴾*but the faithful have a more ardent love for God*﴿[323]

Upon the servant's return to the ranks of the righteous, he distances himself from what incites the anger of God ﷻ and diminishes His favor upon him. For the one who does not yearn for His love, his heart is encompassed by the love of others besides Him. This arises from the love of the world,

---

[322] Sūrat Āl 'Imrān, Verse 31.

[323] Sūrat al-Baqarah, Verse 165.

its people, its seekers, and those striving for its sake, which is ultimately the root of every sin and the source of every calamity. This is indicated in what God says:

﴿يَٰٓأَيُّهَا ٱلَّذِينَ ءَامَنُواْ لَا تَتَّخِذُوٓاْ ءَابَآءَكُمۡ وَإِخۡوَٰنَكُمۡ أَوۡلِيَآءَ إِنِ ٱسۡتَحَبُّواْ ٱلۡكُفۡرَ
عَلَى ٱلۡإِيمَٰنِۚ وَمَن يَتَوَلَّهُم مِّنكُمۡ فَأُوْلَٰٓئِكَ هُمُ ٱلظَّٰلِمُونَ﴾

﴿*yā-ʾayyuhā lladhīna ʾāmanū lā tattakhidhū ʾābāʾakum wa-ʾikhwānakum ʾawliyāʾa ʾini staḥabbū l-kufra ʿalā l-ʾīmāni wa-man yatawallahum minkum fa-ʾulāʾika humu ẓ-ẓālimūn*[a]﴾

﴿قُلۡ إِن كَانَ ءَابَآؤُكُمۡ وَأَبۡنَآؤُكُمۡ وَإِخۡوَٰنُكُمۡ وَأَزۡوَٰجُكُمۡ وَعَشِيرَتُكُمۡ وَأَمۡوَٰلٌ
ٱقۡتَرَفۡتُمُوهَا وَتِجَٰرَةٞ تَخۡشَوۡنَ كَسَادَهَا وَمَسَٰكِنُ تَرۡضَوۡنَهَآ أَحَبَّ إِلَيۡكُم مِّنَ
ٱللَّهِ وَرَسُولِهِۦ وَجِهَادٖ فِي سَبِيلِهِۦ فَتَرَبَّصُواْ حَتَّىٰ يَأۡتِيَ ٱللَّهُ بِأَمۡرِهِۦۗ
وَٱللَّهُ لَا يَهۡدِي ٱلۡقَوۡمَ ٱلۡفَٰسِقِينَ﴾

﴿*qul ʾin kāna ʾābāʾukum wa-ʾabnāʾukum wa-ʾikhwānukum wa-ʾazwājukum wa-ʿashīratukum wa-ʾamwālun-i qtaraftumūhā wa-tijāratun takhshawna kasādahā wa-masākinu tarḍawnahā ʾaḥabba ʾilaykum mina llāhi wa-rasūlihī wa-jihādin fī sabīlihī fa-tarabbaṣū ḥattā yaʾtiya llāhu bi-ʾamrihī wa-llāhu lā yahdī l-qawma l-fāsiqīn*[a]﴾

﴿*O you who have faith! Do not befriend your fathers and brothers if they prefer faithlessness to faith. Those of you who befriend them—it is they who are the wrongdoers. Say, 'If your fathers and your sons, your brethren, your spouses, and your kinsfolk, the possessions that you have acquired, the business you fear may suffer, and the dwellings you are fond of, are dearer to you than God and His Apostle and to waging jihād in His way, then wait until God issues His edict, and God does not guide the transgressing lot'*﴾[324]

God ﷻ has also criticized the lovers of the world most eloquently, saying:

﴿وَتَأْكُلُونَ ٱلتُّرَاثَ أَكْلًا لَّمًّا﴾

﴿*wa-ta'kulūna t-turātha 'aklan lamma*ⁿ﴾

﴿وَتُحِبُّونَ ٱلْمَالَ حُبًّا جَمًّا﴾

﴿*wa-tuḥibbūna l-māla ḥubban jamma*ⁿ﴾

﴿*You eat the inheritance rapaciously, and love wealth with much fondness*﴾[325]

---

[324] Sūrat at-Tawbah, Verses 23–24.

[325] Sūrat al-Fajr, Verses 19–20.

Conclusion

Regarding Sins

Let us consider what God ﷻ says in the following verses:

﴿إِن تَجۡتَنِبُواْ كَبَآئِرَ مَا تُنۡهَوۡنَ عَنۡهُ نُكَفِّرۡ عَنكُمۡ سَيِّـَٔاتِكُمۡ وَنُدۡخِلۡكُم مُّدۡخَلٗا كَرِيمٗا﴾

﴿*in tajtanibū kabā'ira mā tunhawna 'anhu nukaffir 'ankum sayyi'ātikum wa-nudkhilkum mudkhalan karīma*ⁿ﴾

﴿*If you avoid the major sins that you are forbidden, We will absolve you of your misdeeds and admit you to a noble abode*﴾[326]

﴿وَٱلَّذِينَ يَجۡتَنِبُونَ كَبَٰٓئِرَ ٱلۡإِثۡمِ وَٱلۡفَوَٰحِشَ﴾

﴿*wa-lladhīna yajtanibūna kabā'ira l-'ithmi wa-l-fawāḥisha*﴾

﴿*those who avoid major sins and indecencies*﴾[327]

﴿ٱلَّذِينَ يَجۡتَنِبُونَ كَبَٰٓئِرَ ٱلۡإِثۡمِ وَٱلۡفَوَٰحِشَ إِلَّا ٱللَّمَمَۚ﴾

---

[326] Sūrat an-Nisā', Verse 31.

[327] Sūrat ash-Shūrā, Verse 37.

﴾*alladhīna yajtanibūna kabā'ira l-'ithmi wa-l-fawāḥisha 'illā l-lamama*﴿

﴾*Those who avoid major sins and indecencies, apart from [minor and occasional] lapses*﴿[328]

Ultimately, these verses indicate that sins are divided into two categories: major and other sins that God termed *sayyi'ah* which generally refers to wrongdoing or transgressions. It is worth noting that this term can encompass both major and minor sins in various narrations and verses. However, in the first verse mentioned, it is used in contrast to al-Kabīrah, which refers to the major sins, so it is appropriate to translate it as "lesser sins."

It is not far-fetched that the verse,

﴿لَا يُغَادِرُ صَغِيرَةً وَلَا كَبِيرَةً إِلَّا أَحْصَاهَا﴾

﴾*lā yughādiru ṣaghīratan wa-lā kabīratan 'illā 'aḥṣāhā*﴿

﴾*It omits nothing, big or small, without enumerating it*﴿[329]

is an indication of the division of sins into minor and major categories. However, some scholars have raised questions about this division, as some consider any disobedience to God a major sin because it involves disobeying Him.

---

[328] Sūrat al-Najm, Verse 32.

[329] Sūrat al-Kahf, Verse 49.

Only sacred Islāmic law can determine what constitutes a major sin and distinguish it from minor sins. Hence, it is very fitting to mention here what the sacred Islāmic law has classified as major sins and then discuss some things that could also be considered major sins but are often overlooked by individuals, to the extent that they might not even consider them sinful.

Regarding the major sins, there are specified indicators in the narrations. For instance, regarding what God ﷻ said in the verse at the beginning of this section:

﴿إِن تَجْتَنِبُوا۟ كَبَآئِرَ مَا تُنْهَوْنَ عَنْهُ نُكَفِّرْ عَنكُمْ سَيِّـَٔاتِكُمْ
وَنُدْخِلْكُم مُّدْخَلًا كَرِيمًا﴾

﴿*in tajtanibū kabā'ira mā tunhawna 'anhu nukaffir 'ankum sayyi'ātikum wa-nudkhilkum mudkhalan karīman*﴾

﴿*If you avoid the major sins that you are forbidden, We will absolve you of your misdeeds and admit you to a noble abode*﴾[330]

[330] Sūrat an-Nisā', Verse 31.

Imām Jaʿfar aṣ-Ṣādiq 🕮 said,

> The major sins are those for which God has made
> Hellfire obligatory.[331]

Notably, the narrations regarding the enumeration of
major sins vary in terms of the number. This variance
might be because some narrations suffice by mentioning
the most prominent and gravest major sins, as there are
different levels among the major sins. We refer to the
explicitly mentioned major sins, regardless of their
hierarchy.

Major sins include the following:

1. Killing a person unlawfully.

2. Disobeying parents.

3. Engaging in usury [ribā].

4. Abandoning one's family after migration [hijrah].[332]

---

[331] Kulaynī, Shaykh Muḥammad b. Yaʿqūb, *al-Kāfī*, Vol. 2, p. 276.

[332] The intended meaning is for a person to leave Islāmic lands and
places where they can know the religious rulings, adhere to the faith,
and go to a place where they cannot do so. After Muslims have
established places where they can seek refuge and openly practice the
rituals of Islām, leaving these places is referred to as *Taʿrīb Baʿd al-
Hijrah* (literally "migration after migration").

5. Accusing chaste women of adultery without evidence.[333]

6. Unjustly consuming the property or money of orphans.

7. Fleeing from the battlefield.[334]

8. Despairing of the mercy of God.

9. Feeling secure from the plan of God.[335]

10. Associating partners with God (polytheism).

11. Committing adultery. It is reported that Imām Jaʿfar aṣ-Ṣādiq ﷺ said,

    > Whoever commits adultery has left the fold of faith.[336]

12. Drinking alcohol.

---

333 This refers to accusing a chaste, innocent person of adultery without any established evidence. This ruling applies to both men and women.

334 Escaping from the enemy after engagement while adhering to the conditions mentioned in the chapter of Jihād in jurisprudential books.

335 It is when a person feels safe from being lured into a trap and is deceived by the illusion of leniency.

336 Kulaynī, Shaykh Muḥammad b. Yaʿqūb, *al-Kāfī*, Vol. 2, p. 278.

13. Theft.

14. Disbelief in God.

15. Neglecting obligatory acts, such as prayer, fasting, pilgrimage, almsgiving, khums, jihād, enjoining good, and forbidding evil.

16. Not following the Ahl al-Bayt ؏ and disassociating from their enemies.

17. Learning, teaching, or practicing sorcery except to repel harm from an innocent person.

18. False oaths. In Arabic, *al-Yamīn al-Ghamūs al-Fājirah* refers to a wicked and depraved false oath. It is called *Ghamūs* because it submerges its bearer into sin and Hellfire.

19. *Al-Ghulūl* refers to embezzlement or betrayal in acquiring spoils and stealing from the spoils before distribution.

20. Giving false testimony and concealing true testimony.

21. Breaking covenants.

22. Severing family ties.

23. Pride and arrogance.

24. Envy.

25. Hypocrisy, ostentation [riyā'].

26. Encouraging wrongdoing and forbidding what is right.

27. Lying.

28. Breaking promises that one must fulfill.

29. Treachery. Yazīd al-Sayyārī reported that he asked Imām Ja'far aṣ-Ṣādiq 🕮,

> What is the status of a person who, in this affair (religion), lies when speaking, breaks promises, and betrays trust?

The Imām replied,

> It is a lower state than disbelief, but not disbelief itself.[337]

30. Obscenity

31. Indecency

32. Cursing a believer

33. Seeking leadership without qualification

---

[337] Ibid., p. 290.

34. Adultery and lacking protective jealousy over one's honor

35. Backbiting[338]

36. Gossiping

37. Altering and omitting from the Book of God and the Sunnah of His Prophet ﷺ

38. Disrespecting Islāmic sanctities

39. Prioritizing worldly gains over religious matters (i.e., pursuing worldly gains through the deeds of the Hereafter)

40. Fanaticism [zealotry, bigotry, or nationalism][339] And racism. It is narrated from Imām Ja'far aṣ-Ṣādiq ؑ:

---

[338] It has been narrated that backbiting is more severe than adultery. It involves speaking about your fellow believers and revealing what God has concealed about them.

[339] Nationalism, which its bearer sins through, has been explained as a person seeing the worst individuals of his people as better than the best individuals of other groups. Simply loving one's people is not a form of nationalism; true nationalism is when one assists one's people in committing injustice.

> One who practices fanaticism or fanaticism is practiced for him has severed the ties of faith from his neck.[340]

And in another narration, he ﷺ said:

> One who practices fanaticism, God will bind him with a faction of the Hellfire.[341]

41. Arrogance[342] as well. In a narration, it is mentioned:

> Whoever enters into arrogance is destroyed.[343]

Understand that arrogance has different levels. One is when a person beautifies their bad deeds, making them appear good in their eyes, becoming pleased with them, and thinking that they are performing righteous deeds.

42. Believing that God ﷻ has favored someone over others.

43. Considering one's good deeds superior, displaying arrogance, and pointing it out to everyone.

44. Seeing oneself as exempt from falling short.

---

340 Kulaynī, Shaykh Muḥammad b. Yaʿqūb, *al-Kāfī,* Vol. 2, p. 307.

341 Ibid., p. 308.

342 Arrogance: It is self-conceit or pride.

343 Kulaynī, Shaykh Muḥammad b. Yaʿqūb, *al-Kāfī,* p. 313.

45. Rebellion or tyrannical transgression [baghī] against the Imām or the Islāmic ruler. It is narrated that Amīr al-Mu'minīn ﷺ said:

> O people, surely rebellion leads its perpetrators to the Hellfire.[344]

46. Injustice [Ẓulm]. Know that injustice has three categories: injustice that God forgives, injustice that God does not forgive, and injustice that God does not abandon. The injustice that is not forgiven is polytheism [shirk]. The injustice that God forgives is people wronging themselves in what is between them and God.[345] The injustice that God does not abandon is the mutual wronging among people,[346] As mentioned earlier.

47. Deception, trickery, and betrayal.[347]

48. Having a double-tongue [speaking insincerely or hypocritically, dishonesty and lack of integrity in one's

---

344 Ibid., p. 327.

345 And it is known that forgiveness is conditional upon certain criteria, including repentance.

346 Kulaynī, Shaykh Muḥammad b. Ya'qūb, *al-Kāfī*, Vol. 2, pp. 330–331.

347 And what is meant by this is committing these actions with a fellow believer or a peaceful Muslim.

speech and interactions with others]. It has been narrated:

> Whoever faces the Muslims with two faces and two tongues, on the Day of Judgment, he will come with two tongues of fire.[348]

49. Harming and belittling the Muslims. It has been narrated from Imām Ja'far aṣ-Ṣādiq ﷺ that God ﷻ said:

> I declare war against the one who harms My believing servant, and I safeguard My anger against the one who humiliates My noble servant.[349]

50. Insulting a believer. It is narrated from Imām Ja'far aṣ-Ṣādiq ﷺ:

> God ﷻ said,
>
> > One who humiliates a friend of Mine has prepared for battle against Me, and I am the swiftest of all in coming to My friends' rescue.[350]

51. Disowning one's lineage. It is narrated that Imām Ja'far aṣ-Ṣādiq ﷺ said,

---

[348] Kulaynī, Shaykh Muḥammad b. Ya'qūb, *al-Kāfī*, Vol. 2, p. 343.

[349] Ibid., p. 350.

[350] Ibid., Vol. 2, p. 351.

> Whoever disowns their lineage, even if it [the lineage] is lowly, has disbelieved in God.[351]

52. Seeking out the faults and shortcomings of the believers. Both Abū Ja'far and Imām Ja'far aṣ-Ṣādiq ﷺ said:

> The closest a person can be to disbelief is when he declares a man as his brother in religion and then counts his unintentional mistakes and slips to disgrace him with them one day.[352]

It is also reported that the Messenger of God ﷺ said:

> O group of people who have accepted Islām with their tongue and belief has not yet purely and freely entered into their hearts, do not criticize the Muslims and do not seek to search into their privacies to find faults in them; for whoever does this, God will then do the same to them, and to whomever God will do such a thing, He may disgrace him even in the privacy of his own home.[353]

53. Defaming a believer. It is narrated that Imām Ja'far aṣ-Ṣādiq ﷺ said:

---

[351] Ibid., p. 350.

[352] Ibid., p. 354.

[353] Ibid., p. 355.

> Whoever debases a believer for a sin will not die before he commits such a sin.[354]

54. Spreading indecency. It is narrated that Imām Ja'far aṣ-Ṣādiq ﷺ said:

    > The Messenger of God ﷺ said,
    >
    > > Whoever spreads an indecent act is like the one who started it, and whoever dishonors a believer for a thing will not die before he commits such a thing.[355]

    What is meant by spreading an indecent act is that the person comes to know of a sin committed by a believer and then mentions it to the general public.

55. Narrating on a believer. This refers to attributing to a believer words that indicate the absurdity of their opinions, the weakness of their intellect, and the foolishness of their nature. It is known that the context of consultation is outside the scope of this ruling, which categorizes it as a major sin. It is narrated that Imām Ja'far aṣ-Ṣādiq ﷺ said,

    > Whoever narrates a story about a believer to tarnish his reputation and undermine his integrity, aiming

---

[354] Ibid., p. 356.

[355] Ibid.

to degrade him in the eyes of people, God removes him from His guardianship to the guardianship of Shayṭān, and Shayṭān will not accept him.[356]

56. Mocking a believer. This involves finding joy in the misfortunes of others. Imām Ja'far aṣ-Ṣādiq ﷺ said,

> Do not express joy at the trouble of your brother [in faith]; God may grant him a favor and transfer that trouble to you.

The Imām also said,

> Whoever rejoices at the suffering that has come upon his brother [in faith], he will not leave this world before going through such suffering himself.[357]

57. Insulting a believer. Insulting involves using foul and offensive language. It does not include false accusations. For instance, if you were to say to someone, "You are a dog," "You are stingy," or "You are despicable," you have insulted them. It is narrated that [Imām] Abū Ja'far ﷺ said,

> Insulting a believer is a gross sin, fighting him is disbelief, eating his flesh [backbiting] is

[356] Ibid., p. 358.

[357] Ibid., p. 359.

> disobedience, and the illegality of consuming his property is like the illegality of spilling his blood [taking his life].[358]

Similarly, it is also reported that Imām Mūsā al-Kāẓim عليه السلام commented on two individuals who were exchanging insults,

> The one who initiates it is more unjust, and his sin and the sin of his companion will be upon him unless he apologizes to the wronged party.[359]

58. False accusation. This is when you suspect or believe something negative about your brother without evidence of his wrongdoing. Imām Ja'far aṣ-Ṣādiq عليه السلام said,

> When a believer accuses his brother [in faith], faith diminishes from his heart just as salt dissolves in water.[360]

In other words, it melts away. It is also narrated that he عليه السلام said,

---

[358] Ibid., p. 360.

[359] Ibid.

[360] Ibid., p. 361.

> Whenever one accuses his brother [in faith] in his religious matters, sanctity, and religious relations will cease to exist between them.[361]

59. Evil assumption. It is narrated that Imām Ja'far aṣ-Ṣādiq ﷺ said,

> Amīr al-Mu'minīn said,
>
> > Deal with the issues related to your brother [in faith] with best interpretations until you receive overwhelming evidence to support the facts. Do not act on [evil] guesswork about a word that has come from your brother [in faith] as long as you can manage to find a place for it in goodness.[362]

Furthermore, God ﷻ has prohibited following assumptions in this verse:

﴿إِن يَتَّبِعُونَ إِلَّا ٱلظَّنَّ وَإِنۡ هُمۡ إِلَّا يَخۡرُصُونَ﴾

﴿*in yattabi'ūna 'illā ẓ-ẓanna wa-'in hum 'illā yakhruṣūna*[a]﴾

[361] Ibid.

[362] Ibid., p. 362.

﴾*They follow nothing but conjectures and they do nothing but surmise*﴿[363]

and

﴿إِن تَتَّبِعُونَ إِلَّا ٱلظَّنَّ وَإِنْ أَنتُمْ إِلَّا تَخْرُصُونَ﴾

﴾*in tattabi'ūna 'illā ẓ-ẓanna wa-'in 'antum 'illā takhruṣūna*﴿

﴾*You follow nothing but conjectures, and you do nothing but surmise*﴿[364]

It should be known that belittling a sin, neglecting it, and considering it insignificant can elevate it to the level of a major sin. Let us revisit a narration cited earlier:

Imām Ja'far aṣ-Ṣādiq ﷺ said,

> Beware of those minor sins that you belittle, for they will not be forgiven.

I [the narrator] asked,

> What are those sins?

He replied,

---

[363] Sūrat al-An'ām, Verse 116.

[364] Sūrat al-An'ām, Verse 148.

> They are the ones which if a man commits, he says: I am prosperous if I do not commit any other sins [i.e., he is not afraid of this sin, seeing it as nothing really bad, and persists in it despite knowing it is wrong, following the mindset: how fortunate I am that it is not worse than that].[365]

In another reliable narration, Abū al-Hasan ﷺ said,

> ... Do not consider minor sins insignificant, for minor sins accumulate until they become many.[366]

Ultimately, persistence in wrongdoing turns a minor sin into a major sin.

Imām Jaʿfar aṣ-Ṣādiq ﷺ said,

> With persistence, no sin is minor.[367]

Imām Muḥammad al-Bāqir ﷺ explained persistence by saying,

> Sinning without seeking forgiveness from God nor resolving to repent, that is persistence.[368]

---

365 Kulaynī, Shaykh Muḥammad b. Yaʿqūb, *al-Kāfī*, p. 287.

366 Ibid.

367 Ibid., p. 288.

368 Ibid.

And Imām Jaʿfar aṣ-Ṣādiq (عليه السلام) said,

> No, by God! God does not accept any servant's obedience to Him while he persists in disobedience against Him.[369]

Overlooked Sins

Among this category of sins are the following:

1. Believing that one is fulfilling what is obligatory upon them and considering oneself innocent, undeserving of any reproach.

This belief is among the blameworthy traits, even if it pertains to a specific action, no matter how small or significant, for no one no, one can fully fulfill the rights of worship or the obligations of obedience. From this, we understand that the calamities that befall a person are often the result of the sins committed by individuals, as we will discuss, God willing.

Furthermore, when one believes in their innocence, they may imagine that the transgressions of others are the cause of their misfortunes. This is a consequence of the conviction of one's innocence. God ﷻ said,

﴿وَلَوْ يُؤَاخِذُ ٱللَّهُ ٱلنَّاسَ بِمَا كَسَبُوا۟ مَا تَرَكَ عَلَىٰ ظَهْرِهَا مِن دَآبَّةٍ﴾

369 Ibid.

﴾*wa-law yu'ākhidhu llāhu n-nāsa bi-mā kasabū mā taraka 'alā ẓahrihā min dābbatin*﴿

﴾*Were God to take humans to task because of what they have earned, He would not leave any living being on its back*﴿[370]

Beware, however, of assuming that this implies that the Prophets, Messengers, and Imāms ﷺ are also tainted—God forbid—by sins, as implied by the general meaning of the two aforementioned verses. That is because every movement and stillness of any individual has a profound connection to the entire universe, as indicated by supplications such as,

> O God, forgive me those sins which tear apart safeguards! O God, forgive me those sins which draw down adversities! O God, forgive me those sins which alter blessings! O God, forgive me those sins which hold back supplication! O God, forgive me those sins which bring down calamities![371]

The descent of punishment upon previous nations due to the wickedness of their deeds is a clear example of this. Some calamities befall children due to their parent's actions, such as a child being born mute, deaf, blind, or leprous due to the deeds of their father or a child tending indecency and wrongdoing because of his parents'

---

370 Sūrat Fāṭir, Verse 45.

371 Part of Du'ā' Kumayl.

behavior. The verses are explicit, and the narrations are unequivocal in conveying this meaning. If transgressions become rampant, God ﷻ punishes the disobedient due to their sins. As for the righteous, their ranks are elevated or treated like the infallibles, being lifted from the earth as retribution against the sinners. This is because infallibility deprives people of the blessings and virtues associated with their optional and inherent existence.

God's saying

﴿وَمَا كَانَ ٱللَّهُ لِيُعَذِّبَهُمْ وَأَنتَ فِيهِمْ﴾

﴿wa-mā kāna llāhu li-yuʿadhdhibahum wa-ʾanta fīhim﴾

﴿But God will not punish them while you are in their midst﴾[372]

points to the second aspect, and His saying

﴿وَمَا كَانَ ٱللَّهُ مُعَذِّبَهُمْ وَهُمْ يَسْتَغْفِرُونَ﴾

﴿wa-mā kāna llāhu muʿadhdhibahum wa-hum yastaghfirūna﴾

[372] Sūrat al-Anfāl, Verse 33.

﴾*nor will God punish them while*
they plead for forgiveness﴿[373]

refers to the first aspect.

2. One of the matters that is transgression but is often overlooked is when a person commits one sin and unknowingly becomes a cause for another.

For instance, if someone engages in fornication or homosexuality, it leads to calamities that affect not only the righteous but also all beings as a result of an inevitable process. It is known that the doer of a cause is the doer of the effect. In this case, the adulterer or the homosexual becomes the cause of the calamities that befall people. Yet, they imagine they have not sinned themselves and God ﷻ. God said,

﴿وَٱتَّقُواْ فِتۡنَةٗ لَّا تُصِيبَنَّ ٱلَّذِينَ ظَلَمُواْ مِنكُمۡ خَآصَّةٗۖ
وَٱعۡلَمُوٓاْ أَنَّ ٱللَّهَ شَدِيدُ ٱلۡعِقَابِ﴾

﴾*wa-ttaqū fitnatan lā tuṣībanna lladhīna ẓalamū minkum khāṣṣatan wa-ʿlamū ʾanna llāha shadīdu l-ʿiqābi*﴿

[373] Sūrat al-Anfāl, Verse 33.

﴾*And beware of a punishment, which shall not visit the wrongdoers among you exclusively, and know that God is severe in retribution*﴿[374]

The gravest of these sins that result from other sins is what befalls the Prophets and Imāms ﷺ in the form of various calamities due to the sins committed by people. This includes not only killing, fighting, and multiple forms of harm that the infallibles are subjected to but also diseases and similar afflictions that affect the infallibles due to the corruption of the world and the disturbance of the environment caused by the sins of the sinners.

If dust appears in a room, the first signs of dirt and dust appear on the cleanest and purest objects. Similarly, when the world becomes corrupt and disturbed, the consequences [the afflictions due to this corruption] befall the infallibles due to the sins committed by the disobedient. In this regard, God said,

﴿ظَهَرَ ٱلْفَسَادُ فِي ٱلْبَرِّ وَٱلْبَحْرِ بِمَا كَسَبَتْ أَيْدِي ٱلنَّاسِ﴾

﴾*ẓahara l-fasādu fī l-barri wa-l-baḥri bi-mā kasabat ʾaydī n-nāsi*﴿

[374] Sūrat al-Anfāl, Verse 25.

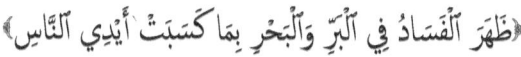

❴*Corruption has appeared in land and sea
because of the doings of the people's hand*❵375

And regarding some transgressors, God said,

❴ٱلَّذِينَ طَغَوْا۟ فِى ٱلْبِلَدِ❵

❴*ᵃlladhīna ṭaghaw fī l-bilādⁱ*❵

❴فَأَكْثَرُوا۟ فِيهَا ٱلْفَسَادَ❵

❴*fa-ʾaktharū fīhā l-fasādᵃ*❵

❴*—those who rebelled [against God] in their cities
and caused much corruption in them*❵376

This is not limited to specific transgressions; it refers to the
disruption of the world's order due to the commission of
sins, and this is referred to in verse:

❴وَإِذَا تَوَلَّىٰ سَعَىٰ فِى ٱلْأَرْضِ لِيُفْسِدَ فِيهَا وَيُهْلِكَ ٱلْحَرْثَ وَٱلنَّسْلَ
وَٱللَّهُ لَا يُحِبُّ ٱلْفَسَادَ❵

❴*wa-ʾidhā tawallā saʿā fī l-ʾarḍi li-yufsida fīhā wa-yuhlika
l-ḥartha wa-n-nasla wa-llāhu lā yuḥibbu l-fasādᵃ*❵

---

375 Sūrat ar-Rūm, Verse 41.

376 Sūrat al-Fajr, Verses 11–12.

﴾If he were to wield authority, he would try to cause corruption in the land and to ruin the crop and the stock, and God does not like corruption﴿[377]

Even in human affairs, human actions cause a person to become a domain for the devil, as God ﷻ stated,

﴿إِنَّمَا ٱسْتَزَلَّهُمُ ٱلشَّيْطَٰنُ بِبَعْضِ مَا كَسَبُوا۟﴾

﴾innamā stazallahumu sh-shayṭānu bi-baʿḍi mā kasabū﴿

﴾only Shayṭān had made them stumble because of some of their deeds﴿[378]

Many of the verses that mention the descent of punishment upon previous nations indicate that it was a result of their deeds, as God ﷻ said,

﴿فَأَخَذَتْهُمْ صَٰعِقَةُ ٱلْعَذَابِ ٱلْهُونِ بِمَا كَانُوا۟ يَكْسِبُونَ﴾

﴾fa-ʾakhadhathum ṣāʿiqatu l-ʿadhābi l-hūni bi-mā kānū yaksibūna﴿

﴾So the bolt of a humiliating punishment seized them because of what they used to earn﴿[379]

---

[377] Sūrat al-Baqarah, Verse 205.

[378] Sūrat Āl ʿImrān, Verse 155.

[379] Sūrat Fuṣṣilat, Verse 17.

and other similar verses. The interconnectedness of human activities and their dwellings with the cosmic order should not be ignored. This negligence renders individuals unaware of the consequences of their actions, making them heedless of the crimes and harm they cause to others.

A person might think that their deeds, compared to others, do not warrant the afflictions that befall people. However, they should realize that this belief is a transgression as it means they are underestimating and belittling what they have committed. Additionally, even a seemingly minor transgression a person commits, if it has contributed to the conditions that necessitate divine punishment, becomes a partner in every small or large wrongdoing that leads to the occurrences of inherent disorders and other consequences in the world. Even the dominance of certain darkness over the state of affairs can result from the commission of transgressions.

Evidence of this notion can be found in the supplication of Imām al-Ḥusayn ﷺ when he was struck by Abū al-Huṭūf al-Juʿfī with an arrow on his noble forehead, causing blood to flow down his face.

Imām al-Ḥusayn ﷺ said,

> O God, You see the state where I find myself among these sinful servants. O God, count them individually; strike them down in multitudes. Do

> not leave one of them on the earth, and never forgive them.

Then he raised his voice,

> O nation of evil, how wretchedly have you treated Muḥammad ﷺ in his progeny! Surely, after me, you will not hesitate to kill a man, and you will not fear the killing. Rather, it will be easy for you to kill him upon your killing of me. By God, I hope that God will honor me with martyrdom, and then He will take revenge on my behalf from you in a way that you do not perceive.

So al-Ḥasīn asked,

> And how will He avenge you from us, O son of Fāṭimah?

He replied,

> He will afflict you with your suffering, and your blood will be shed, and then He will pour down punishment upon you.[380]

---

[380] Al-Muqarram, ʿAbd al-Razzāq, *Maqtal al-Muqarram*, p. 339. Al-Baḥrānī, ʿAbdullāh Nūr-Allāh, *Maqtal al-ʿAwālim*, p. 98. Qummī, Shaykh ʿAbbās, *Nafs al-Mahmūm*, p. 189. Al-Khawārazmī, *Maqtal al-Ḥusayn*, Vol. 2, p. 34.

Adding to this is his ﷺ supplication upon bidding farewell to his son 'Alī al-Akbar, when he said,

> O God, withhold from them the blessings of the earth, disperse them thoroughly, tear them apart completely, make them divided factions, and never let the rulers be pleased with them.[381]

In the same sense, Imām al-Ḥusayn ﷺ also informed them of what would happen if they were to kill him,

> By God, you will not remain after [killing] me, except that you will be afflicted, just as a rider on a horse is thrown in all directions, and you will experience turmoil like the pivoting of a grinding millstone. My father gave me this promise, which he received from my grandfather, the Messenger of God ﷺ.[382]

In his ﷺ supplication at the end of what was previously mentioned, he said,

> O God, withhold the rain from them, send upon them years of famine like the years of Yūsuf, and let

---

381 Al-Muqarram, 'Abd al-Razzāq, *Maqtal al-Muqarram*, p. 312. Al-Khawārazmī, *Maqtal al-Ḥusayn*, Vol. 3, p. 30.

382 Al-Muqarram, Abd al-Razzaq, *Maqtal al-Muqarram*, p. 283. *Tārīkh Ibn 'Asākir*, Vol. 4, p. 343. Al-Khawārazmī, *Maqtal al-Ḥusayn*, Vol. 2, p. 7. Sayyid b. Ṭāwūs, *Al-Luhūf 'alā Qatlā al-Tu*, p. 54, Ṣaydā edition.

> a servant from Thaqīf rule over them, giving them a drink from the cup of bitterness, for they belied us and betrayed us, and You are our Lord. In You we trust, and to You is the ultimate return.[383]

The occurrence of what he ﷺ foretold is evidence of what we have mentioned.

Ultimately, the verses we referred to are sufficient and conclusion in this regard, such as God's saying:

﴿فَكُلًّا أَخَذْنَا بِذَنۢبِهِۦ فَمِنْهُم مَّنْ أَرْسَلْنَا عَلَيْهِ حَاصِبًا وَمِنْهُم مَّنْ أَخَذَتْهُ ٱلصَّيْحَةُ وَمِنْهُم مَّنْ خَسَفْنَا بِهِ ٱلْأَرْضَ وَمِنْهُم مَّنْ أَغْرَقْنَا ۚ وَمَا كَانَ ٱللَّهُ لِيَظْلِمَهُمْ وَلَٰكِن كَانُوٓا۟ أَنفُسَهُمْ يَظْلِمُونَ﴾

﴿fa-kullan ʾakhadhnā bi-dhanbihī fa-minhum man ʾarsalnā ʿalayhi ḥāṣiban wa-minhum man ʾakhadhathu ṣ-ṣayḥatu wa-minhum man khasafnā bihi l-ʾarḍa wa-minhum man ʾaghraqnā wa-mā kāna llāhu li-yaẓlimahum wa-lākin kānū ʾanfusahum yaẓlimūn[a]﴾

﴿So We seized each [of them] for his sin: among them were those upon whom We unleashed a rain of stones, and among them were those who were seized by the Cry, and among them were those whom We caused the earth to swallow, and among them were those whom We drowned. It was not God who

383 Sayyid b. Ṭāwūs, *Al-Luhūf ʿalā Qatlā al-Tufūf*, p. 56. Al-Khawārazmī, *Maqtal al-Ḥusayn*, Vol. 2, p. 7.

wronged them, but it was they
who used to wrong themselves❵[384]

3. Moving on, among the sinful matters that are often overlooked is when a servant blames his Lord when He delays answering his prayer.

This is especially the case if he combines this with the belief that there is no deficiency or shortcoming on his part in his supplication. This may lead them to think or assume that there is a deficiency or shortcoming on the part of the One who answers, and this belief is indeed one of the ugliest sins. That is because such an action implies not trusting God to fulfill His promise of responding to the caller's invocation. Furthermore, entertaining thoughts of injustice or ignorance regarding His attributes is a severe wrong. Beyond this, assuming there is no room for any deficiency or shortcomings in oneself is an even greater transgression.

4. Another such matter is assuming that the deeds one perceives as righteous and valid entitle them to God's favor and elevation of ranks, thus imagining oneself among the ranks of the righteous. Sometimes, when one's eyes shed tears during supplication and worship, one may think themselves akin to God's allies. It is important to understand that all such notions are delusions and ignorance, revealing the ugliness of human nature.

---

[384] Sūrat al-ʿAnkabūt, Verse 40.

5. Among these matters is also presuming that one has earned merit with God and superiority over people by engaging in certain acts, such as performing night prayers and visiting the Master of Martyrs ﷺ and other infallibles ﷺ. Such a person fails to recognize that what they have done is, in reality, a blessing from God ﷻ in terms of divine legislation. Islām and its injunctions, which encompass numerous blessings from God, are bestowed upon us. God ﷻ says,

﴿لَقَدْ مَنَّ ٱللَّهُ عَلَى ٱلْمُؤْمِنِينَ إِذْ بَعَثَ فِيهِمْ رَسُولًا مِّنْ أَنفُسِهِمْ﴾

﴿la-qad manna llāhu ʿalā l-muʾminīna ʾidh baʿatha fīhim rasūlan min ʾanfusihim﴾

﴿God certainly favoured the faithful when He raised up among them an apostle from among themselves﴾[385]

God further blessed such a person by guiding him to Islām and the path of truth, granting him success in performing worship and enabling him to do it. God also protects him from the interference of demons among humans and jinn. Despite this, such a person remains oblivious to what God has done for him and does not hold himself accountable for not soundly benefiting from these blessings. He does not undertake acts of worship that align with God's desires, intentions, and directions. This reflects his ignorance, delusion, and foolishness. Indeed, how generous is God,

[385] Sūrat Āl ʿImrān, Verse 164.

for He does not deprive him of standing before Him, despite his follies.

One of the most prominent indicators of the connection between actions performed by individuals—even if they are done in a state of forgetfulness or heedlessness—and the universe is the requirement of many religious practices to be performed at specific times or under certain conditions. For example, fasting during Ramaḍān, pilgrimage during particular days of the year and at a designated location, the particular direction [qibla] during prayer, and the precise timing for each prayer. For instance, the Fajr prayer consists of two units [rakʿāt] performed at a specific time. In comparison, Ẓuhr and ʿAṣr prayers comprised four or two units, respectively, and the Maghrib prayer consists of three units, all performed at designated times and places. These requirements underscore the intricate connection between religious obligations and contextual considerations in the universe. This emphasizes that the divine mandates and considerations set by the sacred legislator [Sharīʿah] are closely intertwined with the realm of the cosmos and the potential for corruption.

Likewise, some prohibitions are specific to certain times or places, such as the prohibitions within the sacred precincts [Ḥaram], the prohibitions during the state of consecration [Iḥrām], seclusion for worship [Iʿtikāf], and the bans within mosques and other specific locations. Similarly, marriage is prohibited with one woman while permitted with another, is lawful under certain circumstances, and is forbidden under different circumstances. These interrelationships exist to achieve specific benefits and desired virtues, which can only be realized through those conditions and restrictions or because malevolent forces in the universe and corruption can only be averted through specific actions at particular times and places. This may be why it has been said that divine legal rulings exist to secure benefits and avert harm by adhering to them. The command for the prayer of signs [Ṣalāt al-Āyāt] during eclipses and other cosmic phenomena serves to ward off anticipated evils associated with these signs, such as obscuring the sun's light for a certain period with the moon over the entire or parts of the earth or veiling the moon's light from the earth. All of this reveals what we have discussed.

From here, we understand the extent of divine blessings due to people's negligence in fulfilling these obligations, committing prohibitions, and failing to perform worship as required. If a doctor prescribes medicine and it is not taken as directed, what is intended to be beneficial can turn harmful, and what is meant to heal can cause illness. It should not surprise us, therefore, that it is narrated,

> How often a servant recites the Qur'ān, and the Qur'ān curses him.[386]

[386] Majlisī, ʿAllāmah Muḥammad Bāqir, *Biḥār al-Anwār*, Vol. 89, p. 183.

This means that it causes him to move away from God's mercy. Many of these actions, good or bad, have effects and consequences, even if one commits them unintentionally due to legitimate excuses such as forgetfulness or sleep.

From here, we also know the extent of the ugliness and heinousness of the crimes committed by the servant, knowingly or unknowingly, throughout his journey within the realm of servitude. The most dreadful aspect is that the Creator, with His mercy, generosity, compassion, and tenderness, points out to the servant the actions that shield him from the evils of the universe and the corruptions of his conduct and the conduct of others. Instead of thanking his Master for guiding him to these actions and obligating him to them for his protection, the servant perceives them as burdens, hardships, and restrictions through impertinence, ignorance, and defiance. When he does perform some of these actions without adhering to them properly, he considers himself to have attained high ranks, assuming that God is obliged to accept and reward him, which leads to pride and arrogance. This ultimately distances him from the realm of God's mercy more than he ever imagined he was close to it.

Thus, the servant must always be thankful for the obligatory and recommended acts and be grateful for the legislation of prohibitions. For within the framework of the comprehensive Islāmic system, it is indeed a divine favor upon the servants. God says:

﴿لَقَدْ مَنَّ ٱللَّهُ عَلَى ٱلْمُؤْمِنِينَ إِذْ بَعَثَ فِيهِمْ رَسُولًا مِّنْ أَنفُسِهِمْ يَتْلُوا۟ عَلَيْهِمْ
ءَايَـٰتِهِۦ وَيُزَكِّيهِمْ وَيُعَلِّمُهُمُ ٱلْكِتَـٰبَ وَٱلْحِكْمَةَ وَإِن كَانُوا۟
مِن قَبْلُ لَفِي ضَلَـٰلٍ مُّبِينٍ﴾

﴿la-qad manna llāhu ʿalā l-muʾminīna ʾidh baʿatha fīhim rasūlan min ʾanfusihim yatlū ʿalayhim ʾāyātihī wa-yuzakkīhim wa-yuʿallimuhumu l-kitāba wa-l-ḥikmata wa-ʾin kānū min qablu la-fī ḍalālin mubīn[in]*﴾*

﴿God certainly favoured the faithful when He raised up among them an apostle from among themselves to recite to them His signs and to purify them and teach them the Book and wisdom, and earlier they had indeed been in manifest error﴾[387]

He also says:

﴿ٱلْيَوْمَ أَكْمَلْتُ لَكُمْ دِينَكُمْ وَأَتْمَمْتُ عَلَيْكُمْ نِعْمَتِي وَرَضِيتُ لَكُمُ ٱلْإِسْلَـٰمَ دِينًا﴾

﴿l-yawma ʾakmaltu lakum dīnakum wa-ʾatmamtu ʿalaykum niʿmatī wa-raḍītu lakumu l-ʾislāma dīnan﴾

﴿Today I have perfected your religion for you, and I have completed My blessing upon you, and I have approved Islām as your religion﴾[388]

---

[387] Sūrat Āl ʿImrān, Verse 164.

[388] Sūrat al-Māʾidah, Verse 3.

and

﴿يَمُنُّونَ عَلَيْكَ أَنْ أَسْلَمُوا ۖ قُل لَّا تَمُنُّوا عَلَيَّ إِسْلَامَكُم ۖ بَلِ اللَّهُ يَمُنُّ عَلَيْكُمْ أَنْ هَدَاكُمْ لِلْإِيمَانِ إِن كُنتُمْ صَادِقِينَ﴾

﴿yamunnūna ʿalayka ʾan ʾaslamū qul lā tamunnū ʿalayya ʾislāmakum bali llāhu yamunnu ʿalaykum ʾan hadākum li-l-ʾīmāni ʾin kuntum ṣādiqīn[a]﴾

﴿They count it as a favour to you that they have embraced Islām. Say, 'Do not count your embracing of Islām as a favour to me. No, it is God who has done you a favour in that He has guided you to faith, if you are truthful [in your claim]'﴾[389]

From this, we come to understand the secret behind what the Prophet ﷺ narrated, who said,

> Doesn't the one who turns his face away during prayer fear that God will transform his face into the face of a donkey?[390]

This is in addition to what God said in the verse:

﴿فَوَيْلٌ لِّلْمُصَلِّينَ﴾

---

[389] Sūrat al-Ḥujurāt, Verse 17.

[390] Majlisī, ʿAllāmah Muḥammad Bāqir, *Biḥār al-Anwār*, Vol. 81, pp. 211 and 259.

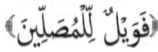

﴾*fa-waylun li-l-muṣallīna*﴿

﴾الَّذِينَ هُمْ عَن صَلَاتِهِمْ سَاهُونَ﴿

﴾*alladhīna hum ʿan ṣalātihim sāhūna*﴿

﴾*Woe to those who pray but are heedless of their prayers*﴿[391]

wherein He condemns them for their neglect of it, even though they are among those who pray—not because they are absent-minded or have left it intentionally, but because they pray while being heedless of what they are engaged in.

[391] Sūrat al-Māʿūn, Verses 4–5.

Advice and Benefits

Consider the following points of advice and benefits to reap from reading all the aforementioned on repentance:

1. It is incumbent upon a person to recognize their actual worth so that they are not afflicted with arrogance when they are granted success in performing some righteous deed or can fulfill an obligation or commitment of a commendable nature. Arrogance can undermine the value of the deed.

2. Responsible individuals must turn their attention inward; they should not imagine that if they were blessed with performing a good deed, it would automatically place them among the ranks of God's righteous servants. If the person performs the deed without feeling a sense of shortcoming and acknowledging that anything he achieves is by the grace of God, his deed can become futile and its value nullified.

3. The acts undertaken by a servant must be characterized by sincerity. One should firmly believe that God's command to undertake obligations and recommended actions is a form of honor extended by the Almighty to empower individuals to discipline, reform, and purify themselves. After all, Paradise is not entered by those whose souls remain impure and unaffected by morally debased qualities. In His wisdom, God has enjoined various forms of worship upon us as a means of self-purification and self-improvement. If you are granted the ability to perform a deed, express gratitude to God.

Be wary of imagining—let alone believing—that your performance of worship fulfills God's rights in the truest sense; rather, thank God for enabling you to accomplish it. Furthermore, it is essential to recognize that every act of worship, if not accompanied by a sincere orientation towards God, becomes a shell devoid of substance. When a servant stands in the presence of God, if their being does not merge with the state of standing before the Supreme Creator of the Heavens and the earth, then that standing is not as it should be.

4. Know that worship plays a significant role in attaining the true station of servitude to the Almighty and fulfilling a fundamental role in sincerity and devotion. Whoever prays or worships out of a desire for Paradise and in pursuit of the abundant rewards promised to the righteous servants of God is driven by self-interest and the fulfillment of personal desires. Such a person is not truly devoted, for they pray, fast, perform pilgrimage, and visit the infallibles ﷷ solely to achieve their goals, including worldly and Hereafter benefits. When the goal of worship is limited to attaining personal desires, one effectively worships oneself. They would not consider worship so significant if they could achieve their desires in this world and the Hereafter without worshiping God.

Similarly, those who worship God out of fear of His punishment and to escape His fire and torment are motivated by self-love and protection for themselves. They do not want pain or suffering for themselves, nor do they accept their souls being ruined or crushed in the layers of divine punishment and the various levels of Hellfire. In reality, they are worshiping themselves and obeying their desires, and it is not far-fetched that this verse applies to them:

﴿أَفَرَءَيْتَ مَنِ ٱتَّخَذَ إِلَٰهَهُۥ هَوَىٰهُ﴾

﴾*a-fa-ra'ayta mani ttakhadha 'ilāhahū hawāhu*﴿

﴾*Have you seen him who has taken his desire to be his god*﴿[392]

True and sincere worship is the worship of free individuals who have liberated themselves from the slavery of their desires and have dedicated their worship exclusively to the Almighty because He is worthy of worship. The two aforementioned categories represent worship from those who remain captive to their selves and desires. May God free us and everyone from such captivity.

We may find it astonishing that some people visit the Master of Martyrs ﷺ or other Imāms and infallibles ﷺ and believe they have a right over these noble figures. This visitor is unfortunate; they are unaware that the one they are visiting has a right over them, as they have been granted the privilege to stand in their presence. Therefore, the

[392] Sūrat al-Jāthiyah, Verse 23.

visitor should first and foremost express gratitude to God for honoring them with the opportunity to visit one of the infallibles. Second, they should thank the infallible for permitting them to enter their revered sanctuary. From this, we should understand that those who neglect worship are undoubtedly in a state of sin and that those who commit forbidden actions or deviate from the path of correct servitude are not only sinning against God but also doing wrong to the infallibles and, indeed, all of creation. That is because all sins hurt the surrounding environment and creations, as evidenced by certain supplications that imply that some sins prevent rain.

In contrast, others darken the space, cause diseases and epidemics, and disrupt the atmosphere with a moral gloom that leads people astray from the path of righteousness. And it is well known that when calamity strikes, it affects and includes both the righteous and the wrongdoers. Therefore, whoever commits a sin or neglects their obligations contributes to these calamities, thereby causing harm to all beings. Indeed, on their shoulders rest the rights of God, His worshipers, and the rights of all creatures. Therefore, if the Exalted God grants the sinner the opportunity, they should turn their attention towards themselves and repent to Him. It is upon them to seek from God, the chance to fulfill the rights of all creatures that they have wronged, as established in their record of actions.

Ultimately, we conclude that calamities, whether natural disasters such as earthquakes, floods, droughts, or afflictions caused by oppressors seizing the rights of Muslims, all stem from the sins of the wrongdoers. God ﷻ created these blessings [worship and good deeds] for His servants, and He does not need any of them. Rather, individuals have brought about these disasters through their deeds, sins, and deviations. God ﷻ said,

﴿بَلَىٰ مَن كَسَبَ سَيِّئَةً وَأَحَٰطَتْ بِهِۦ خَطِيٓـَٔتُهُۥ فَأُو۟لَٰٓئِكَ أَصْحَٰبُ ٱلنَّارِ ۖ هُمْ فِيهَا خَٰلِدُونَ﴾

﴿balā man kasaba sayyi'atan wa-'aḥāṭat bihī khaṭī'atuhū fa-'ulā'ika 'aṣḥābu n-nāri hum fīhā khālidūna﴾

﴿Certainly whoever commits misdeeds and is besieged by his iniquity—such shall be the inmates of the Fire, and they will remain in it [forever]﴾[393]

God also said that

﴿ظَهَرَ ٱلْفَسَادُ فِى ٱلْبَرِّ وَٱلْبَحْرِ بِمَا كَسَبَتْ أَيْدِى ٱلنَّاسِ﴾

﴿ẓahara l-fasādu fī l-barri wa-l-baḥri bi-mā kasabat 'aydī n-nāsi﴾

[393] Sūrat al-Baqarah, Verse 81.

﴾Corruption has appeared in land and sea because of the doings of the people's hand﴿[394]

and

﴿وَلَوْ يُؤَاخِذُ ٱللَّهُ ٱلنَّاسَ بِمَا كَسَبُوا۟ مَا تَرَكَ عَلَىٰ ظَهْرِهَا مِن دَآبَّةٍ﴾

﴾wa-law yu'ākhidhu llāhu n-nāsa bi-mā kasabū mā taraka 'alā ẓahrihā min dābbatin﴿

﴾Were God to take humans to task because of what they have earned, He would not leave any living being on its back﴿[395]

Let us not be deluded and imagine that the infallibles ﷺ were also afflicted by calamities without any cause. As we indicated earlier, sinners' sins cause these calamities and afflictions when they strike. The sinners have wronged themselves, others, and the infallibles ﷺ, who bear the burdens of the calamities resulting from the disobedience of the sinners.

This is our understanding, and all praise be to God, the Lord of all worlds.

---

[394] Sūrat ar-Rūm, Verse 41.

[395] Sūrat Fāṭir, Verse 45.

www.ingramcontent.com/pod-product-compliance
Lightning Source LLC
Chambersburg PA
CBHW030359130626
46549CB00004B/1561
* 9 7 8 1 9 5 6 2 7 6 6 3 3 *